To Amber and Kelly
my daughters
my joy

THE BEST IDEAS COME FROM OTHER PARENTS. . . .

WHAT TO DO WITH ALL THAT ARTWORK ◆ Both my son and I wanted to save all of his artwork, but we couldn't keep everything. We came up with two solutions to our problem. Now, when the refrigerator gets covered with his artwork we take a picture of him in front of it. Then we clear off all his masterpieces from the refrigerator and display some of the artwork in our son's own personal art gallery, the walls of our garage. The photographs provide a permanent but compact record of our own Van Gogh's creations, as well as showing how big he was at the time.

◆

BRUSH YOUR TEETH, UPSTAIRS AND DOWNSTAIRS ◆ To get my two- to four-year-olds to brush their teeth thoroughly, I describe their teeth as having upstairs and downstairs and tell them to be sure to brush every room. We describe the rooms as we brush (e.g., upstairs bedrooms and bathrooms as we brush upper teeth and the kitchen, the bathroom, living room, patio, and garage as we brush the lower teeth). I can keep children brushing for five minutes with this method.

◆

COOKIE SHEET BECOMES A PORTABLE MAGNET BOARD ◆ A cookie sheet can be used for many different activities in the car, especially for long-distance driving: a magnet board (five to ten small magnets offer hours of creative fun), a raceway for small cars and trucks, or a platform to hold Legos or blocks.

IT WORKS FOR US!

PROVEN CHILD-CARE TIPS FROM EXPERIENCED PARENTS ACROSS THE COUNTRY

Tom McMahon

FOREWORD BY
Dr. Remo Cerruti, M.D., F.A.A.P.

Illustrations by Erin Mauterer

POCKET BOOKS
New York   London   Toronto   Sydney   Tokyo   Singapore

The tips in this book have all worked for the parents who submitted them. Children are individuals, however, and not all tips will be suitable or safe as described herein for you and your child. If you have any questions at all, please check with your doctor. In applying these tips, the author and publisher advise you to use your common sense and your intimate knowledge of your own child, and to be sure to keep safety in mind at all times. We cannot be held responsible for the use or misuse of any information in this book.

An *Original* Publication of POCKET BOOKS

POCKET BOOKS, a division of Simon & Schuster Inc.
1230 Avenue of the Americas, New York, NY 10020

Copyright © 1993 by Tom McMahon
Interior illustrations copyright © 1993 by Erin Mauterer

All rights reserved, including the right to reproduce
this book or portions thereof in any form whatsoever.
For information address Pocket Books, 1230 Avenue
of the Americas, New York, NY 10020

It works for us! : proven child-care tips from experienced parents
  across the country / [edited by] Tom McMahon ; foreword by Remo
  Cerruti ; illustrations by Erin Mauterer.
    p.   cm.
    Includes index.
    ISBN 0-671-77733-5 (pbk.)
    1. Child rearing—United States—Miscellanea. 2. Child care—
United States—Miscellanea. I. McMahon, Tom. II. Cerruti, Remo,
HQ769.I836   1993
649′.1—dc20   92-40080
                                                           CIP

First Pocket Books trade paperback printing March 1993

10   9   8   7   6   5   4   3

POCKET and colophon are registered trademarks of
Simon & Schuster Inc.

Text design: Stanley S. Drate/Folio Graphics Co. Inc.
Cover design by Gina Bonanno
Front cover photos by Steven Jones except
  lower left: Jose L. Pelaez/The Stock Market;
  and center: Jon Feingersh/The Stock Market

Printed in the U.S.A.

ACKNOWLEDGMENTS

THANKS TO THE CONTRIBUTORS

First and foremost, I wish to thank all the parents who contributed tips to this book. Without you, this book would not have been possible. Many of your innovative child-care tips have already made a positive difference in my own household. Now, parents from across North America will value them too. Thank you for sharing your experience.

A heartfelt thanks to my family for their understanding and patience while I prepared this manuscript. To my wife, Nancy, for her support, thoughtful advice, proofreading, and editorial comments; and to my daughters, Amber and Kelly, who were constant reminders of the purpose of this project.

I wish to thank a number of other people: Dr. Remo Cerruti, a caring and talented pediatrician whose expert advice is sprinkled throughout these pages, for his dedication to this project; Erin Mauterer, illustrator par excellence; Dennis Ean Roby, for his counsel and editorial advice throughout this project; Paul Dulberg, Florence Grace, and Stacey Lopez—my cheerleaders—for their friendship and encouragement when I needed it most; Eleene Kraft, for her excellent transcription and typing; Sidney B. Kramer, my literary agent, for his guidance; Robin Worthington, an expert columnist, whose writing propelled my project to a national audience; Dr. Neil McCallum, a friend and confidant who assisted with publicity; Jean Hammerback, for her assistance with research; Roger Kendall, for his public-relations savvy; and Claire Zion, my editor, for her belief in this project and her expertise in bringing it to fruition.

A special note of appreciation to the many newspaper editors and reporters (too many to name here) who wrote stories about my parenting project and encouraged their readers to share their tips with me.

CONTENTS

4

LEARNING

5

DEMYSTIFYING DISCIPLINE

6

"PLEASE PICK UP YOUR TOYS"
(Chores for Children)

7

CLOTHES AND LAUNDRY

8

HEALTH AND SAFETY

9

SELF-ESTEEM AND RELATIONSHIPS

10

ON THE GO
(with Children)

11

NIGHTY NIGHT

12

CELEBRATIONS

13

BABY BASICS

FOREWORD

As a pediatrician, I spend a lot of time giving out advice and treatment plans to parents. Taking those directions home and making them work is an entirely different matter, however. It's easy to write a prescription for a medicine, for example, but the prescription doesn't tell a parent what to do if a child refuses to swallow, or spits out the medicine, or swallows it with a smile and then throws up in the parent's lap.

But these are just the kind of problems that *It Works for Us!* helps with. This book provides us with a new, practical, and eminently helpful resource—other parents!

Caring contributors from all over North America have generously shared child-care tips that are "field-tested" and have worked for them. The result is a wonderful compendium of practical strategies for dealing with a wide range of common problems that parents encounter in raising their children.

I have reviewed the tips submitted for the book and I feel comfortable recommending any of them to parents in my own practice. Also, at points throughout the book, I have added specific comments that point out possible hazards or problems that might arise in regard to particular tips. Be sure, however, to always exercise the proper care and good judgment in using any of these tips. If you are unsure about a tip or have questions about its safety or appropriateness, consult your pediatrician before using it. Also, it's important to remember that each child is different and that not all of the tips will work equally well for everyone.

I think you will enjoy this book not only because of the help you get from it, but also because of the pleasure of knowing that this advice comes from the real "experts"—other parents.

—Dr. Remo Cerruti, M.D., F.A.A.P.

A PERSONAL INTRODUCTION

This book is truly unique. Rarely will you find a book with more than two authors; this one has hundreds. And rarely will you find a book so full of practical parenting advice—written by other parents. Parents and grandparents from over three hundred different towns and cities have contributed their experiences to this book. As you will see, their tips are refreshing and innovative. Most of the tips have never been published before. Some are age-old standards that have been tested and proven effective by generations of families. And each tip printed in this book has a parent or grandparent who enthusiastically vouches for its effectiveness.

The idea for this book was born soon after I became a father. My wife and I had just witnessed the miracle of birth, which brought into our lives a beautiful, wide-eyed, redheaded daughter whom we named Amber. We had the typical new-parent jitters—exhilaration tempered by panic. We learned quickly, as most parents do, but we also realized how little we knew about babies and children.

My wife and I had studied many subjects in high school and college, but not parenting. It seemed ironic that we had the least amount of training for one of the most important responsibilities we would ever face. Like many new parents of our generation, we live far from our own parents, making it even more difficult to pick up parenting tips from our own families. And when both parents work, there is little time to simply talk to other parents at the playground, in play groups, or at preschool. So we began reading many of the popular child-care books. They were helpful, especially for quick medical advice and for understanding the ever-changing developmental stages of childhood, but they weren't enough.

Throughout those early days of parenthood, I began to recognize that some of the most useful and practical advice came from other parents and grandparents. Their tips were not only creative, but they worked. For example, my mother had a terrific tip on teething; a coworker offered suggestions for car travel; and a friend showed us a convenient method to make our own nutritious baby food. These tips and others made a positive difference in our lives; they saved time or made an everyday task easier. I began to realize that parents were a resource of experience and wisdom. I started to dream about the possibility of compiling hundreds of their best child-care tips in a book.

In 1990, with encouragement from a few friends, I posted flyers around my community, requesting parents to send me their child-care tips. They responded, slowly at first, with unique solutions to common child-care situations, from potty training to the dreaded bedtime routine. Seven months and two hundred tips later, the media became aware of my project. The *San Jose Mercury News* was the first of more than one hundred newspapers and magazines to publish a story about my quest for parenting tips. Invitations came from radio talk shows, the *American Baby* television show, and even the *Oprah Winfrey* show. But above all, tips were arriving by the hundreds—from parents across North America.

Parents were not only generous with their advice, but they also were excited that someone had asked them to share *their* experience. Friends and relatives eagerly shared their tips, but most came from complete strangers thousands of miles away. The chairperson of a pediatric task force from a medical school in Oklahoma offered his assistance, and a high-ranking county official in Mississippi shared some ideas that were being used in his community. Even some fellow backpackers, with whom I shared a campsite at ten thousand feet in the backcountry of Yosemite, had a few tips to share. One newspaper reporter rang my doorbell for ten minutes before opening the gate to my backyard, only to discover her colleague photographer (and father of five) sharing numerous tips while I scribbled them down. The vast majority of tips I received, whether in a letter or on my answering machine, ended with the same words: "It worked for me."

My wife and I marveled at the creative ideas we heard, and we began using many of them with our own children. We learned how to get our children to quit a favorite activity without a hassle (p. 13) and how to solve an argument between siblings (p. 95). We now have an easy method for recycling our children's artwork while still "saving" it (p. 17), and we have homemade bedtime tapes that are better than any commercial product (p. 216). Our children are safer now when they're in busy parking lots (p. 139), and our bathroom towels are never left on the floor (p. 59). These and many other tips from the book that have worked for our children are now part of our everyday routine.

The tips printed in this book were selected from more than fifteen hundred I received from parents over the past two and a half years. My editor and I selected those which were most innovative, creative, and practical. Some tips were duplicates of ones already received. All tips were checked for safety by our consulting pediatrician, Dr. Remo Cerruti. Any tips received after the manuscript was completed will be considered for the next edition. Yes, we hope there will be a sequel to *It Works for Us!,* so please continue to send me your creative ideas (see pp. 267–68).

The tips are organized into thirteen chapters, which are subdivided by specific topic. Some tips are similar to others in the same section, but with a new or unique twist. If your child doesn't respond favorably to one version of a tip, try another one or add a variation of your own. The contributor's name or initials, city, and state or province are listed with the tip. A few contributors asked that their names not be printed, and a few tips were received without a name; therefore, these tips will only have a city and state listed by them. Dr. Cerruti's helpful "Pediatrician Comments" are signified by the pediatrician logo. My comments, which follow a few of the tips, are distinguished by the "writer at the computer" logo. A dollar sign ("$$") labels tips that can save you money.

I hope you enjoy this book. I also hope it makes parenting a bit easier for you. My main goal from the very beginning of this project has been to offer parents more effective strategies for parenting, which in turn will help us raise happier and healthier children. We parents need all the help we can get, especially from each other, for the difficult and challenging job of parenting.

—Tom McMahon
October 1992

The ultimate success of my life will not be judged by those who admire me for my accomplishments but by the number of those who attribute their wholeness to my loving them, by the number of those who have seen their true beauty and worth in my eyes.

DAVE GRANT, *The Ultimate Power*, 1983

PLAY TIME

◆

Imagination is more important than knowledge.
—ALBERT EINSTEIN

In a child's world, a doll comes to life, wooden blocks are transformed into cities, and a pail of water becomes an ocean of fun. These types of activities—creative play—seem to be the most enjoyable for children and certainly keep their attention the longest. For example, I sometimes pause at my daughters' bedroom door to sneak a peek into their imaginative world. I recently watched my three-year-old put her "babies" to bed. Catching my eye, she held her index finger to her lips and whispered, "Shhh, babies night-night." My six-year-old, only a few feet away, was building a skyscraper with her blocks and Legos. Concentrating with the intensity of an architect, she paused briefly before placing each new piece on the structure. These creative moments stimulate a child's intellectual development, say the child-care experts. And some adults actually credit these early experiences with influencing their career paths many years later.

After repeatedly seeing my children abandon an expensive new toy for the box it came in, I finally learned that simple props found around the house could inspire the best creative play. The abandoned toy could be only one thing, but that simple brown box became their hideout, a crib for their babies, and a "car" to push each other around in. Many store-bought toys, especially the fad toys hyped by the media, can't hold my daughters' attention the same way creative play can. For example, my six-year-old and her friend recently complained of being bored; they had exhausted their toy supply in a matter of minutes. Looking around for something to occupy their time, I yanked the bedspread off my daughter's bed and draped it over three chairs, creating a tent. They shrieked with anticipation, disappeared under the bedspread, and played heartily for two hours. On another occasion, I lined up four chairs and yelled, "All aboard." As they boarded the "train," both girls were shouting out destinations they wanted to travel to. They took turns being the conductor, whose primary job was to take care of a stubborn passenger, our three-year-old.

Arts and crafts are fun and stimulating for young children, and the possibilities of projects are endless. Books, puzzles, games, and television (although, in my opinion, it needs to be used judiciously) are other favorite activities for most young children. Books provide one of the most important activities a child can engage in, from enjoying the pictures to learning how to read (see Chapter 4). Puzzles are another activity that young children are drawn to, from a simple four-piece puzzle for toddlers to a one-hundred-piece jigsaw for older children. Not only are they fun and challenging, but they help children learn sizes, shapes, and colors. Parlor games are fun and have a tendency to bring the whole family together.

To help bring order to the wonderful world of playtime, I have arranged the following activity tips into ten separate sections: Indoor Activities, Pretend Play, Outdoor Fun, Quitting a Favorite Activity, Arts and Crafts, Recyling "Masterpieces," Toys, Coping with Toy Clutter, Storing Toys, and Quick Cleanup. These innovative activities offer hours of fun and adventure for you and your children.

INDOOR ACTIVITIES

RAINY DAY/SICK DAY BOX ◆ For a rainy-day activity or when a child is sick in bed, bring out a special box of toys and games to which your child does not usually have access. *Karin Poe, Fremont, California*

PICK AN ACTIVITY ◆ Decorate a shoe box with your child and place in it strips of paper, each suggesting an activity which you and your child can do together. When your

child is bored or you want to share some quality time, pull
out a piece of paper and have fun. *D.L. Tarsa, Michigan*

A LIST OF THINGS I CAN DO BY MYSELF ✦ Ask
your children to list twenty or more things they can do all
by themselves (reading, drawing, etc.). Save this list and
present it to them the next time they say, "I don't have
anything to do." It reminds them of fun projects they can
accomplish all by themselves. *Rebecca Robinson, San Jose,
California*

TREASURE HUNT ✦ Make up three-by-five cards with
a drawing of easily recognizable places in the house and/
or yard—such as crib, refrigerator, mailbox, etc. Help the
child find the place pictured on the first card, where she
will find the picture card leading to the next hidden card
and the next, etc.; and on to the last place, where the
"treasure" is to be found. *Mr. and Mrs. Roland Giduz,
Chapel Hill, North Carolina*

A GUESS BOX ✦ A small container such as an empty
tissue box or round oatmeal container makes a great guess
or touch box. Take turns with your children placing surprise items in the box. The other person has to guess what
it is by just touching it. It's a fun game and great for language development. *Janice Fonteno, Union City, California*

JUNK MAIL FOR KIDS ✦ Place unopened junk mail in
a colorful shoe box, and save it for a "rainy day" or a
"rainy hour"! When your child announces that he is
bored, hand him his shoe box. He will spend considerable
time opening, examining, and playing with junk mail. Junk
mail often contains colorful stickers as well as interesting
response envelopes which can be filled and licked—the
best part. Almost all junk mail contains forms for filling in
your name, address, and telephone number. This is great
practice for an older child. Make certain that none of this
mail gets posted or you will triple or quadruple your volume of junk mail! *Barbara Allen, Palo Alto, California*

GARAGE FUN ON A RAINY DAY ✦ During a recent
rainy day, I moved the car out of the garage and brought in
all my children's large plastic outdoor toys (small slide,
seesaw, basketball hoop, etc.). Our garage turned into an
outdoor-play area where the children spent the entire af-
ternoon. *Elaine Minamide, San Diego, California*

"POOL" PARTY DURING THE SNOWY WIN-TER ✦ We live in a snowy climate where winters can be long. Sometimes, I fill the bathtub, let the girls put their bathing suits on and get out the popsicles, and let them play in the bathtub. I sit in the bathroom and read the newspaper or a magazine while they are splashing away. *Emily Allen Martinez, Park City, Utah*

"YOU CAN JUMP ON THIS BED" ✦ Instead of throwing away an old mattress, store it on its side in the garage. When children have the urge to jump and tumble, lay the mattress on the garage floor or, better yet, on the grass. *Anonymous, San Diego, California*

$$ INEXPENSIVE BUILDING BLOCKS ✦ At many lumber yards, cabinet shops, or construction sites, end cuts of wood in various sizes and shapes are available at little or no cost. When properly sanded to avoid cuts and slivers, a box of these pieces of wood will provide creative play materials for children to construct towers, bridges, cities, vehicles, figures, or whatever comes into their minds. *Neil McCallum, Fremont, California*

$$ MARBLES ROLL THROUGH PIPE STRUC-TURES ✦ Children love to play and create with pieces of regular PVC pipe and an assortment of connectors. They enjoy connecting the pieces together to make engineering marvels. My children especially enjoyed making curving tubes to roll their marbles through. The pipe and connectors are inexpensive and available at most hardware stores. Buy one or more long sections of pipe and an assortment of connectors (elbows, T's, etc.). Cut the pipe in various sizes that will store easily in a box. *Jim Stuka, Escondido, California*

Only let older children play with marbles. They can be choking hazards for young children.

MOVABLE LEGO STRUCTURES ✦ Our children construct their Lego sets on various sizes of particle boards. Then, if we need to move the structure or clean under it, all we have to do is lift the particle board. The Lego structure always stays intact, and our children don't fuss about having to rebuild. *Lorrie Rubio, Fremont, California*

DEVELOPING MOTOR SKILLS ✦ To help develop your child's large motor skills, arrange the couch's cushions on the floor and encourage him to climb around. Don't be afraid to get down on the floor with him. *Anonymous, Michigan*

$$ CLOTHESPINS ARE ENTERTAINING ✦ For an inexpensive game on a rainy day, try clothespins (not the spring type) and a plastic gallon milk jug. Babies can shake it and toddlers can empty it. Preschoolers can count them and fill and empty the jug. School-age children can make a game out of standing up straight, holding the clothespins close to their noses, and trying to drop the pins inside. *Kim VanGorder, Cary, North Carolina*

"TAKE A WALK ON THE CEILING" ✦ Occasionally, when my children are "antsy," I suggest that they "walk" on the ceiling. To accomplish this, have them look down at a hand mirror as they walk around the house. The hand mirror is held so that it reflects the ceiling. This will give them the illusion of walking on the ceiling. It's especially fun to walk under light fixtures and doorjambs. *Donna Bishop, Stanton, California*

FLASHLIGHT FUN ✦ Purchase a small, cheap flashlight and rechargeable batteries and let a child play games on the walls and ceiling at night. Ever since my grandson could walk, we have played "big Jason, little Jason" by letting him walk towards a wall to see how big and small he gets. We also play chasing light on the wall and ceiling, etc. *Patricia R. Hersom, Walnut Creek, California*

HOLIDAY ACTIVITIES—OUT OF SEASON ✦
Holiday activities can be even more fun to do on non-holidays. For example, I always purchase an extra egg-dyeing kit during Easter. Then, on a rainy day I'll pull out the kit and my children will decorate eggs. My son and I recently decorated the house for Halloween—in February. *Terry LeMonchbck, Pasadena, California*

WHEN ALL ELSE FAILS, TRY A HOME VIDEO ✦
One of the fastest ways of quieting children down is to turn on a home video that contains pictures of themselves or people they know. They will often stop what they are doing and just stand or sit in front of the TV and relive that moment. *Scott Hill, Newark, California*

Hook your video camera to your TV set so the children can see themselves "live" on TV. Watch them entertain themselves.

MAGAZINES ARE FUN ✦
Toddlers love to play with old magazines. When my daughter was a year old, I put her on the floor with about ten old magazines and showed her how she could tear the pages from the book and then tear it into pieces or crumple it into a ball. She had a ball! *Cathy Jones, Cold Spring, New York*

OLD TEXTBOOKS BECOME FUN ACTIVITIES ✦
I let my children play with the old textbooks I had stored in the garage. They can scribble in them, cut out pictures, or just browse through them. Offering books they are allowed to play with cuts down the number of new books that get damaged. *Khush Lodhia, Fremont, California*

TOY CATALOGS ✦
My children love to look at toy catalogs from stores like Sears or Penney's. *Denise Fulford, Southlake, Texas*

Be sure your child doesn't put the magazines in his mouth. Some use lead in their ink.

PHOTO ALBUM FOR CHURCH ◆ We belong to a small county church that does not have a nursery. My three-year-old has quite a time sitting still through an hour-long service. Books and coloring books weren't working long enough, so I purchased an inexpensive pocket-size photo album and filled it with pictures of siblings, grandparents, pets, animals, and neighborhood friends. I change the pictures frequently and only bring it out in church. He loves to sit and look at "his book." (I also take snacks.) *Sheryl Saxton, Tekamah, Nebraska*

INDOOR WATER FUN ◆ Children love to transfer water from one container to another using eyedroppers. Using food coloring, I make each container of water a different color. Children love this activity and it's also good for their eye-hand coordination and color recognition. *Janice Fonteno, Union City, California*

HIGH-FLYING POPCORN ◆ An exciting adventure in cooking for young children is to pop corn *without a lid!* I would put a sheet on the floor of the garage where there was plenty of space, set the electric frying pan in the center of the sheet, add a *tiny* bit of oil and popcorn, and watch the action! Our safety rules required that children could not go *on* or touch the sheet and the popcorn could not pop *off* the sheet. Verbal explanations were given to both the children *and* the popcorn, complete with shaking finger. When all the popping stops, along with delighted screams, the frying pan is removed and the children eat the corn from the outside of the sheet in. A great rainy-day activity. *Fran Thole, Santa Clara, California*

Make sure that an adult supervises the process at all times and keep children at a safe distance. Not recommended for children under three years old.

WINNER PICKS UP THE GAME! ◆ One of the best ideas I have come up with (and one my husband and I still follow every day) is "the winner picks up the game!" In my house, the winner of any game played is responsible for picking up and putting the game away. The winner, still flushed with victory, cheerfully accepts the price of winning. The loser saves face by leaving the room or saying something like, "At least I don't have to put the game away!" This rule has been strictly followed for years in our house. It has eliminated hard feelings after the loss of a game and identified very easily who was in charge of cleanup. *Sue Crockett, Charlton, Massachusetts*

"I CAN'T HOLD ALL THESE PLAYING CARDS IN MY HAND" ◆ My children loved to play cards, but their hands were too small to hold the cards dealt to them. To solve this problem, I turned a shoe-box lid under the shoe box. The children placed the cards between the lip of the lid and the box to make a good card holder. *Kelly Robson, York, Nebraska*

PRETEND PLAY

AN INDOOR TENT ◆ Once or twice a year, I set up my small backpacking tent in the living room for my children to play in. They love to sleep in the tent at night and play "camp" during the day. It keeps them occupied for hours at a time and encourages creative play. If you don't have a real tent, drape a large blanket or sheet over a table. *Thomas Leslie, San Diego, California*

LARGE BOXES CREATE A-MAZE-ING THINGS ◆
I kept five children and the entire neighborhood fascinated
with a room full of large boxes from an appliance store. I
tied the boxes together and made a circle out of them, and
I cut holes from one box to the other and made a tunnel. I
also put in little windows. I put some of the boxes on one
side of the main tunnel and made little trapdoors for the
kids to crawl through. The boxes were heavy enough that
toddlers could crawl on top of them without the boxes falling in. *Dr. W.W. Walker, Gastonia, North Carolina*

STAR IN YOUR OWN MOVIE ◆ If you have a camcor-
der, ask your children if they want to star in their own
homemade movie. It can be a small family production, or
you can invite the neighborhood children over. Older children can write and direct their own script; younger children will enjoy acting out a favorite story or fairy tale. Save
the video for posterity; your children will enjoy it even
more as adults. *Anonymous, Mi-Wuk Village, California*

PICNIC WITHOUT ANTS ◆ To break up the monot-
ony of having to stay indoors due to bad weather or illness,
we have indoor picnics—sometimes with a theme. We
spread a blanket on the floor, bring sandwiches, chips,
fruit, etc. Sometimes I'll pack it up and we will "hike"
around the house to find the perfect spot. We have had
teddy-bear picnics, doll picnics, and Disney Day picnics. To
encourage imagination on these outings, we imagine trees,
creeks, fish, birds, even deer. This can also be done in the
back or front yard. *Stacey Ann Morgan, Oakland, California*

A SUMMER THEME ◆ When school is out during the
summer, I have my children choose a special theme to
keep them occupied during their months off. This year it
will be Indians, and we will be doing all kinds of reading
and activities—even building our own authentic tepee.
They get excited about each summer's theme and generate
a lot of the ideas and projects themselves. *Audrey Swanton, Brewer, Maine*

**HOMEMADE TOWN FOR LITTLE CARS AND
TOYS** ◆ My little boys grew up during the time of Hot
Wheels, so I drew them a town on the back of Naugahyde.
This town had our house and all the neighbors' homes that
they knew, the school, the grocery store, the church, the

gas station, and the fire station. It was about four feet wide and about six feet long. I made it very colorful. This was a place where my little boys played for hours with their Hot Wheels. When they were through we could just fold it up and put it away. It also kept the Hot Wheels together, so that they weren't all over the house or lost. *Marlyn Lovell, Garden Grove, California*

OUTDOOR FUN

FUN IN NUMBERS ✦ Plan a two-month calendar of fun activities with three to five other moms (or dads). Each parent selects one or two activities that they plan and organize. Field trips and activities are more fun when shared with friends. *Kathleen Waters, Fremont, California*

A MAGNIFIED WORLD IS FASCINATING ✦ Purchase an inexpensive magnifying glass, and a whole new world will appear for your children. They will enjoy looking at various items through the magnifying glass. My grandson was worried about our regular ant invasions until I bought him a magnifying glass (at age three) to study insects. Also, we respect insects, animals, and people and kill insects only when we cannot catch them to let them outdoors. *Patricia R. Hersom, Walnut Creek, California*

CORNMEAL DELIGHT ✦ Our house has a back deck instead of a yard, so my three-year-old's outdoor play is somewhat restricted. I filled a small tub with cornmeal and put it on a bench. It was just the right height for her to stand next to the tub and play in the cornmeal. She loved the feel of it on her fingers, digging in it, and "cooking up" all sorts of delights. *N.M., Mi-Wuk Village, California*

JUNIOR CARPENTER ✦ My husband found that my daughter could feel helpful in his workshop if he let her pound nails into a sturdy cardboard box. The nails go in easily and she feels competent. It's also great for her motor skills and coordination. *Anonymous, San Diego, California*

 Always provide adult supervision—and watch those fingers.

WATER-BALLOON YO-YO ✦ Here's an idea for a fun summer toy—it's a water balloon yo-yo. The trick is to put only a very little water in the balloon. The ones we got were inflated to about the size of a navel orange, and about one-fourth to one-third of that was water. Then a ten-inch length of rubber-band type cord was tied to it with a finger loop on the other end. It was a very big hit with all ages, and we still have one intact in January that was purchased in October. *Karen Cutter and Stephen Robison, Belmont, California*

HUNTING FOR TREASURES ✦ When my children were two and three years old, they enjoyed carrying a small plastic pail with them on walks to collect treasures. Our walks were more delightful and relaxing for me since we slowed down considerably to hunt for, study, and discuss the treasures. Sometimes we would later glue the treasures to colored paper or cardboard (such as from a cereal box). *N.K.M., Palo Alto, California*

GO PAINT THE HOUSE ✦ To keep preschoolers busy during the summer, I would send them outside with a bucket of water and a paintbrush. They could paint the steps, the house, and the sidewalk. When they turned around, the paint was dry and they could start over again. My adult kids still talk about how Mom sent them out to paint the house. *Colleen Weber, Merna, Nebraska*

THE LITTLE GARDENER ✦ Children love to play in dirt, so I provide them with a large container full of new potting soil, small plastic planting pots, plastic flowers, and plastic scoopers. Children love to fill the planting pots with soil and plastic flowers. *Arlene Stocking, Fremont, California*

RICE IS BETTER THAN SAND ✦ I empty a large bag of rice in the middle of a large blanket or pour it into a large box for my children to play with. They enjoy it more than they do sand. *Marilyn Stein, Hampton, Virginia*

PLASTER-OF-PARIS CANDY MOLDS ✦ Here's a fun activity that I have found to be a big hit with kids as young as three years old right up to teenagers. I take small candy molds (available in many kitchenware and hobby stores), which come in different designs, and fill them with plaster of paris (two parts plaster to one part water), let them harden for one hour, then pop them out. They can be painted right away, but it's best if you let them dry out for a few days in the sun. Then let the kids paint them with watercolor paints. Young kids just enjoy the activity of painting the little figurines. Older children might want to have a hole carefully drilled in the top and turn them into necklaces or ornaments, attach a magnet to the back for refrigerator art, or even imbed a pin in the plaster before it hardens to make a piece of jewelry. The candy molds come in an assortment of characters including all holidays, dinosaurs, sports, animals, even Teenage Mutant Ninja Turtles! I have made Halloween molds and given them out Halloween night instead of candy with a printed admonition stating they are NOT to be eaten, only painted! I have never known these not to be a hit. *Karen Cutter and Stephen Robison, Belmont, California*

BUBBLEOLOGY ✦ My son and I came across a great recipe for big bubbles: 1 cup Dawn dish detergent, 1 gallon of water, and 1 cup of Karo syrup (the light-colored or clear kind). Mix it all in a bucket, and then use tin cans (with the top and bottom cut out) to make great bubbles. The larger the can, the larger the bubble; the big institution-size cans made the biggest and best. The Karo syrup works like glycerin and may be less expensive. *Debbie G., North Carolina*

$$ HOMEMADE WAGON ✦ Put casters on four corners of a wooden or plastic box which is pulled by a rope and you have yourself a wagon. The revolving motion of the casters on this wagon allows for more tricks than a store-bought wagon. *Bill McMahon, Spokane, Washington*

RAINY DAYS ARE FUN—OUTSIDE ✦ Instead of staying indoors on a rainy day, I put my children's rain gear on and let them go outside. They release some of their energy by jumping in puddles and splashing in the rain. When they're finished, I give them a warm bath, then serve them cocoa. *Teena Hubbard, Irvine, California*

QUITTING A FAVORITE ACTIVITY

THE FIVE-MINUTE WARNING ✦ No matter what the activity in which a child is engaged, he or she has the right not to be abruptly interrupted to do something else. Just think about it; would you like someone to whisk you away from something enjoyable to do something odious? Just as you have the right to be informed, so does a child. Remind your child that a change in activity will occur. Then let him know when he has fifteen, ten, and five minutes to complete whatever it is he is engaged in before the new activity. *Adrienne Pelker, Santa Cruz, California*

"IT'S TIME TO GO" ✦ Children have a tough time leaving a favorite activity such as the playground at the park or the local swimming pool. Now, instead of nagging or complaining, I simply tell my children that it's time to leave. If they don't leave immediately, I clock the number of minutes it takes them to quit. The next time we do that same activity, I make my child wait for the same number of minutes before starting that activity. For example, if my son takes ten minutes to get out of the pool after asking him, he has to wait ten minutes before getting in the pool during the next visit. *Mary Lea McAnally, Stanford, California*

Make sure the child is old enough to understand time and responsibility.

"ON YOUR MARK, GET SET, GO" ✦ When my children are playing at the park or engaged in a particularly interesting activity, I give them a five-minute warning so they can finish up what they are doing and prepare themselves to go. Then, when it is time to go, I say "On your mark, get set, go!" and we all run to the car. This way, leaving is fun, too, and they do not linger at the park. *Sherry Niger, Bountiful, Utah*

A BIRD WHISTLE FOR KIDS ✦ My father started a family tradition years ago by calling us children with a beautiful-sounding bird whistle. Now I use it for my children. The children respond more positively and quickly when they are called with the whistle than when we yell for them. *Mary Lynne Rasmussen, Oshkosh, Wisconsin*

"THE TIMER SAID YOU MUST GO HOME NOW" ✦ When the neighbor children come over to play, they usually give me a message—"I can stay for an hour." I set my stove timer, then when it is time to go home, I say, "The *timer* said you must go home now." It has saved a lot of arguments because a child can't plead with a timer. *Patti Potts Johnson, Omaha, Nebraska*

LEAVING A FAVORITE PLACE ✦ From a very early age, my son threw a fit whenever I came to pick him up from Grandma's house. It was hard for him to abruptly stop whatever he was doing and get out to the car. I finally started using the pickup techniques used by his preschool. At preschool, the kids are all sitting by the door, ready to go and waiting for their parents to arrive. Then the teacher walks them to the parent's car and helps them get in. So now, I call Grandma just before I leave and they finish their activity and clean up. He is ready and waiting for me. When I pull up, Grandma walks him to the car, and away we go. *Kathy Tubbs, San Jose, California*

ARTS AND CRAFTS

CRAFT BOX ✦ I filled a large flat box with "throwaways" from my home and treasures from the craft store: berry baskets, paper-towel and toilet-paper tubes, Styrofoam meat trays, different-shaped spangles, doilies, feathers, plastic eyes, glitter, different-shaped wooden beads, and glue sticks. My five-year-old daughter and her friends have spent hours creating gorgeous masterpieces. A craft box also makes a wonderful gift for a child. *Marie Levie, St. Paul, Minnesota*

 Be careful that a young child doesn't have access to small items he could swallow or choke on.

STAMP DAY ◆ I save all free stamps, like Christmas or Easter Seals, and any free stickers which I receive. Every once in a while, we have what we call "Stamp Day." I give my kids a piece of paper, and they can lick the stamps or place the stickers in any design they want. They have fun and it doesn't cost a thing. *B. Goke, Roselle, Illinois*

$$ CHILDREN LOVE TO MAKE GREETING CARDS ◆ Instead of sending store-bought cards to your relatives, make your own cards with construction paper and a recent photo of your child. The caption can be as simple as "Someone wants to wish you a happy birthday!" *D.L. Tarsa, Michigan*

COUPONS FOR MOM ◆ Children love to cut things out, so I let my children cut out coupons for me. It saves me time too. *Carol Smead, San Jose, California*

$$ PLAY DOUGH RECIPE

2 cups flour	3 tablespoons oil
2 cups water	4 teaspoons cream of tartar
1 cup salt	

If using powdered paint for color, add to flour prior to mixing. If using food coloring, add to water prior to mixing. Then add all ingredients together and cook, at medium heat, till sticky and gathers in a big lump (will pull away from the sides of the pan). Cool and knead out lumps. *A.S., Fremont, California*

NATURE COLLAGES ◆ My preschoolers enjoy gluing treasures (pebbles, leaves, twigs, etc.) which they collect outside onto colored paper or cardboard. I cut up cereal boxes for an ideal weight of cardboard. *Nancy Lee, Pasadena, California*

A COLLAGE OF PHOTOS ✦ Looking at a photo album of himself or herself is an excellent quiet activity for a toddler, one which always calms ours. I recommend covering the pictures with transparent contact paper. I arranged my daughter's album in approximate chronological order so she can watch her own development. I also included pictures of her family and friends. *Melanie Lawrence, Portland, Oregon*

CARTOON COLLAGE ✦ After we finish using a parenting or children's magazine, I cut out all the pictures and illustrations of cartoon characters. I paste them on a large white board and hang it in my toddler's bedroom. It makes a fun, colorful, and inexpensive picture and my toddler loves to point out all his favorite cartoon friends. *Patricia A. McMahon, San Diego, California*

YOU CAN DRAW ON THIS WALL ✦ If your child loves to draw and prefers doing it on the walls, tack up a large sheet of butcher paper on an accessible wall to provide an acceptable drawing area. *Peggy Crane, Cupertino, California*

REMOVING UNWANTED CRAYON MARKS ✦ The product Soft Scrub works great to remove unwanted crayon marks on plastic toys and other items. *Beth Weis, Buffalo Grove, Illinois*

"TELL ME ABOUT YOUR ARTWORK" ✦ I love to admire my children's art projects, but I cringe when they show me a drawing and ask, "Daddy, do you know what this is?" I usually guess wrong. "That's a great-looking gorilla," I once said admiringly. "But Daddy," my daughter replied with a frown, "that's not a gorilla—that's you. Can't you tell?" Since then, my wife has taught me to respond to their drawings by saying, "Tell me about it," instead of trying to guess. *Thomas Leslie, San Diego, California*

NECKLACES YOU CAN EAT ✦ My son likes to make necklaces on yarn using Froot Loops or Cheerios which he enjoys eating as much as making. *Debra Randall, East Haven, Connecticut*

RECYCLING "MASTERPIECES"

WHAT TO DO WITH ALL THAT ARTWORK ✦
Both my son and I wanted to save all of his paper artwork, but we couldn't keep everything. We came up with two solutions to our problem. Now, when the refrigerator gets covered with his artwork we take a picture of him in front of it. Then we clear off all his masterpieces from the refrigerator and display some of the artwork in our son's own personal art gallery, the walls of our garage. The photographs provide a permanent but compact record of our own van Gogh's creations, as well as showing how big he was at the time. *K.T. Hom, San Jose, California*

MEMORIALIZING THREE-DIMENSIONAL ART-WORK ✦ Some artwork is more difficult to save than others, especially the large three-dimensional pieces frequently crafted at preschool or kindergarten. I would put my child on the couch, surround him with his latest art-work, and take a picture. I would keep the picture of the child with his artwork in an album. Since I had a picture of the artwork, I wouldn't feel pressure to save the originals. It was fun to do and we still enjoy the photos. *Kim Griffey, Shelbyville, Indiana*

STORAGE TRUNK SAVES "MASTERPIECES" ◆ Save precious art and craft projects, selected schoolwork, report cards, etc., in an inexpensive storage trunk, available at most discount stores. You can store the trunk in your child's closet or in the garage. Years later, you and your child will have a great time looking through the memorabilia. Just make sure they take it with them when they move out. *Anonymous, California*

TAKE A PICTURE OF THAT LEGO STRUC-TURE ◆ My six-year-old builds very detailed structures out of blocks or Legos that he is very proud of. Often, his two-and-a-half-year-old brother comes along and knocks down the creations, causing major grief to my older child. He even asked me if we could glue his creations together so they couldn't get knocked over. I explained that block and Lego creations are not permanent, and if we glued them together he couldn't build more things. Now, I take photos of my son's creations, which do make his creations permanent. *Robin Bunton, Fremont, California*

$$ ARTWORK WRAPPING PAPER ◆ Use children's artwork as wrapping paper for friends' birthday gifts—the gift is the artwork too. *Pamela Nakaso, Fremont, California*

HANGING CRAFT PROJECTS ◆ Three-dimensional art and craft projects can make beautiful decorations. We hang fishing line from the ceiling and attach our child's art masterpieces to it. This is better than taping or pinning things to the wall. *Patricia R. Shamshoian, Fremont, California*

A STRING OF ART ◆ A fun and simple solution to display artwork is to attach string or twine between two nails or cup hooks on the walls in your children's bedroom and hang their masterpieces with clothespins. *Tracy LaVelle, Fremont, California*

STORING LARGE CREATIONS ◆ Children's artwork mounds up fast. Save the large pieces by rolling them up and storing in large cylinder containers (available in mailing-supply stores). *Carol Smead, San Jose, California*

BEDROOM ART GALLERY ◆ Instead of decorating your child's bedroom walls with posters and fancy pictures, let her hang her own masterpieces on her walls. She will have the pride of seeing her own artwork displayed, and Mom will have an uncluttered refrigerator door. *Melody Mueller, Fremont, California*

WORTH FRAMING ◆ To encourage my children's creativity, I purchased a few inexpensive acrylic box-style frames for their drawings. Every few days or weeks, we change the pictures in the frames. My children are encouraged by the compliments they get from guests who visit their toy room. *Angie Satterfield, Patriot, Indiana*

ARTWORK UNDER GLASS ◆ Display children's artwork under glass on top of a table or desk (at home or work). *Anonymous*

$$ ARTWORK BECOMES STATIONERY ◆ We have found a way to recycle the multitude of art projects our children bring home. The small paintings and drawings make enjoyable stationery and greeting cards. *Polly Morehouse Griffith, Santa Rosa, California*

◆◆◆

TOYS

◆◆◆

$$ MAKE YOUR OWN BABY GYM ◆ To make an inexpensive "baby gym" (cost is $3–4) buy a ten-foot length of ¾″ or ½″ PVC pipe, four 45-degree elbows, and two T's. Cut the pipe into the following pieces: four 2-foot sections for the legs, one 18″ piece for the cross bar, and four 1½″ pieces to place between the T's and the elbows. It comes

apart easily and quickly for handy storage. Hang your child's favorite toys on it using Discovery Toys' Boomering Links or a similar product. *D.L. Tarsa, Michigan*

Be very careful that the toys you hang from the "gym" are secured safely and that there are no strings or ropes long enough for the baby to get tangled in.

"REAL" KEY RING FOR BABY ✦ A key ring securely fastening spare keys will fascinate a baby. *Peg Hartley, San Bernardino, California*

$$ TOY PHONES ✦ Don't throw your old phone away; give it to your child as a toy. A "real" phone is more fun than a toy one. *Barbara O'Neil, San Diego, California*

TOY CHAIN LINKS—1,001 USES FOR CHILDREN AND PARENTS ✦ Colorful toy chain links have many uses for children and parents; their only limit is your imagination. They are available in some toy stores and through Discovery Toys. Here are a few creative ideas:

A Parade of Linked Animals ✦ My son attaches the toy chain links to his stuffed animals and makes a parade. Sometimes he attaches them to his waist and pretends he's a horse. *Stephanie Beyer, Williamsburg, Virginia*

Shopping-Cart Seat Belt ✦ When I first put my seven-month-old into the seat of the grocery shopping cart without his car seat, I used toy chain links as a seat belt. I also hung extra links from the "seat belt" chain and hooked up toys that kept him busy and my shopping peaceful. *Donna Carbone, Waterbury, Connecticut*

Safety Latches ✦ Parents can use toy chain links to close off kitchen cupboards and cabinets. *Anonymous, Gurnee, Illinois*

 Be careful of the miniature toy chain links that could be swallowed by children.

**CONSUMER PRODUCTS SAFETY
COMMISSION HOT LINE
1-800-638-CPSC**

TOY EXCHANGE WITH FRIENDS ✦ Before buying a new toy, Nintendo, or computer software, it's always best to try it out to see if your children will really use it. A toy exchange with other families is the answer: trade toys with each other to consider if they would be worth a purchase of your own. Make sure each toy is clearly marked with the name of the owner and the date it must be returned. *Carol Smead, San Jose, California*

PUZZLE PIECES ✦ Children often play with more than one puzzle at a time, which causes havoc at cleanup time as you try to sort out which puzzle piece belongs to which box. To avoid this problem, mark the back of each puzzle piece with a letter, colored dot, or number to identify it as part of a certain puzzle. You or the child will then be able to easily identify the box to which each puzzle piece belongs. *Robert Levie, Durango, Colorado*

$$ BROKEN AUDIOTAPES ✦ Audiotapes are fragile and often get pulled out of their cassettes and too tangled to repair. To avoid having to buy an expensive replacement, make a backup copy as soon as you buy a new tape. *Kim VanGorder, Cary, North Carolina*

$$ BABIES LOVE KITCHEN "TOYS" ✦ We have the high chair in the kitchen, where the baby can watch what's going on and I can give him things to chew or play with while I'm doing dishes or preparing food. At seven months, he particularly likes Tupperware, spoons, measuring spoons, and things that roll around his tray, like large plastic containers with plastic blocks placed inside. Empty plastic yogurt cups make great stacking toys. *P.H., Albany, California*

1,001 USES FOR PLASTIC PAILS ✦ The most used toys in our household, for both our children (ages two and five), are two inexpensive plastic pails. We seem to take them everywhere: on treasure hunts for leaves, twigs, and rocks; to the park and beach for sand play; and even on a recent vacation, where the children were happiest playing and digging in the dirt. The simplest toys—the ones that can be used in many different ways—are often the best. *Anonymous, Wilmette, Illinois*

OTHER KIDS CAN'T PLAY WITH THESE TOYS ✦ This is a trick my mother used when we were little. A lot of times parents wonder why children get upset when other children play with their toys. It's the same thing with adults: if a neighbor wanted to borrow your old beat-up truck, you might let her, but if she wanted to use your brand-new car, you might think twice about it. My parents allowed us to have two boxes of toys, a box of toys that no one else was allowed to touch and a box with toys that we didn't mind sharing with other children. It always worked for us. *K.B., Reno, Nevada*

COPING WITH TOY CLUTTER

CHILDREN'S "GARAGE SALE" ✦ If your children have a difficult time parting with toys that they don't play with anymore, suggest that they hold a garage sale. Help them price each toy, and let them collect the money in their own money box. The proceeds from the sale can go into savings or they can buy new toys. *B.M., Chattaroy, Washington*

RECYCLE TOYS ✦ Children often have too many toys to enjoy all at once and end up creating more clutter than fun. The valuable trick I learned is to take some of the toys and store them in a box out of sight. After a few weeks, when your child needs a bright spot in his day, you can pull out the old toys and they will seem like brand-new fun. I kept at least one-third of our toys recycled that way and found it worked like magic! It also cut down on the clutter. *June Stewart, Salt Lake City, Utah*

ROTATE THREE BOXES OF TOYS ✦ If your toddler has acquired too many toys from loving family and friends, divide them into three boxes, store two up on a shelf, keep one down, and rotate boxes once a month. As the next box comes down, interest increases with the discovery of "new things." Keep two or three favorite toys always available. *Peggy Crane, Cupertino, California*

TWO TOYS AT A TIME ✦ Our son has gotten a lot better at putting his toys away because we only let him take out two toys at a time. When he wants to take out another toy, he has to put the other two toys back. *Debra Randall, East Haven, Connecticut*

TOY EXCHANGE ✦ I keep many of my children's toys in a box in the basement. When the children want to play with something from that box, they must exchange one of their current everyday toys for something from the cellar box. They learn to appreciate everything and keep toys at a minimum in their room. *Marilyn Horning, Fulton, New York*

CHECK-OUT TOYS ✦ Toys can clutter up a child's room in no time. To discourage this, we started a practice of checking out toys from a large cabinet that had a safety lock on it. Each child could check out three toys at a time. When they finished playing with those toys, they could check out three more. The cabinet contained toys (games, puzzles, etc.), but books were always available in each child's room. *Bonnie Lowe, Fremont, California*

WHEN NEW TOYS ARE ABUNDANT ✦ Whenever Christmas or birthdays come, my children receive a lot of toys. I let them play with them for a while and then I take some of them away and put them in the closet. If they get sick or the weather is bad, I take a toy out. They think it's new, and I save money and agony. *Rosary Liggieri, Paramus, New Jersey*

$$ A FRIENDLY TOY EXCHANGE ✦ Box up the toys that your child doesn't play with anymore and trade it for a box of toys that one of his friends doesn't play with anymore. Both kids will enjoy the discarded toys from their friend. *Anonymous*

◆◆◆

STORING TOYS

◆◆◆

$$ BABY-WIPE CONTAINERS ✦ We use empty baby-wipe containers to store all kinds of things, such as Barbie accessories, play money, marbles, etc. We cover the old baby-wipe label with pretty contact paper and put a label on the top as to the new contents. We then shelve them alphabetically. *Sabra Jiwa, Marietta, Georgia*

SHELVES ARE BETTER THAN TOY CHESTS ✦ I got rid of my son's toy box and put up bookcases and shelves. I found that, with shelves, he is a lot neater and has easier access to the toys. *Debra Carangelo, East Haven, Connecticut*

FLOOR - TO - CEILING STUFFED ANIMALS ✦ An excellent way to display stuffed animals in a child's room without using a lot of space is to hang them on a vertical pole. I bought a regular closet pole with two end attachments (just like in your closet) which was the length of the floor to the ceiling. I secured the end pieces (one to the ceiling, the other to the floor) and began hanging stuffed animals with regular cup hooks. If you have a lot of stuffed animals you won't even see the pole. It's a great way to brighten up a room. *Patty Radley, Fremont, California*

$$ HAPPY-MEAL BOXES ✦ We save the "Happy Meal" boxes from fast-food restaurants. Children find many uses for them, including a good holder for their small toys. *Jennifer Bystrzak, Tonawanda, New York*

PICTURE LABELS SHOW WHERE TOYS BE-LONG ✦ Cut out the picture of the toy from the box it came in, and place this as a label where the toy belongs. Even toddlers can put their toys away if they can match the toy with its picture. *Sharon Marriott, Livermore, California*

STACKABLES FOR TOYS ✦ We use stackable baskets (various brands available) for all small toys. They are easy for a child to use and add color to a room. *Pat Remmes, Walnut Creek, California*

FOR ODDS AND ENDS ✦ We store our daughter's small toys and odds and ends that accumulate in an appropriate-sized plastic trash can. There are colored ones to match any decor. This has solved cleanup for our two-year-old. Now she dumps the toys out—plays with them—then dumps them back in! Cleanup is a cinch—just "trash it"! Also, if we can't find some little something, we know we can usually go straight to that trash can to find it. *Sabra Jiwa, Marietta, Georgia*

 Be careful with buckets, pails, and trash cans around infants and toddlers; they can fall in headfirst and be injured.

INSIDE/OUTSIDE TOYS ✦ Together, the children and I determined which toys were outside toys and which ones were inside toys. We made a rule that outside toys had to stay outside and vice versa. To store small outside toys, we kept a large laundry basket in the backyard. *Bonnie Lowe, Fremont, California*

❖❖

QUICK CLEANUP

❖❖

CLEANUP BAG ❖ If you have to clean up in a hurry (say, under five minutes), grab some brown grocery bags. Just tear around the house filling up the grocery bags with everything you want to put away. Stash the bags in the basement or closet and sort them out some other time. This has an added advantage of being attractive to children as a kind of game—who can fill up the most bags or who can do it the fastest. In under five minutes you can have your house looking all shipshape. *Gail Lynch, Washington, D.C.*

SPREAD A SHEET BEFORE PLAYTIME ❖ My mother has a clever idea that speeds up cleaning my three-year-old sister's room. She always spreads a sheet on the floor *before* my sister plays with her toys. Then, when it's time to clean up, she gathers up the corners of the sheet and picks all the toys up at once. *R.G., Waterbury, Connecticut*

This works especially well for small toys such as blocks and Legos.

TOY PICKUP—BY WAGON ❖ When toys clutter the entire house, we pull a wagon around in which we collect the toys to be put away. It sure saves time and steps. *Angie Satterfield, Patriot, Indiana*

TOYS—UPSTAIRS AND DOWNSTAIRS ❖ If the children's bedrooms are upstairs, let them each bring down a basket of toys in the morning and take them back up at bedtime. It saves a lot of trips up and down the stairs. *Kim VanGorder, Cary, North Carolina*

OPEN WIDE FOR THE CHOO-CHOO (Tips from the Kitchen)

◆

A man finds out what is meant by a spitting image when he tries to feed cereal to his infant.
— I M O G E N E F E Y, quoted in *Violets & Vitriol,*
ed., J. Cooper and T. Hartman, 1980

The kitchen and the dining areas are the hubs of most homes, the places where a myriad of activities takes place. My wife and I used to have a kitchen and dining room where the primary activities were cooking and eating, but this changed drastically when we had children. Now, our primary activities are NEGOTIATING ("If you eat all your chicken, one more piece of broccoli, and drink your milk, you may be excused"), PLAYING FOOD GAMES (our last resort is what we call "Disneyland bites": mimicking rides at Disneyland using spoonfuls of food which end up in the child's mouth), and CLEANING (mainly sweeping up crushed Cheerios—that *we* stepped on).

When I think about the word "kitchen" now, I immediately associate it with dirty dishes, endless chores, and my young daughters. Guess which one of the three causes the other two? I marvel at the quickness with which my children can create so many separate messes, scattered around the kitchen floor like little land mines. As a toddler, our second daughter used to throw her plate on the floor (usually with food still on it) to signal that she had finished her meal. Later, she would demonstrate the baby sport of throwing four clean utensils on the floor in the same amount of time it took my wife or me to wash, dry and put away one.

Children are born comedians, and they seem to save their best routines for the kitchen or dining room. It's where our first daughter wore a hat for the first time; unfortunately, it was her upside-down plate of pasta. Her younger sister, as a toddler, was even funnier. She cleverly waited until all eyes were closed during grace before she sneaked food from the plate of her unsuspecting sister. I guess she knew that most of her own food would end up on the floor or at the bottom of her food-catching bib.

The following kitchen tips, ranging from food shopping to preventing kitchen messes, were selected for their convenience and practicality. The first section has some great Food and Kitchen Tips. It's followed by Feeding Baby, The Finicky Eater, and Dining Out.

Bon appetit!

◆

FOOD AND KITCHEN TIPS

A KITCHEN DRAWER FOR KIDS ✦ My mom gave me the idea of giving my young son access to a bottom drawer full of utensils he can play with: big spoons, spatulas, etc. He loves playing with these "kitchen toys," which keep him occupied while I'm cooking. *Beth Hier, Rutland, Vermont*

A FAIR DEAL ✦ To avoid fights and arguments over which child gets a bigger piece of pie, cake, or other item, I have one child divide the piece, while the other child gets first choice. *Craig Jackson, Fremont, California, and J. R., Covington, Kentucky*

LEARNING SHAPES WITH FOOD ✦ My children learned about various shapes by cutting their sandwiches with safe plastic knives. They loved to cut their sandwiches into rectangles, triangles, squares, and numbers. Not only did they learn about shapes, but they ate their food better when it was cut in fancy shapes. *M.R. Kelly, Rawlins, Wyoming*

SELF-SERVE SNACKS ✦ In order to give my two-year-old food throughout the day when I am busy with housework, I leave a small bowl of snacks in the refrigerator. He knows how to open the door, get his snacks, and close the door again. This keeps him busy with little nutritious snacks he likes and also gives me time to get my household chores done. *D.W., Memphis, Tennessee*

PHOTOS KEEP BABY BUSY IN KITCHEN ✦ A good means of entertaining older babies (and helping to give them a sense of their identity and their place in the world) is photographs. We keep an envelope of less-than-perfect snapshots near our daughter's high chair for her to exclaim and giggle over after meals, thus affording us a few more minutes—sometimes many more minutes—to eat in peace. *Melanie Lawrence, Portland, Oregon*

"I WANT TO HELP CUT THE VEGGIES" ✦ When children want to help cut vegetables, let them use a pumpkin-carving knife; it is safe and it does the job. *Arlene Stocking, Fremont, California*

SCISSORS MAKE CUTTING FOOD EASY ✦ Scissors are better than knives for cutting up food in small pieces for children. A nice pair pf kitchen shears works much faster than a knife and fork, especially when cutting up food like pizza or French toast. *Wendy Ericsson, Lansdale, Pennsylvania, and Cathleen Warner, Gap, Pennsylvania*

PIZZA CUTTERS ✦ Using a pizza cutter (wheel type) to cut up children's food (bread, waffles, etc.) in small, bite-size pieces is not only convenient—it's quick. *Lori Nye, Clinton, Utah*

THE REFRIGERATOR IS A GOOD HIDING PLACE ✦ My toddler can't open the refrigerator door because it's too heavy. So when he decides to play with something that is unsafe or something with which he has misbehaved, I put it in the refrigerator. It's better than putting it on a high shelf to which he could drag a chair, climb up, and get the item anyway. *Joyce Serocke, Mission Viejo, California*

FUN PLACE MATS ✦ Knowing the proper way to set a table is an important part of learning table manners. Take a solid-color vinyl place mat and outline plate, fork, knife, and spoon with a permanent black marker. Cover the place mats with clear contact paper. Children enjoy matching up the right utensils on the outlined place mats. And you don't have to set the table. *Debbie Anderson, Fremont, California*

"LAPKINS" GO ON YOUR LAP ✦ Call a napkin a "*lap*kin" as a reminder of where it belongs during a meal. *Tracy LaVelle, Fremont, California*

COLOR-CODED WASHCLOTHS ✦ Keep a few inexpensive washcloths in the kitchen. They work better than a dishcloth on dirty hands and faces. Use a different color for each child to cut down on germs when someone is sick. *Kim VanGorder, Cary, North Carolina*

HOLIDAY TABLE DECORATIONS ✦ On special family days or holidays, ask the children to make decorations and a centerpiece for the table. It's a great way to show their art as a real "centerpiece." *Anonymous, California*

A CANDLE AT DINNER ✦ I've noticed that my children are less fidgety and stay at the dinner table longer when we have a candle on the table. At times, they seem to be mesmerized by it. *Judith Woodland, Lansing, Michigan*

 Use proper caution anytime you use candles around children.

SELF-SERVE BREAKFAST ✦ When my son was a preschooler, he would awaken before dawn wanting his cold cereal and milk. Because he was too little to pour his own milk from a large container, I came up with the idea of pouring milk in a cup and setting it on a low shelf in the refrigerator. Before bedtime, he would help get a bowl of cereal and a spoon ready at his place at the table. Early the next morning, he would eat his cereal and go back to bed. *Jean Bodlak, Emerson, Nebraska*

Make sure the child is old enough (at least four years old) to take responsibility for this task.

MICKEY MOUSE PANCAKES ♦ For a great birthday or anytime breakfast, make one medium-size pancake and then add batter for two smaller "ears." Use a tube of cake-decorating icing gell to make eyes, nose, and mouth. For Minnie Mouse pancakes, add a hair bow and earrings. *Stacey Lopez, Fremont, California*

TIGER PANCAKES ♦ My daughter is a picky eater, but she loves to eat foods in fancy shapes. For breakfast, I place cookie cutters (animal shapes) in the fry pan and pour pancake batter in the cutter. She won't eat plain pancakes, but she will eat "tiger pancakes." *Panna Tailor, Fremont, California*

$$ PANCAKE "COOKIES" ♦ When you have leftover pancake batter, make pancakes out of tablespoons of batter. Put the little pancakes into the oven on a cookie sheet at 250 degrees F. for fifteen minutes on each side. When they are cool, store them in an airtight plastic container. They make excellent, almost sugar-free cookies for teethers through toddlers. Best of all, they come free with breakfast! Sometimes I make up a half batch of batter and make sixty to seventy little pancakes. This makes a two-month supply of cookies for very little money. If you make them ahead, freeze some of them. If they are moist when thawed, put them in a 250-degree F. oven for about ten minutes to rid them of the excess moisture. *Brenda Capone, Stamford, Connecticut*

HOT CEREAL ♦ My two-year-old daughter gets frustrated and often burns her tongue waiting for her hot cereal to cool. Stirring in an ice cube (or two) both cools the cereal quickly and improves the creaminess of the texture. *Nancy Lee, Pasadena, California*

SORRY—KITCHEN IS CLOSED ♦ Our dear ones ask for snack foods all day long. To limit their requests, I put up a big colorful sign which they designed saying "Kitchen is Closed until 5:00 P.M." It works! *Joan Lyboult, Syracuse, New York*

Make sure that children have access to adequate food and liquids after strenuous activities.

KIDS SAY THE FUNNIEST THINGS

When my oldest child was five years old, I caught him with his hand in the canister of chocolate chips. He was quite surprised when I walked into the kitchen and asked him what he thought he was doing. He promptly replied, "I was just going to count them for you." *Linda McKay, Albuquerque, New Mexico*

A LIST OF THINGS TO EAT ⬥ My children were always asking, "What is there to eat?" The refrigerator door always seemed to be open as they scanned the food inside. My solution was to write a list of everything available in the refrigerator (leftovers, sandwich spreads, veggies, fruits, etc.). I left this list on the table with paper plates. If a child ate a particular food item, she would cross it off the list. This new practice also worked effectively when we had houseguests. It gets Mom out of the kitchen. *Judith Schmidt, Crawfordsville, Indiana*

ADVENTURE DINNER ⬥ As working parents with two youngsters, we would periodically look for some respite from meal preparation by the end of the work week. As an alternative to fast-food restaurants we developed the "Adventure Dinner," which consisted of going to the supermarket and allocating each child an amount of money to select and purchase their dinner for the evening. They did not select just "junk food," and learned to pool their resources for sharing, gained some knowledge of food costs and monetary values, and, with their parents' help, information on nutrition. *Neil McCallum, Fremont, California*

PIZZA NIGHT ⬥ For years, each Friday night at our house was "Pizza Night." This was the night my boys knew they could invite a guest (without seeking permission), eat pizza, and have soda with their meal. For this to work, the parent must be committed to upholding this weekly event. It's worth it; it stops begging during the week to have "so and so" eat over, and it stops requests for pizza and soda on weeknights! *Sue Crockett, Charlton, Massachusetts*

PIZZAS ARE FUN TO "DECORATE" ✦ Make your own or buy a cheese pizza. Have each child be responsible for decorating the pizza with one topping. They love to participate. *Robin Bunton, Fremont, California*

"IS THIS A DESSERT NIGHT?" ✦ Our children begged us for dessert every evening after dinner, until my wife and I asked them to pick two evenings a week on which they could have dessert. They picked Wednesday and Saturday. Now, they only request dessert on those evenings, which are extra-special times. *T.L., Mi-Wuk Village, California*

PLAY DOUGH PICKS UP GLASS SLIVERS ✦ When a glass breaks on the floor, it is difficult to pick up all the small pieces and slivers with a broom. I use a small piece of play dough or regular flour dough to pick up the smallest pieces of glass. I even once used dough to pick glass slivers off my son's skin when he had an accident with a glass tabletop. Remember to always throw away the dough immediately after using it. *K.N., Fremont, California*

TONGUE DEPRESSORS ARE SAFER THAN KNIVES ✦ For a young child who wants to spread the butter on his toast by himself, have him use tongue-depressor sticks. *A.V.S., Fremont, California*

HALLOWEEN CAKE ✦ One Halloween, we bought cupcakes with plastic Halloween decorations. I saved the decorations, and my children and I now make a Halloween pumpkin-patch cake every year. We bake a flat single layer cake (orange colored, if possible) and frost with chocolate frosting. Then we use green decorator icing to make "pumpkin vines" on top of the icing. We finish by putting in the "pumpkin patch"—that is the bakery's plastic pumpkins, black cats, and other Halloween decorations. *Nancy Knowlton, Wilmette, Illinois*

 Be careful that the plastic pumpkins aren't small enough to be swallowed or aspirated by small children.

COOKIE ART ✦ My children enjoy painting sugar cookies or piecrust before I bake them. We mix paint out of 1 egg yolk, ¼ teaspoon water, and several drops of food coloring (the egg-yolk-and-water mixture can be divided before adding food coloring to make lesser amounts of several colors). They use watercolor paintbrushes to paint with and I bake as usual. The paint darkens and becomes shiny when baked. We enjoy sharing our "custom" creations as gifts. *Anonymous, Pasadena, California*

COOKIE DECORATING ✦ I have three girls and to prevent fighting over cookie decorating, I divide everything up. Each girl gets the same amount of cookies and an equal amount of each color of frosting in foam egg-carton containers that have been cut apart. They have their own set of Q-tips and clean paintbrushes to apply the frosting and then add various candy decorations. It works great! Everyone has fun and there is no bickering. *Beverly Killion, Anaheim, California*

TREAT BASKET ✦ Children often receive too much candy during the holidays and at other times from relatives and friends. We solved the problem of controlling their eating of all those sweets by buying them each a very special "Treat Basket" where they keep all of their goodies. Each child is allowed to choose a treat from his basket after dinner if he has eaten a good supper. They love having this secret stash (they keep it hidden behind cupboard doors) and have learned to govern and control their own sweet tooths. *Audrey Swanton, Brewer, Maine*

FEEDING BABY

TWO SPOONS ARE BETTER THAN ONE ✦ I feed the baby with at least two small spoons, so that she can grab and hold one while I feed her with the other. The

feeding process goes much faster this way. *Kimberly Weiss, Bloomington, Indiana*

Good trick! It also works when trying to brush your child's teeth. Give him a toothbrush to hold so he won't try to grab yours.

HANG ON TO THAT SPOON! ✦ When feeding a baby under slippery circumstances, a parent will find that a baby spoon is much easier to hang on to if the handle has been bent down and under. *S.B.K., Westport, Connecticut*

DIVIDED DISHES ARE BEST ✦ I recommend using a Tupperware divided candy dish (or something similar) to place food on when your child is learning how to use a spoon. It's plastic and divided into three equal parts with high sides, which makes it easy to scoop food up with the spoon. *Marsha Meckler, Honolulu, Hawaii*

TRAINING CUPS ✦ If your baby's training cup has two holes (one to drink from and an extra one), cover the extra one with masking tape when your child is just starting out. It makes the drink come out slower and means less mess. *Kim VanGorder, Cary, North Carolina*

Make sure the tape doesn't come off and end up in baby's mouth.

PRACTICE CUP DRINKING IN TUB ✦ Frequent spills accompany the new skill of using a cup. I suggest letting the baby practice drinking (with clean water, of course) with a cup in the tub at bath time. This is also a good time for the baby to practice pouring and dumping—a favorite pastime of babies. *Suzie Schmidt, St. Louis, Missouri*

"LET ME HOLD THE CUP MYSELF" ✦ I thought my son would never learn to use a cup. I always held the cup to his lips, but he would refuse it. One day my sister told me how impressed she was that my son drinks out of a cup. "But he has to hold it himself," she said. Sure enough, when I give him a cup now he drinks like a pro. *Chris Stanley, Bloomington, Indiana*

NONSLIP HIGH-CHAIR SEAT ✦ When my kids first started to sit in the high chair, they were constantly slipping under the tray. We solved the problem when my husband put the sponge for the baby bath on the high-chair seat and sat the baby on that. They don't slip, they sit up higher in the chair, and the sponge can be thrown in the washing machine. *Sheryl Saxton, Tekamah, Nebraska*

RUBBER MAT PREVENTS SLIPS ✦ We put a rubber sink mat on the high-chair seat so our baby doesn't slide off. *Karen Platt-Clark, Rochester, New York*

INTRODUCING NEW FOODS TO BABY ✦ If your baby is not very receptive to eating meat for the first time, dunk a spoon of meat into another food that he likes (like bananas or applesauce). This little trick will get him used to the new taste and texture of the meat and within no time the child will readily eat meat without any disguise. *Sherry Broom, Cantonment, Florida*

WON'T WEAR BIB ✦ If your children won't let you put a bib on them, use a larger-size T-shirt to cover their clothes. They're usually more comfortable, and if it's long enough it will cover their shirts and pants. A print of a Disney or Sesame Street character on the T-shirt will make it even more desirable. *Fran Friedman, New City, New York*

COMFORTABLE BODY ARMOR ✦ We really like the hard plastic bib with the permanent pocket but it seemed uncomfortable to our baby. I put a soft cloth bib under the hard plastic bib, for comfort and to catch liquids running down the chin and neck. *Peg Hartley, San Bernardino, California*

$$ ICE-CUBE BABY FOOD ✦ Save money and serve more nutritional food by grinding or blending your own baby food. Make large quantities that will fill a plastic ice-cube tray and place it in the freezer. Once frozen, store the cubes in freezer bags. Defrost one or two cubes in the microwave for a quick nutritious meal. *M. Ring, Concord, New Hampshire*

$$ WEEKLY COOKING FOR BABY ✦ Once a week I sauté three kinds of meat (ground chuck, ground turkey, and chicken), then prepare three starches (noodles, rice, and mashed potatoes) and three vegetables (carrots, peas, and broccoli). I puree each food in the blender to the same consistency of store-bought baby food. I place each food in a separate bowl from which I make combos of the nine foods. Each serving is weighed in seven-ounce portions and frozen in freezer bags. This makes enough for the whole week. I thaw each day as needed. My son loves them! *Mary Hubbell, Urbana, Illinois*

$$ HOMEMADE CHICKEN-SOUP BABY FOOD ✦ To make baby food, I start with a big pot of soup. I usually use chicken, but do occasionally use different meats. I throw in carrots, green beans, and other veggies, then let the soup cook until it gets tender. I spoon out the meat and veggies and blend them in the food processor. I use the soup juice to thin it. Then I spoon it into ice-cube trays, freeze, and transfer the cubes into Ziploc freezer bags for future use. *Doris and Luann Stuart, Fort Pierce, Florida*

PLASTIC CHAIR MAT UNDER HIGH CHAIRS ✦ A plastic floor mat, the kind made for a desk chair (available at office-products stores), is the perfect thing to place under the high chair in a carpeted dining room. It will protect your carpet from food stains and liquid spills. *S.L., Martinez, California*

VINYL TABLECLOTHS PROTECT FLOORS, TOO ✦ A good use for old vinyl tablecloths is to put one under the high chair to catch the drips and spills. When my son got older I would put one down when he used play dough or paint. *Debra Randall, East Haven, Connecticut*

THE FINICKY EATER

Every child will be finicky about food at one time or another, and every parent will at least occasionally experience food battles with their children. Serving a balanced diet is of utmost importance for your growing child, but there are other issues to keep in mind too.

Always make sure that you serve reasonable quantities of food that is appropriate to your child's age and level of hunger. And try not to put too much emphasis on "eating all your food" or "cleaning up your plate." Children have likes and dislikes just like grown-ups. Make mealtime a social event that your child looks forward to, not an event to avoid.

"THAT'S TOO MUCH FOOD" ✦ If you have a child who complains of "too much" food on his plate and he's no longer hungry, try taking the same portions of food and serving them on a larger plate or platter. It works, believe me. The eye often fools the tummy! *Arlene Stocking, Fremont, California*

"YOU HAVE TO TRY TWO BITES" ✦ If my son didn't think he would like some particular food, we had a rule that he had to try at least two bites. If he still didn't like it, he didn't have to eat it again for two months. Then, we would try it again. As he got older, there were very few foods he wouldn't eat. *Anonymous, Orange, California*

SMALL FOOD PIECES ARE MORE APPETIZING ✦ Three- and four-year-olds love quantities. My three-year-old often wanted two pieces of bread when I knew he would only eat one. To avoid a power struggle, I'd cut the bread in half. He'd have his two pieces, and peace reigned in the household. *Carolyn Mosser, York, Pennsylvania*

LET'S MAKE A DEAL ✦ When our daughter was about six years old, she became very finicky about food—driving her mother up a wall with her likes and dislikes. For example, she hated cabbage, but loved coleslaw. My wife finally allowed her to name any three foods that she did not want to eat. At no time and under no circumstances would she have to eat them, but she would have to eat everything else served to her. From that point on, any time our daughter balked at eating something, my savvy wife would say, "No problem, that's one of the three items you don't have to eat." "Oh no," replied our daughter, "I'm not going to waste one of my three choices on this!" And she promptly ate as she should have. Over a period of two years our daughter at no time exercised her right to exempt three foods! She was so concerned and so protective of her three exemptions that she ate normally of everything else served to her! *Fen Seton, North Haven, Connecticut*

RISING TO A CHALLENGE ✦ When I don't think my child has eaten enough of his meal and he wants to be excused from the table, I challenge him to eat more. "I bet you can't eat ten more peas." "Oh, yes I can," he replies as he scoops up the peas. *Cynthia Baird, Fremont, California*

CHILD-SIZE HAMBURGER BUNS ✦ I have found in my many years of teaching preschool that younger children are much less daunted by and more apt to eat a hamburger which is scaled down to their size. So, I use refrigerator biscuits for children's hamburger buns and make small meat patties to match. *Arlene Stocking, Fremont, California*

VEGGIES IN SMALL AMOUNTS ✦ I have found that a good way to get children to enjoy vegetables is to give a three-year-old three beans, three peas, or three corn kernels, a four-year-old four beans, peas, or corn kernels, etc. The children will learn to like these by getting just a few at a time, and they can always ask for more if they finish. It worked with my children and my grandchildren. Now they all eat vegetables. *Marion Fisher, Jamestown, California*

LESS FOOD ON THE PLATE ✦ My one-year-old son is overwhelmed by a lot of food on the plate in front of him and just messes it about. But he will eat for a long time if served one or two bites or pieces at a time. *P.H., Albany, California*

WHEN CHILDREN WANT A SECOND HELPING ✦ If my children want a second helping of one food, but they haven't finished another food on their plate, I have them eat a few bites of the food on their plate first. Ask a two-year-old to eat two more bites, and a six-year-old to eat six more bites. *Janet Dudey, Fremont, California*

"IF YOU WANT A SECOND SERVING . . ." ✦ After serving a small amount of each food item for a meal, ask the child to eat all (or some) of his first servings before he can have a second serving of his choice. The key to this being successful is to give *small first servings. Julia Kiely, Irvine, California*

CHILDREN LOVE FROZEN VEGGIES ✦ Children who are not fond of cooked vegetables will often eat veggies when they have been frozen hard. Frozen veggies have a different taste and texture than their cooked counterparts. *Julie Cochran, Lakewood, Colorado*

APPEALING VEGGIES ✦ For the veggies that our children don't care for, we get out the different salad dressings, pour a little of each in different bowls, and enjoy quite a feast, dipping away. I have found that melted cheese will make almost any veggie more appealing. *Angie Satterfield, Patriot, Indiana*

Let them also discover the wonderful natural flavor of veggies—without the high fat content on top.

GREEN FRENCH TOAST (OR GREEN EGGS AND HAM) ◆ Help for a fussy eater. Put green food dye in the egg mix before making French toast. It makes eating more interesting. *Gail Lynch, Washington, D.C.*

PINK MASHED POTATOES ◆ Children will eat pink mashed potatoes. Add a tiny bit of food coloring; it really works! *Donna Sanson, Fremont, California*

IS IT A MUFFIN OR IS IT ZUCCHINI? ◆ I cleverly disguise vegetables in tiny bite-size muffins made with a little sugar, whole-wheat flour, and egg substitute. They are highly nutritious and great tasting. Moms and dads love them too! *Vicki Schrimmer, Irvine, California*

GROWN-UP TASTE BUDS ◆ When my son was little, he didn't want to try new foods. He would ask, "Did I ever have this before?" and I would quite often say, "Yes, you did, but you didn't like it. Only adults like this. Maybe your taste buds are developed now enough so that you will like it. So try just a little, and if you don't like it, then we'll wait until you are older because taste buds develop at different rates." Since he always wanted to be grown up, he was always willing to try to see if he had grown up enough to like this certain food. *Ginger Alderson, Albuquerque, New Mexico*

MY DAUGHTER WOULD NOT DRINK HER MILK ◆ Upon turning two, my daughter, Lauren, began inventing "stall" techniques to delay bedtime. What a treat it was when Mommy invented her own "stall" technique, suggesting Lauren could have some milk prior to tucking in. (Lauren is not a milk drinker.) Making it as attractive as possible, Lauren could have her choice of a special cup and straw and even sit up on the counter! Each day my daughter asks for her milk at bedtime. And sometimes to make it more special, I join her with a cup of milk of my own. *Julie A. Beard, Felton, Pennsylvania*

 Don't forget to brush your child's teeth before bedtime, or the nasty cavity bugs will go to work while she sleeps.

FUN NAMES FOR FOOD

We've found that our children will eat some foods they otherwise wouldn't eat if we give them a "fun" name: pork and beans is called **"cowboy beans"**; tuna is **"chicken of the sea"**; and sloppy joes are **"Barbie's barbecue."** *Carol A. Nelson, Memphis, Tennessee*

◆

Peanut butter rolled up inside lettuce leaves are called **"rock and roll lettuce."** Chicken wings are called **"pterodactyl wings."** Add mayonnaise to broccoli to create **"snow-covered Christmas trees."** *A.V.S., Fremont, California*

◆

To get kids to eat broccoli, I tell them that they are **little trees.** *Ann Hersey, Vista, California*

◆

My children enjoyed calling split-pea soup **"seaweed soup."** *Deanna Stemm, Fremont, California*

◆

My children wouldn't eat peas until I called them **"bird eggs in the nest"** (peas in a cavity of mashed potatoes). *Ann Horvatich, Merrillville, Indiana*

CHILDREN ALWAYS EAT FANCY FOODS ✦ Years ago when my daughter was little, I used my hors d'oeuvres cutters to cut out some fancy shapes of bread and cheese— she loved it. Whenever I had young children over for a special-occasion lunch, I would put out bread, bologna, thin-sliced ham, sliced bananas, etc.—anything I could cut with a cutter. They, and now my grandchildren, enjoyed cutting their own lunches into fancy shapes. You can also use number or letter cutters to spell their names. Keep a toothpick or something similar on hand to poke out the food from the little cutters. Use a cutting board at the table. *Mrs. Charles L. Osborn, Los Altos Hills, California*

A "SURPRISE MESSAGE" ON THEIR PLATE ✦ Occasionally, I would serve dinner on paper plates. Before serving the food (always in reasonable quantities), I would write a surprise message on the bottom of the plate (you get first selection for TV tonight, you can skip your chore tonight, etc.). If they ate all their dinner, they were allowed to read the surprise on the plate. It sure motivated them to finish their dinner. *Honey Bentley, Laingsburg, Michigan*

DINING OUT

RESTAURANT FUN ✦ When taking a child to a restaurant, bring along some small toys or a coloring book and crayons to keep the child occupied until dinner is served. *Sam Crescente, Glendale, New York*

TOYS ONLY FOR THE RESTAURANT ✦ A friend of mine has discovered a great way to have a peaceful dining-out experience with a toddler. She has a bag of Hot Wheels cars that is only accessible to her toddler son when they dine out. Since he's not able to play with these often, he doesn't get bored with them quickly, and his parents are

able to have a pleasant experience at the restaurant.
Sherry Broom, Cantonment, Florida

ICE CUBE ON DINNER TRAY ✦ When eating out
with a baby, give the baby an ice cube on the high-chair
tray. It saves the waitress from having to clean up cracker
crumbs. Babies are fascinated watching it change from ice
cube to water. It keeps the child occupied and makes for a
relatively easy cleanup. *Marilyn Summerford, Virginia
Beach, Virginia*

Watch carefully so the baby won't choke on a small
cube.

A QUARTER FOR ORDERING WATER ✦ I give my
daughter a quarter if she orders water at a restaurant.
That way, she drinks something better for her, we save
money on a soft drink, and she thinks she has got it made
because she gets paid for drinking water. *Sharon Arnold,
Lexington, Kentucky*

RESTAURANT NAPKINS ✦ I bring along clothespins
when we go to a restaurant. I put the restaurant table napkin around my child's neck and clip it on like a bib to protect the clothes from getting soiled. *Elyse Screnci, Brooklyn, New York*

EATING OUT WITH CHILDREN ✦ When going to a
restaurant which requires a waiting period, we go into the
lounge and order an appetizer for the child. The child will
quietly eat the appetizer and sip on a glass of juice as we
relax with our calm child. When our name is called, sometimes up to an hour later, we go into the restaurant and
since an appetizer for an adult really is an entire meal for
a child, the child can at that point enjoy a leisurely time
over a dessert while the parents eat their dinner. We have
taken children to very fancy restaurants and this has kept
them very calm. *Lisa Beard, Annapolis, Maryland*

3

ADVENTURES IN THE BATHROOM

◆

'Tis easier to prevent bad habits than to break them.

— BENJAMIN FRANKLIN, *Poor Richard's Almanac, 1745*

My two-and-a-half-year-old sat perched on her potty seat, gripping its front splash guard with her left hand while her right hand banged away on the roll of toilet paper hanging next to her. I sat opposite her on the cold, hard porcelain rim of the tub, waiting for the facial expressions and distinctive sounds that would mean success was near. But those hoped-for signs never came. By the time I gave up in frustration, most of the roll of toilet paper had unraveled into a surprisingly neat pile on the floor. This scene, or a similar one, is replayed in most households as we parents try to conquer one of the true milestones of childhood (and parenthood): potty training.

My wife and I wasted many hours in fruitless waiting like that described above, frustrating ourselves and both our daughters in the process. We had mistakenly assumed they were "ready" for toilet training when they really weren't. Perhaps we were overanxious ourselves, or we listened to other parents who claimed potty success with *their* child at twenty months or less. Or maybe we were just tired of changing all those diapers.

Our experience has taught us that it is better to relax and wait, because no matter what you do, your child will potty train at her own pace and in her own way. So it is important to follow the child's lead instead of setting the pace. A key sign of potty readiness is for the child to be able to anticipate having a bowel movement or urinating. And when you do

46

begin training, keep in mind that setbacks are both normal and common.

Of course, potty training is not the only "adventure" that occurs in the bathroom. Don't miss the sections with tips on "Staying Dry Through the Night," "Personal Hygiene and Grooming," and "Bath Time." There are even some suggestions on making your bathroom more convenient and practical for your children to use. Dental-care tips are listed in Chapter 8 (Health and Safety).

◆

POTTY TRAINING

DIAPER LIMIT ◆ The week before I decided to try going to underpants, I told my son that I only had a week's worth of diapers left for the daytime and after that time he could only wear diapers at night. So every day we would count down how many diapers were left. After they were all gone he was told that he had to wear underpants. We spent the next couple of days in the kitchen so that if there were some accidents it really didn't matter. We had all kinds of fun things planned. Potty training only took two days. *Lynne Bassett, Fremont, California*

NO MORE DIAPERS ◆ During the first weeks after she was potty trained, our two-and-a-half-year-old daughter would still ask for her diapers, which were stored in the garage. I asked her to pick one of her younger friends still in diapers to whom she could give her leftover diapers. She did so, and we made a grand occasion of her presenting the diapers to her friend. She felt so grown-up. She never asked to wear her diapers again but instead spoke proudly of how she had given her diapers to her friend. *N.K.M., Palo Alto, California*

A POTTY ROLE MODEL ✦ Children learn by watching, so take them with you when you use the bathroom. I started doing this when my children were infants. I have three kids and they were all potty trained by the time they turned two. Even if I got them a training seat, they wanted to go into the bathroom. They knew what the bathroom was for. *Lucy Bodola, Yonkers, New York*

A YOUNGER FRIEND INSPIRED SUCCESS ✦ Our two-and-a-half-year-old son had no interest in becoming potty trained until he met Elizabeth, who was already potty trained at two years old. He suddenly became interested in the toilet and became potty trained almost entirely by himself. Peer role models at least inspire interest in new things. *Peg Maddocks, Los Gatos, California*

A PICTURE IS WORTH A THOUSAND WORDS ✦ I had little luck potty training my daughter until I pinned up a poster in the bathroom. In the middle of the plain white poster was a photo of my daughter sitting and smiling on her potty seat. Each time she was successful on the potty, she was allowed to pick a colorful sticker and place it on the poster. She loves stickers and enjoyed filling up the poster with them. She knew what she was being rewarded for since the picture of her on the potty was the focal point of the poster. *Anonymous, San Diego, California*

MAGIC TOILET WATER ✦ My daughter, once potty trained, decided it was entirely too much effort to stop playing and go to the bathroom. We went through months of frustration with "accidents," which were really sheer laziness or lack of interest on her part. Then one day I purchased a blue toilet-bowl cleaner which is installed in the tank. When we arrived home from the store, my daughter showed great interest in this new gadget. She shrilled with delight when the water magically turned from clear to a beautiful dark blue. Since I had not previously used these cleaners, she had many questions about the purpose of this new installation. I told her this was "magic water" for kids who tinkle in the toilet, and each time she went potty in the toilet, the water would change from blue to green. The look on her face was one of excitement and marvel. As it turned out, it was "magic water." And for two thousand flushes we heard screams of delight, "Mommy, Daddy, look, I turned the water green!" From that day forward, she would run in from outdoor play, explaining as she whirled past me, "I'm gonna go turn that water green." I'm proud to say this simple procedure prevented all accidents and as the magic wore off, the habit became established. *Jeanne R. Watts, Omaha, Nebraska*

KIDS SAY THE FUNNIEST THINGS

My three-year-old daughter has learned how to use her own potty, but has not shown any interest in the big toilet. One day I walked into the bathroom and there she was—on the big toilet. I said, "What a big girl!" She replied, "I didn't want to get poopoo in my potty." *K. Sheldon, Newbury Park, California*

BOTTOMLESS TODDLER ✦ When potty training our son, we found it useful to let him run around bottomless outside (I do stress outside). This allowed him to relate the appropriate body part to the discharge. It did get a little messy at times, but it proved to be very effective. *Polly Morehouse Griffith, Santa Rosa, California*

JUST TURN ON THE FAUCET ✦ My mother toilet trained my son quickly by turning on the faucet as he stood in front of the toilet and asking him to make water run just like the sink. *V.L.C., Santa Clara, California*

RUNNING BATH WATER "INSPIRES" SUCCESS ON POTTY ✦ I always sat my child on the toilet seat while I ran the bath water. The sound of the water "inspired" my child to perform on the potty. It worked great. *Rita Wilson, Fremont, California*

"JUST LIKE MOMMY" ✦ After she was potty trained, our daughter would feel bad when she would have an accident. When an accident occurred, I would tell her the story my mother had once told me about an accident I had had in grand proportions when I was very little. My daughter always laughed and felt better about herself knowing that Mommy had had the same problem! *Nancy Knowlton, Wilmette, Illinois*

POTTY TIMER ✦ Children don't like to be asked if they need to go to the potty, and parents often forget to remind them until it's too late. I suggest setting a timer to ring, and when it does, it is potty time. That way Mom or Dad is not the heavy "making" him go. *Barry Fellner II, Hilliard, Ohio*

POPSICLES WORKED FOR ME ♦ My child would never sit on the potty until I offered him a Popsicle. Now, whenever he sits on the potty chair I give him a Popsicle. He sits there until he finishes his Popsicle—and almost always "delivers" for the potty. *Anonymous, Santa Rosa, California*

TARGET PRACTICE ♦ At times, toilet training can be a frustrating endeavor. While a child may understand the mechanics of what is expected of him, he may find little incentive to put this knowledge to use. A friend of mine offered a novel solution for little boys. Place a few Cheerios in the toilet bowl and let him make it a game of "target practice." This can make toilet training fun and improve his accuracy at the same time. *Susie Norton, Manhattan, Montana*

SINK THOSE SHIPS ♦ I tell little boys to pretend that the Cheerios are ships that must be sunk. *Jerry Hancock, Davidson, North Carolina*

HIT THE PAPER ✦ When potty training our son, my husband would throw in a square of toilet paper into the toilet and say "Hit it first." That helped our son improve his aim and not spray it all around the room. *Karen Peters, Garden Grove, California*

A MOVING TARGET ✦ To potty train a male child, I put a Ping-Pong ball in the toilet and told him to try to hit it. Little boys are quite entertained by this. Of course, you need a little fishnet next to the toilet so that you can fish the Ping-Pong ball out later. *Adrienne Yingling, Raleigh, North Carolina*

TARGET PRACTICE WITH A TIN CAN ✦ My son was hard to potty train until I handed him a little tin can as a target. After that, he could hold the can himself and perform. *Ms. Jean Nielsen, Cut Bank, Montana*

STAND ON YOUR LUNCH BOX ✦ My son became frustrated using public rest rooms because he was too short to reach the top of the toilet bowl. My husband and I would hold him up next to the toilet, but he couldn't relax enough to urinate. My solution was to always bring his lunch box with us when we were away from home. I would place the lunch box on a paper towel next to the potty so he could stand on it and be high enough to use the potty. It worked great! *Patty Saunders, Huntington Beach, California*

DON'T FORGET TO PUT DOWN THE TOILET SEAT ✦ If one of my two little boys left the seat of the toilet up I would call them from whatever they were doing to put it down. They learned quickly. I never had to ask my husband because he got the idea from seeing me enforce a polite rule. Both boys now are thoughtful husbands. *Florence Grace, Fremont, California*

A REWARD OF M & M's ✦ M & M's worked great for my children as a reward for potty success. *M.J., New York City, New York*

A PARTY SONG FOR POTTY SUCCESS ✦ Our son was almost three years old and still having trouble potty training. He would go for days without having a bowel movement and we were afraid this was affecting his health.

Finally we came up with the idea of having a party for him if he went. Every time he would have a bowel movement in the potty, we would put a candle in a cupcake and sing "Happy Poop Day" to him. He thought it was great. Since then, friends have tried it with their children and it worked for them too. *Chris Bloomquist, Lincoln, Nebraska*

"ON DUTY" POTTY TRAINING ◆ It seemed too much of a burden for our young children to be aware of bodily functions *all* day as soon as they put "big pants" on. So, we let the kids wear their training pants about an hour at first and then asked if they wanted to go "Off Duty" and wear a diaper. After a while, we waited two hours; then we waited all morning. My daughter decided that she could be "On Duty" even at night after a couple of weeks. We suggested that she try over a nap time first, but agreed that she could try whenever she was ready. *Barry Fellner II, Hilliard, Ohio*

EVERY HOUR, ON THE HOUR ◆ I got this tip on potty training from a mother of seven children (three sets of twins and a single birth). When it came to potty training my child at age two, it took two days and that was it. I took his diapers off him the day I began training him, and, every hour on the hour, I put him on the potty. He was able to understand what I was doing and by the end of the first day, he never wet his pants. My friend said it worked for all seven of her children. She stayed home for the two days and didn't go shopping or do anything else which might disrupt the hourly schedule. *Lindie Gibson, Livingston, Montana*

PRACTICE POTTY TRAINING ◆ When going on outings children get excited and don't want to stop playing to use the rest room. Suddenly they will have an accident, which is embarrassing to them and a hassle to you. To avoid this, take the child to the rest room often, maybe every hour or so, with you. Explain that you're going to the potty and want him to go with you just for the company. When you are in the rest room, tell him to just practice going potty. Most of the time a child will actually use the potty because he doesn't feel like he is being forced to go. *Patty Reafsnyder, Garden Grove, California*

CHOICES AND CONTROL—THE KEY TO POTTY SUCCESS ◆ My two-and-a-half-year-old son was reluctant to sit on the potty for bowel movements. After getting fed up with soiled underwear, I offered him an alternative to the potty. If he felt a bowel movement coming and didn't want to use the potty, then he was to ask for a diaper. He would wear the diaper until he was finished, and then he would change back to underwear. After a few days of this (when he was sure of himself and comfortable with the current situation), I asked him to try to use the potty. I told him, "If you can't do it there, then we'll put on the diaper." I also told him that I would stay with him or give him his privacy (this gave him some control), whichever he preferred. He sat on the potty, waited a few minutes, and asked for his privacy. He succeeded and has been fine ever since. A few times I had to remind him that "Timmy can do it." The positive results came soon after I offered him choices which gave him some control over the situation. *Joan Nurge, Fremont, California*

TV TRAY NEXT TO POTTY ✦ When my three boys were being potty trained, they didn't want to just sit on the potty, so I put a TV tray in front of them with books or colors to keep them from getting bored while sitting there. They were usually successful with their potty training. *Cindy Staudt, Westminster, Colorado*

TOYS FOR THE POTTY CHAIR ✦ To offer my son an incentive to sit on the potty, I had a plastic colander with special toys that we kept in the bathroom. He could play with these toys only while sitting on the potty. *Jayme Trolle, Fremont, California*

One of the tricks to this tip is to keep rotating the potty toys. If a child gets bored with the toys, the incentive will cease being effective.

POTTY-TRAINING INCENTIVE ✦ Purchase several small inexpensive toys. Show the child the bag of toys and tell him that when he uses the potty (for its intended purpose) he can pick a toy out of the bag. He was trained in three days; of course there were still accidents but this idea really motivated him. *Marlene D. Gerber, Livermore, California*

THE POTTY FAIRY ✦ Before the Potty Fairy visits your house you will need a calendar with large blocks for the days of the week, colorful stickers, a few inexpensive (under a dollar) toys, and a few pairs of fancy big-girl panties or big-boy pants. When your child is ready to start potty training, tell her that for each time she goes to the potty without having an accident, the Potty Fairy will bring a small gift as a reward. Also, explain that for each day she has a "perfect" record she will get a sticker to put on the calendar and will be able to wear big-girl panties the next day. Immediately after each potty success, present her with a small gift (that you have stashed nearby) from the Potty Fairy. Tell her that you and the Potty Fairy are very proud of her. Praise is very important! After she is potty trained, tell her that the Potty Fairy left her a graduation present and declared that she is OFFICIALLY POTTY TRAINED. *Dick and Debra Keller, Fremont, California*

"I DON'T WANT TO FALL IN" ✦ When potty training my children, I would put them on the toilet backwards facing the tank instead of using a potty chair or potty seat on the toilet. That way, they could climb up and feel secure, and they didn't fear falling into the toilet. They could hold onto the tank if they had to. We also did not need a potty seat when we are out at a public rest room. Facing backwards is especially good for boys because it prevents spills. *Theresa Stroben, Carlsbad, California*

BIG-GIRL PANTIES INSPIRED SUCCESS ◆ To inspire my two-and-a-half-year-old daughter to be successful with potty training, I took her to the store and showed her some panties with Minnie Mouse on them. She loved them and wanted me to buy them for her. I told her she would have to be successful at potty training for a few days in a row before I would buy them. She soon succeeded, and I took her to the store, let her pick out the exact pair of panties she wanted, let her pay for them and even carry the bag home. I showed her how soft they were. We washed them, and she took them out of the dryer. She hasn't had an accident since because she doesn't want to mess up her new panties. *Kelly Granade, Lynn Haven, Florida*

POTTY TRAINING GIRLS ◆ When potty training our daughters, our pediatrician told us that the best way to teach them to wipe after urinating was to have them go "pat, pat, pat" with the toilet paper, instead of wiping hard and causing irritation. *Tracy Bauch, Milwaukee, Wisconsin*

POTTY TRAINING ON THE ROAD ◆ Here is a wonderful solution to traveling short or long distances in a car with a toddler who is in the midst of potty training. Purchase a child's potty seat with a lid and place it in the back of the car or trunk with a supply of wipes, toilet paper, and disposable diapers. When nature calls, place an opened disposable diaper over the bowl and put the top seat down to keep the diaper from slipping. Have the child use the potty and wipe. Then, simply fold up the diaper and dispose of it later. This has prevented many accidents from happening. Also, it is often better than using dirty rest rooms while traveling. *Tracy LaVelle, Fremont, California*

 Be sure to pull off to the side of the road and stop for this activity, as you will have to take yourself and your child out of safety restraints.

"WHO UNROLLED THE TOILET PAPER?" ◆ I came up with this simple solution to a toddler's urge to unroll the toilet paper onto the floor. If the roll is placed with the paper coming off the backside of the roll rather than over the top, your child can bat away at the roll to his heart's content and the roll just spins without releasing any paper. It's not until about five years of age that your child will figure out he needs to spin it in the opposite direction, long past the time he has an interest in doing so! *David E. Mann, The Woodlands, Texas*

SQUEEZE THE ROLL ◆ To make it more difficult for a child to pull all the toilet paper out, squeeze the roll before you put it on the holder. *Jill Nelson-Johnson, Urbandale, Iowa*

"STAYING DRY" THROUGH THE NIGHT

"MOMMY, I WET MY BED" ◆ Hearing this comment at 3 A.M. signifies the beginning of a twenty-to-thirty-minute routine: taking off the wet sheets, remaking the bed, and cleaning up the child. The worst part is remaking the bed. To avoid this step, I place two complete sets of sheets and rubber pads on the bed before my child goes to bed. After a bed-wetting accident I remove the wet sheets, leaving the second layer of dry sheets and rubber pad on the bed. The child gets to go back to bed immediately, making it easier for him to go back to sleep. *Alisa Johnsen, Chico, California*

LATE-NIGHT SLEEPING BAG ◆ When our child wanted to sleep with us or when he wet his bed, we put a sleeping bag on the floor by our bed and let him sleep there. When he wet the bed, it gave him a second bed so we didn't have to change bedding in the middle of the night. *Susan VanValer, La Cañada, California*

EXTRA DIAPER PROTECTION AT NIGHT ◆ I had trouble with my son's disposable diapers leaking during the night. It was frustrating to know that, if I could just keep him dry, he'd sleep through the night with no problem. Then one day I inserted adult bladder-control shields inside his nighttime diaper. It works great—no more leaks! *Jackie Gress, Fremont, California*

THE WEE-WEE ALARM ◆ A few catalog stores (Sears, for one) sell a device that works well for persistent bed-wetting. It is very simple; an alarm goes off the second urine hits the pad. It only takes a few days for the child to start waking up when he or she has a full bladder, and before an accident. Children react favorably to it. *Laurette Looney, Sparks, Nevada*

 Bed-wetting is a normal phase of the potty-training stage and often a frustrating time for children and parents. There are a myriad of causes—and just as many solutions. Try some of the simpler strategies before using a mechanical device such as the one listed above. And don't hesitate to talk to your child's doctor for additional information and guidance.

"STAY DRY" SURPRISE BOX ◆ My son had a hard time staying dry through the night. I made a "stay dry" box by covering a shoe box with wrapping paper (contact paper would also work) and filling it with little toys and treats. If he stayed dry through the night, he would get to select one prize. It kept him dry for a month straight the first time we tried it. A "stay dry" box can be a great motivator if there is not an underlying physical problem. *Jodi V. Wilding, Centerville, Utah*

✖◆◆✖

PERSONAL HYGIENE AND GROOMING

✖◆◆✖

DON'T FORGET TO WASH YOUR HANDS ◆ After children master potty training, teach them to wash hands after going to the bathroom. It takes very little soap and water and any doctor can tell you how important it is. *Patricia R. Hersom, Walnut Creek, California*

REINFORCE GOOD HABITS ◆ To reward our sons for washing their hands after using the bathroom, they get to pick out a sticker, which they can place on a paper plate we have taped to the bathroom mirror. It gets the job done! *Carol A. Nelson, Memphis, Tennessee*

A LOW BATHROOM MIRROR ◆ Install a small mirror below the medicine cabinet so little ones can use it when brushing their teeth and combing their hair. *Carolyn Mosser, York, Pennsylvania*

One small square mirror tile (available in most hardware stores for $3) can be used for this. It can be mounted on the wall with mounting-tape squares (if appropriate for your wall surface) at your child's eye level.

THIS IS THE WAY WE WASH OUR FACE ◆ When wiping up baby after eating—since babies hate to have their faces washed—sometimes it helps to sing. Even a simple song like "This Is the Way We Wash Our Face" makes it a lot easier to wash baby's face. *Wendy Ericsson, Lansdale, Pennsylvania, and Cathleen Warner, Gap, Pennsylvania*

BATHROOM "BASKET BUNNY" ◆ The morning routine around our house used to be hectic; our children were constantly asking my husband and me to find their grooming products: styling gel, spritzer, sunscreens, etc. So I completely cleaned out the cabinet under the bathroom sink, where I placed a basket for each child with all the items that they needed to get ready in the morning. To emphasize the importance of keeping the baskets neat and orderly, I initiated the "Basket Bunny." Occasionally, when the children weren't around, the Basket Bunny would inspect the baskets and reward neatness by leaving a note, a quarter, or a new item they needed. This worked so well that I did the same organizing of my own bathroom supplies; no one was more surprised than me when I received a quarter from the Basket Bunny. For the past nine months the bathroom baskets have remained neat and clean. *Stacy Krimetz, Livermore, California*

A TOWEL FOR KIDS ◆ When hanging a towel on the towel rack for small children, use an extra-long towel that reaches almost to the floor. Put snaps on one end of the towel or use safety pins to hold it to the towel rack. The long end of the towel will hang over the front of the rack

and the short end will fasten to the rack near the top. You could install a lower towel rack for the small children, but then the towel will still end up on the floor. *Hugh Heydt, Omaha, Nebraska*

FEARFUL OF HAIRCUTS ✦ A friend of mine's daughter was fearful of getting her hair cut, so her mother drew her a picture of her getting a haircut and a picture of her eating ice cream. She explained that they would celebrate her haircut by going out for ice cream. They both looked at the pictures many times before the actual haircut, and soon the daughter began to associate the haircut with ice cream. Her daughter had no fear throughout the haircut; it went as smooth as ice cream. Visual pictures often work much better than lengthy explanations. *Rebecca Robinson, San Jose, California*

"NO WIGGLE" HAIRCUT ✦ When I was a young lad, I was very ticklish. Giving me a haircut was something more than most barbers would or could endure. More than one struggled to give me a haircut and then told my mother they couldn't finish the job. Finally, we met a barber (and an expert armchair psychologist) who carefully listened while Mom explained my problem and then said, "You just leave him to me. I'll take care of it." I was busily reading a comic book, oblivious to what was taking place. "You're next, Wade," he said, and motioned toward the barber chair, adding, "and bring another comic book with you." I did just that, and the barber said, "Now Wade, I want you to read that new comic book carefully because after the haircut I am going to ask you three very important questions about it." I did just that, or tried to, and the barber finished the haircut before I could finish the comic book with nary a wiggle or twitch. *Wade Misko, Lincoln, Nebraska*

CUTTING A TODDLER'S HAIR ✦ When a toddler's hair needs a little trim at home, sit him in a high chair with very small finger foods such as Cheerios on the tray. By the time all those little circles are conveyed to the mouth and eaten one at a time, you can finish trimming. Also, if your child gets used to having haircuts at home, (hopefully) the first trip to the barber or hairstylist will not be scary. *Peggy Gilbreth Nipper, Omaha, Nebraska*

TV DISTRACTS FEAR OF HAIRCUT ✦ Put a toddler in a high chair in front of her favorite TV show. She will watch the program instead of wiggling. *Janet Johnstone, Fremont, California*

xxxxxxxxxxxxxxxxxxxxxxxxxxxxxxxxxxxxxxxxxxxxxxxxx

BATH TIME

xxxxxxxxxxxxxxxxxxxxxxxxxxxxxxxxxxxxxxxxxxxxxxxxx

NEWBORN WHO DOESN'T LIKE TO BATHE ✦ When my baby came home from the hospital, she did not like sponge baths and did not like the bathtub. I found that running the water in the sink while I was bathing her calmed her down and gave her something to listen to. This has worked every time I have given her a bath. She doesn't fuss or get mad. *Linda Bennett, Centre Hall, Pennsylvania*

SHOWERING WITH BABY ✦ Whether it's her first or third child, if a mother wants to take a long shower, what is she to do with a screaming child? I use an infant seat, preferably one with a rocker handle, strip the child down, put a towel on the seat, and set the child in it. I take my shower and, when the child cries, I can peek out of the shower curtain and talk to him. When it's the child's turn, I pick him up, shower him, and put him in the towel. Then I have time to dry myself off, do my hair, whatever. The baby is in the bathroom with me and doesn't care how long I take. When my older child got too big for the seat, I put bathroom toys in a little box for him to play with while I was in the shower. *Brigitte Kimball, Chapel Hill, North Carolina*

NO-SLIP TUB ✦ My sister has a practical method for bathing babies who can sit up by themselves but who slip in the tub. I put my daughter in a plastic laundry basket in the tub. The water flows in and out. My daughter can hold on to the sides of the basket and her toys are still in reach. *Barbara Sheehy, Kensington, California*

No matter what method you use to make your child's bath a safe and pleasant experience, never leave your child alone in the tub, even for a short moment.

$$ TUB TOYS ◆ Instead of buying expensive bath toys, use a few plastic containers and spoons. My daughters have more fun in the tub with things from my kitchen than with true toys. *Nancy Lee, Pasadena, California*

Make sure that things from the kitchen do not have small parts that may come loose or break off during play and be swallowed or aspirated.

FUNNY HAIR DESIGNS DURING SHAMPOO ◆ When my child was one to two years old, he had a great fear of having his hair washed. Bath time was an immense struggle. We tried everything. Finally, there happened to be a hand mirror on the counter, and after we got the shampoo on, I asked him if he would like to see what his hair looked like. He thought that was the funniest thing.

We took turns making different designs and he would look in the mirror. It ended the battle at bath time. *Cindi Everts, Napoleon, Ohio*

WASHING HAIR ✦ To get your little girl (or boy) to be happier while washing her hair, you can give her a "My Little Pony" or some other toy with hair and let her wash its hair while you're washing her hair. *Jennifer Bystrzak, Tonawanda, New York*

MAGIC SHAMPOO ✦ When my daughter was young, shampooing was a problem. I used to pretend that the shampoo was magic which, when I sprinkled it on her hair, gave me the power to look through the strands of her hair and see different cartoon characters, Disney characters, and people in our family. I would say, "Oh my gosh, look who I see in there!" while I was shampooing, rinsing, and parting her hair. *M.H., Huntington Beach, California*

NO MORE TEARS ✦ My daughter didn't like to have her hair washed. So while she was in the bathtub, I laid her down on her back and poured water over her head from a plastic glass or bowl, being careful not to get any water on her face. We lathered her up and she played hair-style with the shampoo. When it was time to rinse, she lay down again and I poured water over her head, again being careful not to get water on her face. I realized that pouring water over her face caused her to lose her breath and frightened her. *Sharon Zanoni, Penn Valley, California*

BATH GOGGLES ✦ We have found it helpful to allow our son to wear swimming goggles while having his hair washed. It keeps water and soap out of his eyes. *Angie Satterfield, Patriot, Indiana*

A SHAMPOO VISOR ✦ My son hated to have his hair washed until I bought an inexpensive visor hat that keeps soap out of his eyes. He wears a small plastic visor hat and also keeps a dry washcloth over his eyes. I tell him to close his eyes tight and tilt his head back. The water rolls down his back, and the visor prevents soap and water from getting into his eyes. *Sandi Poznanski, Howard Beach, New York*

NON-SPLASHING INFANT ✦ When our daughter was an infant, my wife would bathe her in the kitchen sink.

It worked great except for all the splashing; my wife got soaked and so did our kitchen. So I offered our daughter a wafer cookie to hold in both of her hands while my wife bathed her. She was so busy holding and sucking on the cookie that she completely stopped splashing the water. The key is to keep their hands occupied with something enjoyable during the bath. *C.T., Worcester, Massachusetts*

4

LEARNING

◆

Every child is born a genius.
— R. BUCKMINSTER FULLER

Children love to learn, and they have all the natural ingredients to prosper at it. They're inquisitive and enthusiastic about new things. All they need is stimulation and guidance. That's where we parents come in. The other evening my six-year-old, who is in the first grade, was frustrated and wanted to quit working on her writing project. She and her classmates were each writing their first book (only one hundred words). My daughter had titled her story "The Dark Walkway"; it was about a little girl walking home one night through a scary walkway. To stimulate her interest in the project, I asked her to put her coat on and grab her flashlight. We walked out to the dark walkway near our home that she was writing about. She became so stimulated with ideas for the rest of her story that she raced back into the house and eagerly started to work on her project again.

To instill a passion for learning in children, it's important to follow our children's lead instead of pushing our own interests. Find out what they're drawn to, then provide enrichment materials and activities for that subject. For instance, a curiosity about dinosaurs might prompt a visit to a museum or the public library. Also, teachers (both preschool and primary) often have clever ideas and educational resources to share.

An appetite for learning often has its roots in a love of books. Parents and educational experts alike claim that an early interest in books sets the stage for a lifetime appreciation of reading. Dozens of parents wrote to me, each asserting that their routines of stories contributed immensely to their child's love of reading as an adolescent or adult. One parent touts a letter received from her teenager who was at summer camp. Instead of requesting candy and other snacks like many of the other kids, he wrote, "Send more books."

Many of the tips in this chapter offer creative ways to make learning fun and stimulating. If you have a difficult time prying school information out of your child, I suggest you read the tips beginning with What Did You Do in School Today? (p. 72). School Mornings offers some great suggestions for getting little ones out the door in the morning. Learning in the Car has tips for turning a boring trip of errands into a lively learning session. And For Love of Books offers practical ways to encourage an early appreciation of reading and books. Chapter 11, Nighty Night, also offers some clever ideas on books and reading in Bedtime Rituals.

◆

LEARNING TIPS

"MOMMY, WHY IS . . . ?" ✦ When you are being driven crazy by the question "Why?" resist the temptation to answer the question. Instead, look at your child and say, "Why do you think?" If you answer the question, you have done all the thinking for the child. By challenging him, you do several things. You show him respect by asking his opinion. You increase his capacity for thinking on his own and help him develop common sense. When I have done this, it is amazing the answers I have heard. Almost each question was answered correctly, and great discussions have come out of using this method. It is a tool you can use to help build a young person's confidence. Another plus is the "Why?" questions will taper off. Instead of asking "why" all the time, the child will start to think for him/herself and bring up subjects for discussion rather than ask obvious questions. *Teddy Heard Orr, Charlotte, North Carolina*

TEACHING NUMBERS AND LETTERS TO TODDLERS ✦ Put magnetic numbers and letters on the refrigerator and go through them with the child as often as you can. You can just use one letter or number at a time, or you can make words. *Patricia R. Hersom, Walnut Creek, California*

WALK OR SKIP TO NUMBER 9 ✦ To teach numbers or the alphabet, write numbers or letters on colorful pieces of paper or on pieces of paper cut out to resemble feet. Place the numbers or letters in a large circle and have your child stand in the center of the circle. Ask her to walk or skip to certain numbers or letters. It's a fun way to learn. Offer prizes or rewards for correct responses. *Samantha Hoyt, Fremont, California*

WOODEN LETTERS ARE GREAT LEARNING TOYS ✦ My mother did a wonderful thing for me as a child. She got me some wooden letters, not blocks but cutout letters. You can get them now in either wood or plastic. I played with them like toys and when I would ask what one was she would tell me. I learned all my letters before I was two. *G.L., Rochester, New York*

LEARNING COLORS, SHAPES, AND NUMBERS ✦ To help a child learn colors, shapes, and numbers, pick a different color, shape, or number each day and focus on that new item throughout the day. For example, if you pick the color "red," you can serve cranberry juice, a red apple, or pancakes with strawberry syrup. Later in the day you can look for red items around the house or while shopping. Having a focus or theme each day is not only fun, it's an effective learning technique. *Janice Fonteno, Union City, California*

UNDERSTANDING TIME ✦ The concept of time is very difficult for my young children, especially when counting time until an event will take place. I found that it was easier for them to understand how many "bedtimes" or "nighty nights" rather than "days" there were until a certain event. For example, "In four nighty nights we will go to Grandma's house." *Anonymous, San Diego, California*

WHAT PRINCIPALS WANT PARENTS TO KNOW

- Listen and talk with your children, paying consistent attention to questions and feelings.
- Show pride in your children's academic growth and accomplishments.
- Regularly encourage children with their schoolwork.
- Instill a strong work ethic in children.
- Help children perceive themselves as capable problem solvers.
- Give priority to schoolwork, reading, and other academic activities over nonacademic endeavors.
- Set standards and expectations for your children.
- Help with homework when needed.
- Encourage regular discussions with your children and find opportunities to enlarge vocabulary and sentence patterns.
- Get to know your children's academic strengths and weaknesses.
- Make frequent use of books, newspapers and periodicals.

Reprinted with permission from the National Association of Elementary School Principals and World Book Educational Products

LEARNING COLORS ◆ Babies can discriminate colors very early (eight to twelve months) if they are taught to do so. I used different-color balls and would roll them to the baby. I would say, "Here comes the red ball," or ask "Where's the green ball," or "Roll the blue ball to Mommy." Start with two very different colors, then add more colors as your baby progresses. *N.S., San Jose, California*

OFFER CHOICES ◆ By offering choices to children, we are teaching them to be individuals as well as demonstrating our confidence in them. The choices can be simple, such as, "Do you want to brush your teeth first or put your pajamas on? Do you want to sit on the couch or on the chair?" Before offering choices, make sure that you can live with either choice they select. Learning the value of making good choices now will help them make the right choices in adolescence and beyond—when I'm not going to be there. *Florence Grace, Fremont, California*

LEARNING WITH LAUNDRY ✦ Both my daughters loved to hand me clothes to put in either the washer or dryer. I used this activity to teach colors and names of clothing. As they handed me something, I would name the item and its color or colors, and they would practice saying the words after me. I sometimes would also include the item's owner, e.g., "Kelly's pink shirt." *Nancy Knowlton, Wilmette, Illinois*

EARLY INTEREST IN COMPUTERS ✦ Our computer has a screen saver which has geometric designs, flowers, etc. that come onscreen when a computer is left unattended. Children can press a key and the design changes. Our thirteen-month-old daughter loves to sit on our laps and play with the computer this way. It keeps a child entertained for a few minutes and teaches hand-to-eye coordination. *Brenda Kiba, Milpitas, California*

LEARNING ABOUT SAVING AND SHARING ✦ When my children do chores around the house they earn money. Each child has his own bank account in which each one deposits a share of his money. At Christmas or birthday time, they have their own money with which to buy their siblings a small gift and still have money left for themselves. The idea is to get them to save and to share. *E.M.M., Starkville, Mississippi*

AN EARLY LESSON IN SAVING MONEY ✦ I took my girls to the bank to open savings accounts when they were barely old enough to write their names on the account application—eight, I suppose. Then I encouraged them to deposit monetary gifts from grandparents as well as a portion of their allowances and any other earnings they had. I pointed out that when there was something special they really wanted, the money would be there for them to use, and they could continue to build the account so that, when they were old enough to want a car, or needed savings to help fund their college education, they'd have the resources. They were given allowances based on the assumption that they would contribute to the welfare of the household by cleaning up after themselves—e.g., carting toys to their rooms and putting them away, making their beds, and putting dirty clothes in the hamper. If they wanted to earn extra money, I would hire them to do age-appropriate jobs. This early lesson—the power of saving— has instilled in them as teenagers the value of money and the benefits of saving. *Caroly Jones, Albuquerque, New Mexico*

MUSIC, MAESTRO! ✦ When my five-year-old began piano lessons (at her insistence), I worried about becoming a "practice nag" and taking all the fun out of music lessons. To avoid becoming a witch about practicing, I began requesting "piano concerts" from her instead of reminding her to practice. As much as possible, I make the request for my benefit, e.g., I tell her that I would like to listen to some music while I put my feet up for a few minutes or while I'm washing dishes. *Nancy Lee, Pasadena, California*

MAKING GEOGRAPHY FUN ✦ We have a globe in our den which our children love to spin and play with. We started off by teaching easy-to-recognize continents (like Australia), then we introduced various countries. Our two children (ages three and six) enjoy having us quiz them by asking, "Where is South America?" or "Where is Italy (the country that is shaped like a boot)?" or "Where is the equator?" *Anonymous, San Diego, California*

LEARNING TO RIDE A BIKE ✦ When you are teaching your child how to ride a bicycle, take him to an open

place instead of having him ride along the sidewalk or street. That way the child can concentrate on balancing without worrying about the bicycle going in a straight line. The perfect place is a baseball infield. The child can ride anywhere he wants and all you have to do is follow along behind. If the child does fall, the baseball field is softer than the street or sidewalk. *Brian Hupp, Satellite Beach, Florida*

ONE TRAINING WHEEL—A CONFIDENCE BUILDER ◆ My daughter had a hard time learning to ride her bike until someone suggested putting one training wheel back on. One training wheel gave her the feel of riding on her own, while at the same time offering a sense of security and balance. After one week of practicing with the training wheel, my daughter had gained the skill and confidence she needed to ride without assistance. *Sharon M., West Nyack, New York*

PREPARE FOR INEVITABLE FALLS ◆ Have the child wear knee pads and gloves to cushion inevitable falls when training on a two-wheeler. *Tracy Bauch, Milwaukee, Wisconsin*

BIKE HELMETS ARE COOL ◆ My children are not allowed on their bikes without wearing a bike helmet. We showed them pictures of professional bike riders—all wearing helmets. We let the children pick out their own helmet as long as it met or exceeded the safety standards. Some come with neat-looking covers, others have sticker kits that jazz up their appearance. Gradually, many of the other kids in our neighborhood are buying and wearing them too. *Linda Lane Miller, Sterling, Virginia*

 Bicycle injuries are one of the most common injuries to children. Getting your children used to proper protection for physical activities should start early, before they progress to more intense or risky activities.

LEARNING ABOUT WEIGHTS AND MEASURES BY BAKING ◆ Children can learn about counting by helping you count the number of spoonfuls or cups you

need for baking. Older children can actually learn more complicated forms of weights and measures. It's a fun way to learn calculations—and the reward is what pops out of the oven! *Rita Wilson, Fremont, California*

PRESCHOOL WEATHERPERSON ◆ At preschool, my grandson made a simple weather map showing the weather with a simple dial in the middle. Each morning he determines the weather outside and then points the dial at the description best matching the weather. *Pat Remmes, Walnut Creek, California*

LEARNING HELPS DIMINISH FEARS ◆ Thunder and lightning can be very scary to children. Just having them cuddle in with Mommy and Daddy may help, but our kids still hear the big booms and try to hide under the covers. I took my daughter to a location of the house where we could see the lightning, turned off the lights, and we sat there and watched together. I then talked to her about how "magical and special" thunder and lightning was; how it danced across the skies; how it would make pretty pictures with light. Then it would clap as if to say how good it looked. I would point and say "Look" and "Oooohhh" for each lightning strike. It wasn't very long before she was pointing them out before I could. *Scott Hill, Newark, California*

SPECIAL BOX TO CALM FEARS DURING THUNDERSTORMS ◆ My children are afraid of thunderstorms. I have made up a special box with crayons, coloring books, paper, and small toys from cereal boxes. During thunderstorms, we take the box out and play with it. That is the only time they can play with the box, so it makes the storm and the box extra special. *Jean Sinkko, Norfolk, Virginia*

"WHAT DID YOU DO IN SCHOOL TODAY?" ◆ To get children to talk about their day at school, you must ask them very specific questions: "What did you learn in math today?" or "Who did you play with at recess?" Asking, "What did you do in school today?" usually prompts a response of "Nothing" or "I don't remember." *N.S., San Jose, California*

LOOKING FOR LONG ANSWERS ◆ Try to ask questions that cannot be answered with yes or no. This gives them a chance to express themselves and encourages them to speak in complete sentences. Development of oral language is a great beginning of self-expression. *L.S.J., Fremont, California*

THREE QUESTIONS ABOUT SCHOOL ◆ To stimulate conversation during dinner, we ask everyone to tell three things that happened at school or work that day. We all enjoy hearing about each other's day. *Anonymous, California*

HOMEWORK CLIPBOARD ◆ Each of my children has his own clipboard for homework. They attach their homework to the clipboard and hang it on the wall immediately after arriving home from school. A pencil is attached to the clipboard with a string. We always know where the homework is and the clipboard is convenient to take in the car or to the baby-sitter's. *Carol Smead, San Jose, California*

EARLY PIANO LESSONS ◆ My five-year-old daughter often came with me to my piano lessons. During the week between the lessons I would help her learn a *very short* exercise which she would be allowed to play for my teacher at the end of my lesson. She was very proud to do so and couldn't wait to begin real lessons herself. I also believe that watching me practice and receive instruction has provided a model for her own efforts to learn new skills. *Anonymous, Wilmette, Illinois*

BEAT THE HOMEWORK CLOCK ◆ If your children don't seem interested in doing their homework, make a game of it. Have them estimate how long each homework activity (reading, spelling, etc.) will take. See if they can beat their own projection, as long as it's reasonable and they don't rush through their work. It's a motivator! *Rebecca Robinson, San Jose, California*

CLEAN UP THE PARKS . . . ◆ When our boys were three and five years old, we did "litter patrol" in a public park from time to time. We would take our own trash bags to put the garbage in. We would talk about how much better the park looked when the garbage was in the proper place and how the animals were safer when the garbage wasn't on the ground or in the trees and bushes. We kept the refundable cans and bottles we found. The kids seem to enjoy this activity and it taught responsibility in many ways. *Koleen Tompkins, Salem, Oregon*

A-MAZE-ING LEARNING GAME ◆ Set up the family room like a maze, making tunnels out of pillow cushions and creating lanes out of blocks, etc. Using a chalkboard, write out simple questions for your children to answer. The first child who guesses each correct answer gets to run through the maze first. You can also use numbers, alphabet letters, pictures of familiar items, etc. *Karin Poe, Fremont, California*

NEW CHALLENGES EACH BIRTHDAY ◆ We used each birthday as a milestone in order to encourage our son to accomplish something new. There seems to be a psychological shift that occurs on a birthday which allows him to do or try something that he was reluctant to do only a few days prior. For his third birthday, he was to be completely potty trained; his fourth, to get dressed all by himself; his fifth, to tie his own shoes. *Audrey Swanton, Brewer, Maine*

A LESSON IN GIVING ◆ I always bring my son with me when I volunteer at the local homeless shelter. He helps with the meals and plays with the children at the shelter. He has learned the importance of helping people who are less fortunate than himself. *Robyn Pappas, Peoria, Arizona*

TEACHING CHILDREN TO SWIM ◆ I have three boys ages twelve, seven, and four, and all three of them were swimming by the age of two. When they were able to sit up by themselves, I filled the tub halfway and dropped a handful of nickels and dimes in. I told my boys to go underwater and retrieve as many coins as they could. Later that evening we would take those coins and buy ice cream with them. When they took swimming lessons, they were never afraid to put their heads underwater. *Peter Dolan, Bronx, New York*

 Starting early to get your children used to water activities is a good idea, but don't assume that they are "water safe" just because they aren't afraid of the water or can swim. Always supervise.

SCHOOL MORNINGS

THE EVENING BEFORE SCHOOL ✦ On school nights, we set out our son's clothes, backpack, and any other thing he wants to take to school. Then in the morning he has a routine of first eating breakfast, then getting dressed, and if time permits, doing an activity of his choice. This routine sure helps the morning to go smoothly. *Debra Randall, East Haven, Connecticut*

DRESSED AND READY TO GO—THE NIGHT BEFORE ✦ Toddlers and preschoolers are sometimes difficult to dress during the busy morning routine. Sometimes I dress my children in sweat suits or other comfortable clothing for bedtime. Then, they're ready to go in the morning. It's a real time saver on those mornings when you have to get out the door quickly. *Debra Kassarjian, Fremont, California*

KIDS SAY THE FUNNIEST THINGS

When my daughter was in kindergarten (she is now in the second grade) she asked me one day, "Mommy, am I a following person?" "What is a following person?" I asked. "Well," she replied, "the teacher always says, 'Would the following people please line up,' and she calls my name." *Randi Beckerman, Sharon, Massachusetts*

A CHORE FOR BEING LATE ✦ Getting children out of the house and to school on time was a real challenge until we implemented a new rule: If the children are not out of the house by 8:15 A.M. (school starts at 8:30 A.M.), they have to do an extra chore after school. *Mary Lea McAnally, Stanford, California*

DON'T FORGET YOUR SCHOOL SUPPLIES ✦

Getting my two elementary-school-age children out the door on time each morning is a real challenge. I have two lists posted by the door, one for each child. They list everything each child needs to bring to school: backpack, bike helmet, lunch, homework, etc. Before leaving the house, they have to look at each item on the list and nod their head that they have that item. *Mary Lea McAnally, Stanford, California*

"I DON'T FEEL LIKE GOING TO SCHOOL" ✦

Sometimes my child says he doesn't feel good and would like to stay home from school, but he doesn't appear to have any symptoms. I tell him that he can stay home, but he will have to rest all day in order to get better, and he can't play with any of his friends. After hearing this, he usually jumps up and gets ready for school. *Lori Nye, Clinton, Utah*

XXX

LEARNING IN THE CAR

XXXXXXXXXXXXXXXXXXXXXXXXXXXXXXXXXXXXXXXXXXXXXXX

LEARNING ON THE GO ✦ I use the three-mile com-mute to the baby-sitter's to teach my kids new things. At first, when they were learning to talk, they would recite the names of the people at the baby-sitter's. As my son grew older we progressed to calling out colors and types of ve-hicles. "I see a blue truck." "I see a yellow bus." From there we progressed to "Green light means go" and "Red light means stop." Now that he is three, he can identify what a stop sign looks like and he can spell "S-T-O-P." We are working on "At a stop sign, look left, look right, no cars—go." I found this kind of interaction has helped save my sanity and improve my driving habits by making me more aware, especially on those hectic mornings when we are late. I feel good when I get to work because I know I've spent at least some time daily helping my kids to learn. *Terri Murphy, Redwood City, California*

HABLA ESPANOL? ✦ My daughter has a series of learn-to-speak-Spanish tapes from her weekly Spanish class. We play them as we drive in the car. It makes er-rands less tedious for her and avoids the struggle of mak-ing her take time out from play to listen at home. Plus, I'm learning with her! *N.K.M., Palo Alto, California*

CAR GAMES FOR FUN AND LEARNING ✦ My chil-dren and I love to play word games in the car because it's fun and it makes the time go by faster. We challenge each other to make a rhyme about a topic, or we try to name opposites or synonyms of words given. It's also a great way to introduce new words into a child's vocabulary. *Maureen Compton, Fremont, California*

SPELLING WORDS TO GO ✦ I use the car time, ei-ther on errands or long drives, to quiz my children on their homework, especially things they have to memorize. This works great for spelling lists, the months of the year, state capitals, etc. The children love to practice in the car and it

makes the driving time go by fast. *Bonnie Lowe, Fremont, California*

>>

FOR LOVE OF BOOKS

>>

READ TO YOUR BABY ◆ When the baby is only two to three months old—start reading to her! She may be squirming and impatient, but by four or five months, she'll be helping you turn the pages. It is *never* too early to start. *Erin M., Fremont, California*

PERSONALIZED PICTURE BOOKS ◆ The next time you visit a farm or zoo, take photos of the different animals. Include your child in as many pictures as possible. Mount the photos in a small three-by-five mini-album that has plastic sleeves to protect the pictures. Write the name of the animal on a label and place one on each page. This has helped my two-year-old son interact with our friends and relatives—he explains each picture with enthusiasm. He has also learned to recognize different letters and words. He's three now, but it's still one of his favorite books. *Terri Murphy, Redwood City, California*

PRESCHOOLERS CAN READ, TOO ✦ Pre-readers can quickly learn to read certain words in a storybook. Pick out one to three words that appear multiple times in the story, such as names or easy-to-read words such as "dog." Teach the child how to say and identify those words. Using your fingers to track the words in the story, prompt your child to repeat those special words you identified earlier. He will stay involved in the story better while learning an important new skill—reading. *Rebecca Robinson, San Jose, California*

READING PRACTICE ✦ I have my eight-year-old son read to his six-year-old sister. She loves it and my son improves his reading skills. *Janice Bednarik, Phoenix, Arizona*

TRACK WORDS WITH YOUR FINGERS ✦ As you read to your child, point to the words as you say them. This helps children understand the meaning of these funny symbols (letters) and helps them to memorize the meaning of simple words. *Anne McCallum, Fremont, California*

USE YOUR CHILD'S NAME ✦ To encourage your child to listen to a storybook, substitute your own child's name for the character's name written in the book. *Diane Welch, Alameda, California*

READING RITUAL ✦ When my child started first grade his bedtime was 8:00 but I would allow him to stay up an additional thirty minutes to read books. He would jump at the chance to remain up a little longer even though it may not-have been to do exactly what he wanted. This has turned out very well: he is now seventeen years old and reads several hundred books a year. *Vicki Nance, Atlanta, Georgia*

BOOKS FOR NAPS ✦ While I was raising my three children, I believed in good naps and would put them in their crib with a pile of books. We would read a few, then I would leave, and they could look at books as long as they wanted. But when I checked on them—nine times out of ten—I would find them sound asleep with a book tented over their little faces. Even my active child! All of my children have grown up and still love to read. *Koni Sundquist, Duluth, Minnesota*

BEDTIME READING ◆ After a certain time in the evening, approximately thirty minutes before their bedtime, the only activity I would allow would be to read books in their beds. It settled them down for bedtime, but more important, it promoted a lifelong appreciation for books. *Anne McCallum, Fremont, California*

SHUT OFF THE TV AND BRING ME YOUR BOOKS ◆ Every evening for one half hour the television and radio are turned off and my son brings me his books. He has quite a selection but I have read his favorites so many times that he can now read them to me. It is a relaxing time for me, I get to spend uninterrupted time with my son, but most important, he absorbs these books like a sponge and is learning so quickly, I am amazed. *Theresa Grotheer, Brooklyn, New York*

AN HOUR OF NINTENDO FOR AN HOUR OF READING ◆ For older children who are addicted to Nintendo, allow them to play the game for the same amount of time they read each day. So, if your child wants to play more Nintendo, it is a great motivator to read more. *Claudette Beamon, Hamden, Connecticut*

MAKE A BOOK FOR YOUR TODDLER ◆ Buy or use an old photo album and cut pictures out of magazines (colors, cars, animals, flowers, babies, and toys) that fascinate your child. *Janette Totherow, Anadarko, Oklahoma*

5

DEMYSTIFYING DISCIPLINE

◆

*The family is a court of justice which never shuts
down night or day.*

— D E   C H A Y A L , *Sens Plastique*, 1949

Although discipline is probably the most controversial as-
pect of child rearing, and one of the most frustrating for
parents, it is also one of the most important for a child's
development. Parents discipline their children to teach them
responsibility, to protect them from danger, and to instill
socially acceptable ways of behaving. The ultimate goal is to
have our children become self-disciplined. As parents, we
hope that effective discipline during childhood will lead to
good judgment and responsible behavior in adolescence and
beyond.

There is no one model of discipline that has been univer-
sally accepted; children are unique and respond to different
approaches. Even children within the same family may need
to be disciplined in very different ways.

A consequence for disobeying a rule is usually some form
of punishment, ranging from a stern look to a physical spanking. A verbal scolding is all some children need for a minor
infraction. Other proven tactics include isolating the misbe-
having child for a short time, either by making her go to her
room or sit in a corner, or restricting her from a valued
privilege. Most child-care experts recommend spanking only
as a punishment of last resort, which should not be excessive
and should be restricted to the buttocks so you don't hurt
the child. Also, never shake a baby; it can cause serious injuries or even death. Excessive punishment of any kind, physical or mental, can be detrimental to your child's development.

Always try to match an appropriate punishment to the
misdeed; never give a severe punishment for a minor infrac-

tion. Whatever the punishment is, you should administer it immediately after the undesirable behavior. Some parents wait for a considerable amount of time before punishing their child, which creates confusion for the child as to which behavior is being punished. This is especially true for very young children.

The best discipline approaches are well balanced; misbehavior is punished and good behavior is actively reinforced. Reinforcements for children should vary according to their individual preferences (toys, favorite activities, etc.), but all children appreciate words of praise or encouragement, a smile, or a reassuring hug from a parent.

Sometimes we reinforce our child's misbehavior without being aware of it. For example, recently my daughters sneaked up behind me in the backyard and sprinkled me with water. I asked them to stop, but I was also chuckling. They took my laughter as permission to continue sprinkling water; I had given them a mixed message. They didn't stop until I clearly (and loudly) told them how I felt about being soaked. By that time, their feelings were hurt, and I felt like a heel. If a parent occasionally reinforces misbehavior, it will be very difficult to stop that behavior from occurring. In fact, a behavior that is sporadically approved is the most difficult to stop. For example if you occasionally give in to your toddler's tantrum for not buying her a toy at the grocery store, be prepared for a tantrum every time you pass the toy rack. Rest assured she will remember being reinforced with a new toy the last time she threw a tantrum. At this point, a parent will have to suffer through many future store tantrums by completely ignoring them until they stop.

Discipline is also taught indirectly through our own behavior. The best way to teach discipline is to be a good role model for your children—to practice what you preach. Children love to emulate their parents, and they usually don't discriminate between our good and shady sides. I'll never forget how embarrassed I was when our baby-sitter took me aside and, in a scolding tone, told me that my toddler was reciting a four-letter word. "Gee, I wonder where she could have learned that," I replied as her glare intensified. A lesson learned.

Discipline is a lifelong process for parents and child alike. As parents, the more disciplined we become, the more we can instill it in our children.

The following tips are a mix of several refreshing new approaches to discipline, as well as some of the clever old standards. There are four sections in this chapter: Discipline Tips, Time-out and Corner Time, When There's Two or More of Them and Only One of It, and When Siblings Argue.

But first, here's one discipline tip that works for me—in three easy steps.

1. Explain Your Rules Clearly

Children need firm limits; they actually find security in having boundaries. Explain your rules clearly and in a way the child can understand. For instance, to avoid misunderstanding, I often ask my six-year-old to repeat what I have explained. Of course, don't expect too much from your toddler; she cannot comprehend the meaning of rules and limits.

Children will respond better to rules if you explain the importance and reason for the rule. Try to remember how you felt when your parent gave you the old "because I told you so" explanation.

2. Explain the Consequences

If your child balks at one of your rules or requests, explain what the consequence will be for not obeying. This offers your child a choice and, at least in our house, limits the verbal arguments. For example, my wife recently asked my daughter to pick up her toys by noon the next day. If she didn't, my wife explained, "I'll pick them up, but you won't see them for three days." This gave my daughter a choice: either pick up the toys or face the consequence.

3. Be Consistent

My daughter decided to test my wife by not complying with her request to pick up the toys. As promised, promptly at noon the next day, my wife boxed up the toys. My daughter, wide-eyed in disbelief, watched silently as her mother disappeared with the toys. Since then, my daughter has picked up her toys when faced with a similar decision.

This example illustrates a key concept about discipline which babies have learned by their first birthday: A rule is not a rule unless it is enforced consistently. They quickly and skillfully learn how to test their parents and how to determine which rules they must take seriously.

◆

DISCIPLINE TIPS

CREATIVE PROBLEM SOLVING ✦ When our daughters come to us with a problem, ranging from spilled juice to a sibling dispute, we take two steps: (1) We repeat and acknowledge the problem, and (2) we ask, "What can we do about it?" The child usually has the answer and can solve the problem herself. This also fosters independent thinking and problem-solving skills. *Tracy LaVelle, Fremont, California*

KIDS WILL BE KIDS ✦ Children get into trouble when they are put into situations where they are not allowed to be children. I learned this important advice from a Montessori nursery school my daughters attended. Keeping that in mind gave me a little bit more understanding and patience when confronted with temper tantrums at the checkout line at the grocery store, emotional meltdowns in restaurants, etc. *Emily Allen Martinez, Park City, Utah*

"FIRMNESS WITHOUT ANGER, FIRMNESS WITHOUT ANGER" ✦ To ward off responding in anger to my child's actions, I chant in my head, "Firmness without anger." That little chant takes care of a lot of problems. It sure helps me to put things in perspective before I act. *M.B.B., San Antonio, Texas*

WHEN ANGRY, HIT A PILLOW ✦ To help control those feelings of anger, beat on a pillow. It's a good outlet for tension and nobody gets injured. Even children can be taught to use this outlet as an alternative to hitting someone or throwing something. *N.S., San Jose, California*

IT'S NOT A LAUGHING MATTER ✦ When one of my children did something wrong but very silly, the parenting books always advised to never reprimand while laughing. However, sometimes I couldn't help laughing. I overcame the dilemma by telling my girls that it was funny ONCE but it wouldn't be funny again. Both of my girls understood and usually never did it again. *Nancy S. Jamison, Newtown Square, Pennsylvania*

COUNT TO THREE ◆ If my child doesn't follow directions as he's told, I give him one more chance by saying, "If you're not doing what you're supposed to be doing by the time I count to three, you'll be disciplined." If you're consistent with following through with your promise, you'll see results. It's as simple as one, two, three. *Ed Isenberg, Fremont, California*

ICHI-NI-SAN ◆ To get the immediate attention of my children, I count to three in Japanese: *ichi-ni-san*. My children know I'm serious when they hear these three words. *Carol Smead, San Jose, California*

WHISPERING GETS A CHILD'S ATTENTION ◆ An effective way of getting a child's attention is to whisper. If the situation is getting out of control, go over, put your hand on the child's shoulder, and whisper softly. The child will stop to listen. *Dawn M. Dempsey, Toledo, Ohio*

"HOW COME?" ◆ I have learned that children respond better to the question "How come?" than "Why?" *Edward Lott, Sykesville, Maryland*

SHARING FEELINGS CALMS A TANTRUM ◆ When one of my children threw a tantrum, I'd speak to him lovingly, get down and pick him up in my arms, and encourage him to explain his feelings. Verbalizing feelings really helps to calm a child. *Carolyn Catell Mongillo, North Haven, Connecticut*

YOU WEREN'T A GOOD LISTENER ◆ Instead of telling a child that she is "bad" (i.e., a bad person) when she does something I don't like, I say that she is not a "good listener" today. I then praise her when she is a "good listener." I even forewarn my child before going to a particular place that I expect her to be a "good listener." When we sit her in a chair or have quiet time away from others due to negative behavior, we say, "You were not a good listener, so you must have time away." *Ruthie Schneider, Lorain, Ohio*

GRUMP BUMPS ✦ When a child is crabby we tell him he has "grump bumps" on him as a fun way to make him aware of how he is acting. *Jeff LaVelle, Fremont, California*

THE WHINING BAG ✦ When confronted with whining, I let the child know that I'm interested in what he has to say, but I don't want to listen to his whine. So I would offer him the "whining bag" (a plain paper bag), which he could whine into. The concept of the whining bag is so silly that the whining quickly changes to giggles. *Janet Dudey, Fremont, California*

SAVING FACE ✦ Use compromise to get young children to cooperate. If they want you to read more before bed say, "Let's compromise, I'll read *one* more book." After the book, if they want another, remind them that they agreed to one more and put them to bed. Knowing that I've given in a little (but not too much), I find that my children feel I'm taking their needs into consideration and they cooperate. If we're at the beach and it's time to leave and they want to play in the sand, I say, "Let's compromise. You can build one more sand castle and that's it!" But you must not let them manipulate you beyond your agreement. *Alana D. Emmet, Yonkers, New York*

THE BIG "NO" SHEET ✦ I'm a single parent and father of three children. My situation requires that I get maximum cooperation from the children in order to survive—and to flourish. I strongly object to corporal punishment and must therefore employ other means to make the children do what I want them to do. I have developed a listing which is prominently displayed in my kitchen. It is entitled in bold letters "The Big No Sheet," and each child's name is shown at the top of separate columns. When I ask one of the children to do something and he or she refuses to do it, I write in their column both a "NO" and what is needed to get this "active No" removed. When a child makes a request of me, I check "The Big No Sheet." If he has a "NO" under his name, I give it back to him, e.g., "No, you can't have a pajama party," "No, you can't go to the mall with your friend," and "No, you can't borrow my camera," etc. My response will be "No" to each and every request he makes until the required chore is completed. Since implementing this rule, I now receive much more cooperation from my children. *F.C., York, Pennsylvania*

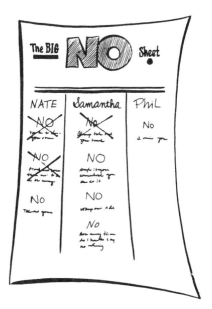

DISCIPLINE—DON'T HUMILIATE ✦ When possible, discipline your child in private. Children often become so humiliated and embarrassed by being punished in public or, worse yet, in front of friends, that they won't listen or respond to the discipline. *T.L., Mi-Wuk Village, California*

FIND THE HUMOR—EVEN IN ANGER ✦ I have learned to try to find the humor in things—especially those difficult moments we all have raising children. Sometimes other parents can see the humor in a personal situation that I can't. The other way to cultivate a sense of humor is to write down what your child has done to make you so angry. Then go back to it later and try to make it an amusing anecdote or poem. You could save it in a journal to give to your child when he is older. Finally, I tell myself to look in the mirror every morning and say out loud, "I love this child with all my heart. Having him or her in my life has brought me immeasurable joy. Growing up is very difficult. My job is to show my love every day, to encourage and praise at every opportunity, and to be a gentle teacher of right and wrong. Whatever I do today, I will do with love." *Mary Plante, Pompano Beach, Florida*

ASK ME NICELY ✦ The following advice came from a child and I gladly followed it: "Ask me nicely—don't tell me. And say 'thank you.' " It still works after forty years. *Maureen Wemken, Secaucus, New Jersey*

TEMPER TANTRUMS ◆ An important rule to follow when dealing with temper tantrums, especially the child's first one, is to ignore it. If it's not reinforced, even by your attention, it probably won't occur again. *N.S., San Jose, California*

WHEN FRUSTRATED—HUG ◆ Whenever you are really angry and frustrated with your child, do something very nice for her. Cuddle her, and read her favorite story to her, take a walk with her, or give her a bath. Giving your child a gift of love and pleasure is a great way to remind yourself how special she is and how insignificant her transgression was. *Donna J.W. Katzman, Atlanta, Georgia*

A BALANCED APPROACH ◆ The older our children got, the more we found ourselves criticizing and correcting their behavior. We made a rule for ourselves that for every negative comment we made to each child, we had to make a positive, commending, or appreciative comment. We found that positive rewards for the slightest good behavior work much better than negative ones. All sorts of side benefits have resulted from the positive comments, such as an increase in the child's self-esteem, love and respect for parents, and enjoyment of work. *Ron Burda, San Jose, California*

DON'T OVERDO THE WORD "NO" ◆ Instead of always saying "NO" to your children, occasionally say "I wouldn't do that," or "Are you sure you want to do that?" Save the word "NO" for those times when you REALLY mean it. "No" is more effective if a child doesn't hear it all the time. *Florence Moorman, Buffalo, New York*

POSITIVE SUGGESTIONS ◆ Give children stickers, surprises, special entertainments, etc. as rewards for being good. Kids are better when a parent gives positive suggestions. Instead of saying "If you don't . . . , you can't . . . ," say "If you do . . . , you can . . . ." *Gwen Braecklein, York, Pennsylvania*

A PLEASANT ACTIVITY FOLLOWS AN UNPOPULAR REQUEST ◆ The key to getting my toddler to cooperate with me is to word the request in a positive way. Whenever I have a request that he will probably react negatively to, I try to focus on what we will do after the disliked task is completed. For example, I'll say, "Let's go brush our teeth so we can read a book and get cozy," or "Let's wash your hands so we can eat," or "Let's change your diaper so you can go outside." *Wanda Nevin, Walnut Creek, California*

OFFERING ALTERNATIVES ✦ Whenever I have to take away something or say "no" to my thirteen-month-old daughter, I always make sure that I offer her something that she can have as an alternative. For example, "No you may not play in the refrigerator, but here are some pots and pans for you to play with." She tends to have fewer temper tantrums with this approach. *Betsy Rutherford, Livermore, California*

LIMITING TV TIME ✦ Each Sunday my son and I sit down and review the weekly TV section of the newspaper. Together we determine what is worth watching during the week. I tape most of the selections so he can watch them at a time that is convenient—after all homework and chores have been completed. The Discovery Channel offers terrific educational shows. *Robyn Pappas, Peoria, Arizona*

IS THAT YOUR BEST SCREAM? ✦ When your child is crying loudly and uncontrollably, ask her to kindly scream louder because she is not doing a very good job. Usually she will stop to think about what you have said. *Tina Schefield, Hamden, Connecticut*

BRIEF ISOLATION FOR A TODDLER ✦ Brief isolation has worked to discipline our two-year-old. She will periodically throw a frenzied tantrum if one of her requests isn't granted immediately. We warn her that we will put her in the crib if she doesn't stop crying, hoping that she will recover on her own. If she continues her spectacle, we put her in the crib until she calms down. Since beginning this discipline, the tantrums have occurred less frequently. *Thomas Leslie, San Diego, California*

"THAT'S OK, ACCIDENTS HAPPEN" ✦ I was cleaning and had a bucket of water on the floor when my little three-year-old dumped it. He ran off feeling bad about having made a big mess. I gave him a towel and told him, "All of us make accidents. I have done it myself lots of times. But it's how you handle it after that counts. So here is a towel; you can help me clean it up." Afterward, I praised him for being a good worker. *Janice Shumway Cluff, Manti, Utah*

"DON'T TOUCH THOSE KNICKKNACKS" ♦ We have many items (knickknacks, planters, etc.) in our house that were off limits to our children. At a very early age we taught our children not to touch these items. They saw them daily and had no problem. However, when our granddaughter came along, everything in our house was new to her—she had not seen these things every day. When she reached the stage of walking around the furniture, her first inclination was to "touch" and "take" everything within her sight. So, as we watched her approach to touch something, Grandma would put her on her lap, and Grandpa would be the "gopher." Grandma would say, "See?" and if she was agreeable to that "thing," Grandpa would bring it over and Sherrie would hold it and touch it and "see" it. When she could feel that it was cold and hard and not very interesting to play with, it satisfied her curiosity. When she started talking, she would take us by the hand and point to an object and say, "See?" and we would play the game with her. But she never touched an item without us with her. Sure made having a grandchild in our knickknack-cluttered house a whole lot easier. *D.J.L., St. Paul, Minnesota*

SHOW YOUR LOVE, EVEN IN ANGER ♦ Never let your children doubt your love for them, even for a moment and especially when you're angry. You can be angry at their behavior, but be sure they know you still love them. *Florence Grace, Fremont, California*

CLASSICAL MUSIC CALMS TEMPERS ♦ When tempers begin to flare at our home, I turn on calming (usually classical) music to help relax everyone. *Sherry Niger, Bountiful, Utah*

"IF YOU'RE GOING TO FUSS AND SCREAM, DO IT IN YOUR OWN ROOM" ♦ When a child aged two or more has a temper tantrum, try to be calm but firm, lead him to his room, and put him inside. Tell him he can come out when he is quiet. When he quietly comes out, CHEERFULLY ask him if he is done screaming. If so, then tell him to go play or do what you had asked him to do. Don't sound mad or mean, as it is all over. It wasn't long when just being told to "do that in your own room" was enough to quiet my children. *Diana A. Ingersoll, Hawthorne, Nevada*

TAKE A DEEP BREATH ◆ At times when our child is crying so hard that we can't understand what he's saying, I tell him to take a deep breath, count to three, then blow it out. He does this twice. This usually calms him down so he can let us know what's troubling him. It sure beats repeating "Stop crying" to no avail. *Terri Murphy, Redwood City, California*

"I AM GOING TO MY ROOM" ◆ Disciplining my son was a challenge. When all else failed and we needed some time out, I sent myself to my room for five to ten minutes, locked my door, and read a book. If, while I was in my room, he wanted to express his anger by kicking the door, that was acceptable. The expression of anger never lasted longer than two to three minutes. *A.V.S., Fremont, California*

✖◆◆✖

TIME-OUT AND CORNER TIME

✖◆◆✖

STANDING IN THE CORNER ◆ We don't believe in physical discipline, but needed an unpleasant alternative to objectionable behavior. Standing in the corner works best for us because kids hate to be bored, there is always a corner nearby (even in public), and the punishment can be tailored to fit the behavior. We use one minute for reminders (forgetting) and longer times for serious behavior by older children. A cheap timer kept near the best corner is helpful. If the child leaves the corner, the timer is started all over at the beginning. It worked well up to the age of twelve years. *Ron Burda, San Jose, California*

AGE DETERMINES THE LENGTH OF CORNER TIME ◆ Limit the time in the corner to as many minutes as the child's age. For example, a three-year-old sits three minutes, a six-year-old sits six minutes. *Ruthie Schneider, Lorain, Ohio*

SIT ON IT ◆ To make sure your child stays put during "corner time" or "time-out," have him or her sit on something (e.g., a leaf, piece of paper, etc.) Don't let him or her move off of it during the time-out. *A. Mercurio, Long Beach, California*

CARPET REMNANT MARKS THE SPOT ◆ Use a small square of carpet remnant as a place where a child sits during a time-out. *Theresa Blanca, Fremont, California*

THE "QUIET CHAIR" ◆ We use what we call the "Quiet Chair." Our child has to stay there until the time-out is over. *Andrea Rainey, Greer, South Carolina*

"GOOD GUY, BAD GUY" PARENTS ◆ In order to avoid one parent appearing to be the "bad guy" and the other the "good guy," the parent who puts our daughter in the corner also gets her out. *N.K.M., Palo Alto, California*

THE "TDH" SYSTEM ◆ Discipline in our house is handled by saying "Okay, if you are still doing that after the count of three, then it's time for a TDH." "TDH" means Time-out, followed by Discussion, and then a Hug and affirmation that it was the BEHAVIOR that was bad, not the child. We try to say things like, "That is inappropriate behavior," or "That behavior is unacceptable." *Audrey Swanton, Brewer, Maine*

WHEN THERE'S TWO OR MORE OF THEM AND ONLY ONE OF IT

"WHOSE DAY IS IT?" ◆ When our two daughters were young, they always argued about who would be the first to do certain things. One day I suggested to them that one would take odd days and the other would take even days. From that day on, whether it was a privilege or a chore that required one person to do it, the simple question was, "Whose day is it?" Even now, in their thirties and facing the question of who will do what, the girls turn to each other and ask, "Whose day is it?" They must have thought it was successful because they now use it with their own children. *Louis Wells, Indialantic, Florida*

BIRTHDAYS DETERMINE ODD-EVEN ✦ Children's birthdays are a good way to pick odd-even days. If your children's birthdays happen to both be on odd or even days, a flip of a coin could determine who gets to be the important decision maker on odd days and who on even ones. *Shirley Vaughan, Hobart, Indiana*

OLDER SON IS EVEN ✦ I decided that my older son was "son number one" and the younger son was "son number two." Since one is an odd number and two is an even number, all odd-numbered days were "number-one son's" days and all even-numbered days were the "second-son's days." *Peggy Gilbreth Nipper, Omaha, Nebraska*

"WHOSE DAY IS IT" SETTLES MOST ISSUES ✦ My family uses the odd-even method to determine whose turn it is to shower first, monitor the TV remote control, sit in Daddy's favorite spot when he's not around, and more. *Nancy Leddy, North Haven, Connecticut*

ONE PRIVILEGE, THREE CHILDREN ✦ While on a three-day vacation, my three children constantly argued about whose turn it was to do just about everything. I allowed each child one day of the three days to have all the privileges. It worked like a charm, and I have continued to do it at home. At the beginning of each month, I put all three of their names on each day on the calendar, rotating their names by one every day. Whenever there is a disagreement about which TV program to watch, who sits where at the table or in the car, who may read the newspaper first (the person who brings in the paper gets first refusal), we check the calendar to see who's at the top of the list that day. I also check the calendar when I need help. I'll ask, "Who's at the bottom of the list today?" and that person helps. *Hazel Woodsmall, Santa Ana, California*

"IT'S MY TURN TO SIT IN THE FRONT SEAT" ✦

My two daughters frequently argue over who gets in the front passenger seat of our car. Our rule is: whoever sits in front on the way to our destination, sits in back on the way home, and vice versa. The only problem is trying to remember at the end of the day who was sitting in the front first. *Theresa Harrington, Daly City, California*

TOSS A COIN ✦

When my daughters, who are four and six, would argue over things like whose turn it was to sit in the front seat of the car, I would toss a coin and whoever won the flip would get to sit in the front seat and the other would get the coin. That usually placated both of them. *Diana Merkel, North Haledon, New Jersey*

"THE TOY IS TAKING A TIME-OUT" ✦

If two or more children argue over a toy or book, the item itself should take a time-out. The children soon learn that it's better to share than to not have the item at all. *Sharon Marriott, Livermore, California*

A TIMER FOR A POPULAR TOY ✦

If children argue over who's going to play with a favorite toy, set a timer to limit the amount of time each child can play with that toy. *Theresa Blanca, Fremont, California*

TWO CHILDREN, ONE TV ✦ We had two children (seven years apart in age) and one TV, so Saturday cartoons were a hassle. I wrote out the names and times of shows, cut them apart, and put them in a bowl. Each child drew alternate strips. They negotiated for time and swapped time slots in order to see one-hour shows. This taught sharing. *Nina Martin, Norman, Oklahoma*

"I'M THINKING OF A NUMBER" ✦ When my children rent videotapes, each wants to play his tape first. I think of a number, then ask them to guess what it is. The child whose guess is the closest to my number gets to watch his video first. If the children are young, pick a number within range of their knowledge (1–10, for instance). For older children, create a large range (1–100, for instance) so they will have to figure out who's closest. Not only does this game settle arguments, it teaches counting and arithmetic. *Patricia Lopez, Fremont, California*

SHARING MADE EASY ✦ If there is a sharing problem with an item like an outdoor swing, I let each child have a turn while the other one and I count to perhaps twenty or by tens to a hundred. This also helps them with their counting skills. *Sherry Niger, Bountiful, Utah*

✖✦✦✖

WHEN SIBLINGS ARGUE

✖✦✦✖

BACK-TO-BACK PUNISHMENT ✦ During spats between my brother and me, it wasn't uncommon for Mother to send us outside with instructions to sit under a shade tree with our backs to each other. We were told we had to stay in that position and could not look at each other. Of course, only a few minutes would pass before we were peeking at each other, giggling, and soon best of friends again. *Frances Best, Lincoln, Nebraska*

EYE-TO-EYE APOLOGY ✦ A friend of mine has a creative way to stop her two boys from arguing or fighting. She makes them sit on the floor closely facing each other with their legs crossed. They have to sit there until they apologize and make up. It really works. *Cynthia Baird, Fremont, California*

FROM QUARRELING TO LAUGHTER ✦ Having three small boys at home seems to produce a lot of quarreling. To help curb some of it, I make the two that are arguing or fighting sit face to face and stare at each other (this could work by itself because they almost always burst into laughter). Then each one must tell the other what he himself did wrong. They then shake hands or hug. This works and seems also to teach them that it takes two to fight. *Jodi V. Wilding, Centerville, Utah*

A FRIENDSHIP CIRCLE STOPS ARGUMENTS ✦ Children sometimes argue over a minor problem and spend a great deal of time trying to figure out whose fault it is. When this happens, I have them form a circle, shake hands with each other, and say, "Let's be friends." If it is a major problem, we all sit on the floor and talk, taking turns to air differences. *Joan Lyboult, Syracuse, New York*

"YOU CAN RESUME YOUR ACTIVITY AFTER YOU RESUME BEING CIVIL" ✦ If my children fought or argued, I had them sit in the living room facing each other. When they became civil to one another again, they could resume whatever it was they'd been doing. This worked fabulously. *Carolyn Catell Mongillo, North Haven, Connecticut*

IF YOU TATTLE, SAY SOMETHING GOOD FIRST ✦ When either of my boys came to me to tattle, I would write what he had to say on the blackboard only after he had told me something good to write about his brother. It usually took so long to think of something good that he couldn't remember the bad thing. The habit of tattling fizzled out, which was my object in the first place. *F.R., Brighton, Illinois*

IT'S TIME TO CLEAN THE BATHROOM ✦ When older children bicker with each other, tell them that "It's time to clean the bathroom." That way, if one of them starts whining and complaining and picking on the other one, the other one will say, "Look, we'll have to clean the bathroom if you keep this up, so let's stop now!" *Emily Oberlag, West Chester, Ohio*

KIDS SAY THE FUNNIEST THINGS

I was recently trying to determine which one of my children had broken something. Of course, they all answered "I didn't do it!" Later that evening my six-year-old told me that when she grew up and got married she would only have one child. "That way," she said, "I will ALWAYS know who did it." *Peggy Maxey, Enid, Oklahoma*

REPARATIONS ARE BETTER THAN APOLOGIES ✦ When one child hurts another in some way (hitting, destroying something they have built, etc.) I ask the child to "make the other child feel better." This may involve a hug, rebuilding the Lego structure, or whatever would rectify the situation. *Linda Yazzolino, Newark, California*

GO TO YOUR ROOM AND WRITE ✦ When my two children fight, I make them go to their room and write a list of reasons why they love the other sibling or why they should be nice, etc. I have them do writing assignments to make them stop and think why they should be good to each other. *Sharlene Fallsman, Denver, Colorado*

IF YOU CAN'T ACT CIVIL, YOU CAN'T TALK TO EACH OTHER ✦ My brother and I were three years apart, and we argued and fought a lot until my father implemented a new rule. When my father caught us arguing, he tried to resolve our conflict by asking us what the problem was. If we continued our argument and accusations, he would forbid us to talk to one another for a certain length of time (it could be hours, or a day, or up to two days) until we could be reasonable with one another and treat each other with respect. My brother and I found the discipline of not being able to talk to each other unbearable. Siblings do not realize how much communication there really is between them. We would sneak around my father trying to communicate with each other while we were being disciplined. We learned very quickly to talk out our differences in a more humane manner instead of shouting and hitting each other. I feel the value of positive communication was well learned between my brother and me. *J.K.S., Castro Valley, California*

ONLY WRITTEN COMPLAINTS ARE ACCEPTED ✦ Now that my children have reached the age where they can be left alone for a few hours, I return home to hear a litany of complaints from each child about their siblings' behavior while I was gone. This practice of tattling on each other has subsided considerably since I instituted a new rule: If you have a complaint about your siblings' behavior while I'm gone, write it out on paper. Only written complaints will be acted on. This new practice has filtered out all the frivolous complaints and little annoyances; only the big issues are worth writing about. Besides limiting the tattling, this new rule has inspired writing practice, and the notes will be a fun legacy to pass on to the children when they are older. *Kathy Stokes, Winnipeg, Manitoba*

6

"PLEASE PICK UP YOUR TOYS" (Chores for Children)

◆

Cleaning your house while your kids are still growing is like shoveling the walk before it stops snowing.

— PHYLLIS DILLER

If there were an Olympic event for creating the greatest mess in a house in the shortest amount of time, my three-year-old would win a gold medal and my six-year-old would win silver (and probably miss the gold herself by only 1/100 of a second). All kidding aside, I am truly amazed—and on rare occasions even impressed—at the speed with which my children can scatter their toys around the house. I first realized that our home would never again be neat and orderly soon after our oldest daughter learned how to walk. Now, five years later and with only a faint memory of order in my life, I don't even flinch upon hearing the thunderous sound of hundreds of plastic Legos being poured onto the carpet. Nor do I yelp loudly and wake the entire family when I step barefooted on a "lost" Lego during a late-night visit to the bathroom. I'm becoming a seasoned veteran!

I would be delighted if my children picked up their toys without being reminded, but they seem to find doing other household chores more enjoyable. Our three-year-old, for instance, likes setting the table and helping to rinse the dinner dishes. Our six-year-old loves to assist with cooking and baking, and she also helps her younger sister with many tasks. And, of course, there are "fun" activities like sorting laundry or helping wash the car. It doesn't matter what the task is

99

(as long as it's appropriate for a child's age) or whether it is performed perfectly. Doing some form of chores enables a child to contribute to the household and instills a sense of family responsibility.

When children complete a chore successfully, especially if it's a new task to them or they do it spontaneously, let them know how proud you are. Recently, for example, my six-year-old daughter surprised us by picking up all her toys without being asked. My wife and I made a point of thanking her and giving her a big hug, but I also wanted to do something special that would encourage her to pick up her toys again without us begging her. So, after my daughter went to bed, I made a colorful certificate that read, "THANK YOU FOR CLEANING YOUR ROOM. THIS CERTIFICATE CAN BE REDEEMED FOR A SPECIAL REWARD FROM DAD." It was signed, "*The Cleaning Bunny.*" My daughter loved it and has since received more certificates—not every time she cleans her room, but frequently enough to encourage her to keep her toys picked up. She now offers similar certificates (redeemable from big sister) to our younger daughter.

Many of the following tips offer creative ways to assign chores, turn boring tasks into "fun" activities, and employ imaginative rewards. (Chapter 1, Play Time, also offers some practical tips relating to chores. See the sections Coping with Toy Clutter, Storing Toys, and Quick Cleanup.)

CHORE TIPS

CHORES HELP THE WHOLE FAMILY • Do not ask your children to please put away the dishes for "me." They will grow up with the attitude that they are doing all tasks for "Mom," instead of making the house run smoothly for everyone. Instead, say something like, "Let's all take a job and do it and get this place looking good so we can all have time for ourselves and so no one person will have to do all the tasks." *Ruthie Schneider, Lorain, Ohio*

COMMUNITY (HOUSEHOLD) SERVICE ✦ An idea that has worked well for us involves community service (never housework or chores—these are very heavy-sounding words!). The name of each room in our house is placed in a bag. Every other week, alternating with our housekeeper, we clean a room at a time. One child draws the room we will do together from the bag. Certain tasks belong together, such as dusting stair rails, table, and mantel or vacuuming chair and sofa, etc. The child who did not draw chooses which task he or she prefers to do. When we finish a room, we repeat the draw with the other child drawing a room from the bag. We limit our housecleaning on this day to two hours. With all of us working together, not only do we have some terrific conversation, the kids are getting educated in caring for things in our house and we all know exactly how much time we will be spending on a task that I, personally, dislike to do very much. *Stacy Krimetz, Livermore, California*

FAMILY-HISTORY LESSON DOING CHORES ✦ If your children help you with chores around the house, talk about where some of the objects or family heirlooms came from. This will help your children understand the importance of these objects and teach them how to care for them. Family heirlooms help children understand their family history, which it is never too early to learn about. *Florence Moorman, Buffalo, New York*

START AT AN EARLY AGE ✦ Start chores and a sense of responsibility at an early age. It is unrealistic to think that all of a sudden, at age thirteen, children will become young adults who willingly do chores. At three, my children *chose* a little chore to do on a daily basis and started to remove their own plates from the dinner table. At times, it seems more work than it's worth, as you could clean the table off three times faster! But the patience required is well rewarded as they get older. *Audrey Swanton, Brewer, Maine*

A MORNING CHORE BOARD ✦ To increase my six- and three-year-old daughters' independence in getting ready for the day, I made a "chore board" for each child. I took a wooden plaque of sufficient length, glued on a picture to represent each chore, covered the board and pictures with a clear liquid sealer, and screwed in a cup hook at the top of each picture. The girls helped me choose the pictures from magazines. As each child completes a chore, she covers the chore's picture by hanging a wooden heart on the cup hook. (We found the hearts at the craft store — be sure to space your cup hooks so that the hearts fit!) If all her hearts are hung by the time we need to leave for school or the timer goes off (on the weekends), she gets a sticker to paste on a piece of paper which tells her how many stickers she needs to earn a predetermined treat. They are enthusiastic, our conversation focuses on hanging hearts instead of nagging about chores, and the chores get done! The three-year-old has even surprised me by making her own bed. *Nancy Knowlton, Wilmette, Illinois*

FIVE-MINUTE WARNING ♦ To get children to clean up after playing, I would give them a warning that cleanup time was near. In five minutes, I would tell them to clean up. I noticed that they would fuss less if they had a warning. *Roberta Dunaief, Coconut Creek, Florida*

THE BIGGEST MESS WINS ♦ One of the tricks I use to get my daughter to pick up her room is to have her count the number of things she puts away. She proudly reports to me (and with not a little amazement) the large number of toys and other things she picked up. *Anonymous, Pasadena, California*

HOUSECLEANING ASSIGNMENTS ♦ As my working day got longer and as the children got older, we agreed to a cleaning system that kept the house clean and orderly. We divided all the chores in three equal amounts and each of us was given three assignments per week. Each Sunday the chores were listed on pieces of paper and we held a drawing. If someone drew the same chore three weeks in a row, he was allowed to negotiate a trade or bargain with each other. Everyone in the family must keep his or her own room clean and also turn in the clothes for the laundry. (Mom's in charge of the laundry.) This system works great. The house is kept in order and clean, and when an area or chore is not clean, you know who is responsible. The children also make sure everyone in the family respects their assigned area by reminding them to pick up after themselves. They learned responsibility and respect for each other. *Joyce Richardson, Pinecrest, California*

"POST-IT" NOTES FOR REMINDERS ◆ Children sometimes need reminders for things to do: chores, school activities, family responsibilities, etc. I use "Post-it" notes which are color-coded for different topics (yellow for school, blue for chores and responsibilities, and green for family and social activities). The children take the notes and place them on certain items that will help them to remember that chore or activity. They work great! *Elaine Womboldt, Lansing, Michigan*

ROUND AND ROUND IT GOES, WHICH CHORE YOU WILL DO, NOBODY KNOWS ◆ To make work fun, draw pictures or list the names of different chores on a plain paper plate. Divide the plate into pieces of pie-shaped triangles, listing a different chore for each triangle. Hold the middle of the plate down with your thumb or attach it to a piece of cardboard so it will spin. Draw an arrow pointing at the plate, which signifies the "winning" triangle. Ask your children to spin the plate to see which job they will be responsible for. Include one space that says "Day Off." Children love to play the "Work Game." *Carol Smead, San Jose, California*

CHORES ON PING-PONG BALLS ◆ I assign household chores on Ping-Pong balls, which my children select from a jar each Saturday morning. It makes chores into a fun process. *Janet Dudey, Fremont, California*

SONGS FOR CHORES ◆ Singing during chores makes them fun. My children and I change the words (depending on the chore) to "This is the way we clean the table, clean the table, clean the table . . . '' The children sing along and the chores seem less painful to do. *Sharon Marriott, Livermore, California*

DAILY HELPER ◆ Being the mother of ten children, I have had to throw out most of my schedules and assign them one day a week that they are my helper or buddy. We go around and I try to teach them to do certain jobs. They do their chores and at the end of the day I give them their allowance for the week. That has helped to eliminate trying to concentrate on so many children and jobs at a time. *Marcia Harward, Fountain Valley, California*

STOP TOY CLUTTER ◆ Have children put one toy away before getting out another. This stops toy clutter and makes picking up easier. *Florence Moorman, Buffalo, New York*

PICK UP YOUR TOYS OR LOSE THEM FOR A DAY ◆ If my children didn't pick up their toys, I would confiscate the toys for a day or longer. The next time I asked my children to pick up, they were more motivated to comply. *Anonymous, Sunnyvale, California*

A "RANSOM BOX" ◆ When my children were growing up, they often left their toys out after playing with them. I would remind them to pick them up. If they didn't, I put them in the "Ransom Box." To get them back, they had to pay a nominal fine out of their allowance or do an assigned task or chore. They learned to keep their toys picked up. *Ila Kohl, Fremont, California*

DO A CHORE, GET A TOY BACK ◆ When my children leave their toys out so I have to pick them up, I put them in a box. On Saturday, the children have to complete one chore for each toy they want back from the box. *Linda Crosby, Fremont, California*

UNLOAD THE DISHWASHER ◆ My four- and six-year-old unload the dishwasher every day. A friend gave me the idea of putting my dishes in the lower cupboards so the kids can reach them. The few things that store up high or require special handling are put on the counter for me to put away later. *Beverly Killion, Anaheim, California*

A BACK-SAVING IDEA ✦ When emptying the dishwasher, I often let my children carefully hand me the items to put away. Not only do they get the satisfaction of helping, it saves me a lot of bending. *Polly Morehouse Griffith, Santa Rosa, California*

THE PINT-SIZED "DUST BUSTER" ✦ My three-year-old likes to "help" me around the house. When I am ready to dust, I put his old mittens on him and spray them with dust spray. He does a pretty good job wiping down the furniture and it keeps him busy and out of mischief while I'm cleaning. *Sheryl Saxton, Tekamah, Nebraska*

"I DON'T FEEL LIKE IT" ✦ When asked to do something, my eight-year-old would often reply, "I don't feel like it." So when he asked me to do something for him, I told him "I'm sorry, I don't feel like it today. Remember that's what you tell me?" After a few times of this, he got the drift. *Marilyn Horning, Fulton, New York*

KIDS SAY THE FUNNIEST THINGS

My four-year-old stepdaughter was playing in the same room I was in when I heard a heavy sigh. When I asked her what was wrong, she replied, "Oh, I just didn't know being a real person was going to be so difficult." *Kevin Bemis, Tecumseh, Michigan*

A DEADLINE TO COMPLETE A CHORE ✦ Once you set up a list of chores that you feel is reasonable according to the skills and schedule of each child, set a deadline for when you expect these chores to be completed (before going to bed, 3 P.M. Saturday, etc.). Let the children know what the consequence will be if the chores are not done by the deadline. It's also a good idea to remind them once or twice. I would not let my children do a privilege activity until their chores were completed. *Gina Cox, Naperville, Illinois*

"STAY IN YOUR ROOM UNTIL YOUR CHORE IS DONE" ✦ Tell your child that she must stay in her room until a specific chore (picking up toys, etc.) is done. The first time you try this she may stay in her room for hours protesting. Soon, however, she will quickly get her chore done so she can play. *Melissa Burton, Fort Lewis, Washington*

"I DIDN'T GET RESPECT UNTIL I ... " ✦ I've often felt like Rodney Dangerfield—"I don't get respect." My kids can sometimes seem like a hurricane, making messes as they move through our home. Then, there I am left to clean up. When I asked the boys (ages two, five, and eight) to pick up and help me put the house back in order, I was told by each that "I didn't do it." One day while they were watching TV, I went to their room and made a big mess with their toys. This included the large bucket of Legos. I told them they had a big mess in their room to pick up. When they went up wondering what I was talking about, they were indeed met with a large mess. I asked them in a very calm voice to please pick up. This time they really didn't make the mess and were very quick to tell me so. "But Mom, we didn't make this mess, why should we pick it up? It's not fair." I simply stated, "Now you know how I feel." They got the message. *Marilyn Horning, Fulton, New York*

"TIMED" CHORES ✦ To encourage my children to clean their room I would set my timer, then announce, "Clean your room until the timer goes off." Ten to fifteen minutes of steady work goes a long way. Make it fun by playing a children's-song tape while they work. Always praise their work. *Florence Grace, Fremont, California*

"TIME TO CLEAN UP" SONG ✦ When it's time to clean up after activities, I sing, "It's time to clean up, it's time to clean up and put all the toys away." Then I name all the chores that need to be done. For example, I sing, "Let's put all the books away, let's put all the crayons away, let's put all the play dough away," etc. Singing during chores makes it fun for the children. *Janice Fonteno, Union City, California*

PICK UP TOYS UNTIL THE SONG IS OVER ✦ Occasionally I challenge my children to pick up all their toys before a certain song is over. They always love a challenge so they scurry around, racing to complete their task before the song is completed. This also works for chores. *Rebecca Robinson, San Jose, California*

"IF YOU CAN RUN A GAMEBOY, YOU CAN RUN A MAYTAG!" ✦ When my stepchildren were about eleven years old, I taught them to do their own laundry. From that day on, it was their responsibility. We give advice now and then on stains, sorting, and special garments. At first they complained; now they brag to their friends that they know how to do laundry. *Deb Skillstad-Rost, Omaha, Nebraska*

> Don't forget to teach conservation too! Older children and teens love to wash just one article of clothing through a whole wash-and-dry cycle just because they want to wear that particular item.

"WHO KNOWS WHERE THIS BELONGS?" ✦ To get my children to help me pick up their toys, I ask them, "Who knows where the puzzle belongs?" or "Where do the crayons go?" They usually pitch in to help and it gives them great pride to know the answer. It's kind of tricky, but it works. *Carol Smead, San Jose, California*

CHORES ALWAYS SEEM MORE FUN AT BEDTIME ✦ We noticed that our daughter was very willing at bedtime to do some otherwise dreaded chore. So once in a while, on a Friday or Saturday night, I allow her the treat of staying up late and cleaning her room, practicing the piano, doing her homework, or some other activity which needs to be done. *N.K.M., Palo Alto, California*

SORTING SOCKS ✦ To add a little life to that tedious laundry chore, I let my children help by sorting the socks. It's fun to watch their minds work and they seem to enjoy the sense of accomplishment. *Polly Morehouse Griffith, Santa Rosa, California*

A SURPRISE IN THE LAUNDRY BASKET ✦ Once I fold and place the clean clothes in the laundry basket, I encourage my four- and five-year-old daughters to put their laundry away. They know that if they put all their clothes away they will find a surprise at the bottom of the basket. *Tracy Bauch, Milwaukee, Wisconsin*

CHILDREN LOVE TO HELP WITH LAUNDRY ✦ Have your toddlers help you hang out the laundry. Let them hand you clothespins and the clothes as you hang them to dry, or let them help you pin the clothes on the line. *Janette Totherow, Anadarko, Oklahoma*

BEHAVIOR CHARTS ✦ I had little success in having my daughter pick up her toys until I made a game of it. Using felt pens I created a daily chart which had spaces to place colorful stickers. She received a sticker to place on the chart if she put her toys away. She was excited to get a sticker for her chart and even more elated to receive a special reward for acquiring five stickers. *Thomas Leslie, San Diego, California*

WHAT TIME IS CONVENIENT FOR YOU THIS WEEKEND? ✦ Whenever I had a hard time getting my sons to clean their room or help with chores around the house, I would ask them what time would be convenient for them over this next weekend to clean or do their chores. This was a close-ended question and they would say something like "Oh, eleven o'clock." I would then respond, "Oh, eleven o'clock on Saturday. OK, that sounds good." They felt they had a choice and I knew that it was going to get done because they had made the agreement. It does work. *Maureen Jones, Madison, Connecticut*

FIRST ONE DONE WITH HER MESS WINS! ✦ A trick I use to get my daughter to pick up is to challenge her to a "cleanup" race. We race to see whether she can clean up her room faster than I can clean up the kitchen after dinner. *Nancy Knowlton, Wilmette, Illinois*

THE COOPERATION STORY ◆ I made up a song to help my two-year-old daughter help pick up her toys. It is called "The Cooperation Song." The words are very simple, It's just: "Cooperation, that's our game, Cooperation is the name of our game. You help me and I'll help you and we'll get things done faster too." I have three daughters, seven, four, and two years old. Now the seven-year-old makes fun of the song, but I still find her singing it to herself when she is cleaning up her room. *Michelle Stephens, Toledo, Ohio*

A PENNY EARNED ◆ My preschooler went through a time of using LOTS of Scotch tape, and I found myself irritated by how much she wasted. I finally had her earn her own tape by doing tasks around the house in exchange for money to buy the tape (such as handing the clean dishes to me from the dishwasher or helping me make a bed). She then had her own tape and was not constantly raiding my supply. She also acquired some useful household skills and perhaps some understanding of the connection between working, saving, and buying things. I actually got the idea from her preschool, which asked each year that children "earn" the money to buy a food item to donate to a feed-the-hungry program. *Nancy Lee, Pasadena, California*

CALENDAR CONTRACT ◆ My daughter needs to do eye exercises with my help three times each week. Getting her to do them was a battle until I gave her her own calendar. At the beginning of each week, we look at her calendar together and choose the three days on which we will do her eye exercises. Then we both initial the days. Now my daughter usually reminds me to do the exercises on the days we've agreed to do them. After each two weeks of us both keeping our commitments to exercise, she gets a small treat. *Karen Schmidt, Redmond, Washington*

PAYDAY FOR CHILDREN ◆ All of my children have jobs depending on their age. Fridays, without fail, are paydays—small amount of money, school supplies, a special snack, etc. Payment is based on output and age and is chosen from several options. Ambition, self-worth, responsibility, value of money, and decision making are lasting assets. At first, they needed gentle reminders that one earns rewards, but they learned quickly. *Catherine Gray, Melbourne, Florida*

FILL A WHOLE PIE—GET AN AWARD ✦ Trivial Pursuit "pie" game pieces (or you can make your own) can become a new game that encourages desired behavior in your children. There are six pieces to a pie. One piece can be earned for every day except Sunday. Parents decide what must be done to earn a piece of the pie. The object is to earn a pie piece every day so that by Sunday you have earned your whole pie, which entitles you to a reward. The rewards can range from just "recognition" and the pleasure of seeing a completed pie, to a favorite dessert, to being allowed to do a favorite activity. *Sabra Jiwa, Marietta, Georgia*

EARNING STARS ✦ We award a star for each time any of our children does his or her chores without complaining. After a child collects ten stars, we reward him or her with a treat, such as making a phone call to Grandma or picking a favorite dinner and helping to make it. *Angie Satterfield, Patriot, Indiana*

PICK UP FIVE THINGS ✦ Before my children could do one of their favorite activities, I would require each of them to first pick up five things (or ten things). It's a great way to get your house picked up quickly—with no complaints. *Florence Grace, Fremont, California*

7

CLOTHES AND LAUNDRY

◆

Out damned spot, out I say!
— WILLIAM SHAKESPEARE, *Macbeth*, 1623

From shopping for new clothes to washing soiled ones, parents spend an immense amount of time with their children's clothing. And beginning when children are as young as two years old, families may experience occasional "clothing wars." In our house these battles center around two issues, choice and comfort. We finally resolved our problems about who should choose what to wear—our daughters or us—after we read Sarah Gerber's tip "Clothing Battles," which suggests letting a child pick an outfit from a few selections of *your* choosing. Giving our daughters this kind of choice lets them feel they are in control, yet their selections are always appropriate. We're still working on the issue of whether our daughters' clothes are comfortable enough. Paying careful attention to their comments about likes and dislikes seems to help a lot.

There is another issue that needs to be brought out of the clothes closet. We fathers have to face up to the fact that dressing little girls is quite a different task from dressing little boys. I have found this out the hard way. First, my wife laughed at me when I put our daughter's panties on backward (both sides looked the same to me!). Then I was embarrassed at our daughter's swimming lesson when a giggling mother pointed out that I had put my daughter's swimsuit on backward (it had *very* weird straps!). Finally, I was saved from the worst possible humiliation by my six-year-old last year. "Dad," she shrieked as I walked out the front door, "You have Kelly's (my three-year-old) party dress on backwards!" (it had straps *and* frills, plus bows that looked like they belonged in the front). I only wish that I had known sooner about Leslie Boyce's tip "Belly-button Underwear."

111

Laundry is a big issue with parents as well. I learned this quickly when, to my surprise, three of the first five child-care tips that I received in the mail pertained to laundry. I imagined my child-care book turning into one about children's laundry. Obviously it didn't, but there are some great tips in this chapter to help with the never-ending chore of sorting, washing, drying, and putting away your children's clothes.

◆

CLOTHING TIPS

BELLY-BUTTON UNDER-WEAR ◆ Our little girl has trouble telling the front from the back on her underwear. We took a laundry marker and painted a belly button on the front so she can match the belly button on her panties with her own belly button. Now she always gets her pants on correctly. *Leslie Boyce, Salt Lake City, Utah*

RIGHT SHOE, LEFT SHOE ✦ Here is how I taught my three-year-old how to put her shoes on the right feet. I showed her her bare feet and pointed out how her big toes came together when her feet were side by side. Then, I took a permanent marker and drew ovals (big toes) on the sides of the soles of her sneakers where her big toes would be and told her the big toes on her shoes should be together just like her own big toes. She's had no problem with any shoes that were marked. *Susan Risner, Denton, Texas*

ARROWS HELP MATCH SHOES ✦ I used a magic marker to put an arrow in the sole of each shoe which pointed towards the middle. In other words, in the left shoe the arrow would point to the right and in the right shoe the arrow would point to the left. That way she was able to put on her shoes without asking for help. *Dan Rogowski, Rolling Meadows, Illinois*

KIDS SAY THE FUNNIEST THINGS

When my son was about four years old, he put his right shoe on his left foot and his left shoe on his right foot. I said, "Danny, you've got your shoes on the wrong feet!" He looked down at his feet, somewhat confused and replied, "No I don't. These are my feet!" *Joan Quinn, Colwyn, Pennsylvania*

SMILEY FACES HELP WITH SHOES ✦ I draw smiley faces on the inside soles of the shoes so that the smiley faces will be facing each other when the shoes are on the proper feet. *Sandy Hultgren-Mabry, Bloomfield, Michigan*

CLOTHING BATTLES ✦ If your child often demands to pick out her own outfits to wear in the morning (even though they might be inappropriate), give her a choice among several alternatives which you have assembled. She feels in control and you feel satisfied that she will be wearing something appropriate. Teach her ways to pick out her own clothes and put yourself in her position and see what she might like to wear. *Sarah Gerber, Plant City, Florida*

DON'T LOSE THE HOODED-JACKET STRING ✦
Weave one side of the string from your child's hooded jacket in and out of a 4-hole button about 1″ to 1½″ in diameter. Tie a knot in the end of the string. Repeat with the string on the other side. This stops the tie ends from slipping through the hood. *Jan Green, Fremont, California*

IF PANTS ARE TOO LONG ✦ If your child's pants are too long, put inexpensive terry-cloth wrist bands on their pant or pajama legs to keep them up so that the child doesn't trip on them. *Lynette Fujitani, San Antonio, Texas*

Make sure the bands are not too tight, and check them regularly.

"HOKEY-POKEY" DRESSING ✦ To make the dressing process easier with my toddler, we sing the "Hokey Pokey" song together using words which are appropriate for the stage of getting dressed which we are at. For example, to put on socks, we sing. "You put your left sock on. You put your left sock on. You put your left sock on, and you shake it all about!" To put on a shirt, we sing, "You put your left arm in." After she shakes her left arm "all about," we repeat with the right arm. Children love it! *Linda Rodgers, Fremont, California*

CLOTHES ON THE FLOOR ✦ To discourage my children from tossing their clothes on the floor, I charge them for each clothing item found on the floor: 10¢ for dirty clothes and 25¢ for clean items. I tally up the total and make them pay me on the spot. After the first two days of this practice they started to keep their clothes where they belonged. *Angie Bryson, Fremont, California*

"I DRESSED MYSELF" BUTTON ✦ Make a button pin for your toddlers or preschoolers that says, "I dressed myself today." They get to wear it on the days that they do so. Kids will get a reminder all day long even from strangers. *Kim VanGorder, Cary, North Carolina*

SKID-PROOF SOCKS FOR NEW WALKERS ✦
When our children were first learning to walk, I would use fabric-paint tubes (the puffy type) to paint designs on the

bottoms of their socks to make the soles skid-proof. *Vicki Schrimmer, Irvine, California*

I CAN PUT MY OWN COAT ON ✦ To teach a toddler how to put on his own coat, have him lay the coat on the floor in front of him, open, with the top of the coat towards his feet. All he needs to do is put his arms in and flip the coat over his head. *Penny Vaughan, Chesapeake, Virginia*

SLIPPERY NEW SHOES ✦ Most girls' shoes are slippery when new. I take a strip of silver electrical tape and put it on the bottom. Then I score the bottom with an ordinary key. No more slips (or at least fewer slips). *Jennifer Bystrzak, Tonawanda, New York*

A quick rub with fine sandpaper works great too.

LOANING BABY CLOTHES ✦ I keep a clothes-marking pen (available at sewing stores) in the baby's room and put our initials on everything we loan out. I have a box in the closet for outgrown clothing to be kept and lent out, and a bag in the closet for clothing to be given away. I have plastic bags (the kind your groceries come in) hanging from hangers in the closet with yellow Post-its on them with the name of the person to whom the clothes will be returned. *Margaret Healy, Albany, California*

Always make sure plastic bags are securely placed away from infants and children, as they can suffocate in them.

CLOSET ORGANIZER ✦ Our three-and-a-half-year-old would want a specific article of clothing and would go through every single drawer, dumping everything out just to find it. We resolved it by installing a closet organizer with the right size hangers so that he can see every single shirt he owns. Put the pants, T-shirts, and shorts on the shelves. This made our mornings much easier because he can now see all of his clothes and easily pick out what he wants. *Lynne Bassett, Fremont, California*

ADD A LOWER CLOSET POLE ✦ In a regular clothes closet, most children's clothes take up only the top space. Install a lower rod so that children can reach it easily. This way the entire closet can be utilized. *Hugh Heydt, Omaha, Nebraska*

Also, clothing rods that hook onto the existing rod can be purchased from most department stores.

LAUNDRY TIPS

FOR THAT FRESH LAUNDRY SMELL ✦ Add ⅓ cup of baking soda to the rinse water to make baby's laundry smell fresh. *D. Martinez, Fremont, California*

WASHING CLOTHES FOR SENSITIVE SKIN ✦ If your child has sensitive skin, add ⅓ cup of vinegar to the rinse cycle of your washer. It will rid soap residue from the clothes. It really works. *Michele Robson-Bermudez, Fremont, California*

LIQUID DISH SOAP ♦ I keep liquid dish soap near the washer and squirt a little on soiled areas (milk, carrots, formula, etc.) before putting clothes in the wash basket. The clothes can soak until wash day, and the results are very good. *Jan Harvey, Fremont, California*

WASHING SMALL ITEMS ♦ Keep a nylon net on a hook near the changing table so you can put those small clothing items (socks, booties, etc.) in it when you undress your child. Put the tied-up net in the washer with the rest of the laundry. *D. Martinez, Fremont, California*

STAIN-FIGHTING FORMULA ♦ This recipe works great on baby bibs and clothes to get out those formula, medicine, burp, and dirt stains that go with having children.

> 1 gallon hot tap water
> 1 cup Cascade
> ¼ cup bleach

Soak clothes for 30 minutes, then launder as usual. Check fabric for colorfastness. *Barbara Carmedelle, Fremont, California*

STAIN STICK TO GO ♦ My friends made fun of me at first when they noticed that I carried a small container of Stain Stick in my purse at all times. But as soon as my toddler spills, the stain stick goes on the spill, and everyone continues with their activities. I can wash the outfit two or three days later, and no more stain. *Lori Krouse, Red Lion, Pennsylvania*

PRESOAK IN THE DIAPER PAIL ♦ After washing a load of diapers, I add about ¾ gallon of hot water, 1 cup of detergent, and ½ cup of baking soda to the diaper pail. The detergent starts working on the diaper stains and the baking soda absorbs most of the odor until I get around to the next load of laundry. *Nancy Stuever, Fountain Valley, California*

NO FABRIC SOFTENERS FOR DIAPERS ♦ Don't add fabric softeners to your diaper load. It makes them feel softer, but it makes them unabsorbent—like fiberglass! *Bobette Pestana, Tampa, Florida*

EXTRA RINSE FOR DIAPERS ✦ For the best wash possible, I put dirty diapers through two wash/rinse cycles. I use Dreft detergent with hot water for the first cycle, then use a cup of vinegar for the second wash cycle, and rinse as usual. The vinegar removes any soap residue left over from the first rinse. *Nancy Stuever, Fountain Valley, California*

CRAYON STAINS ON FABRIC ✦ To get crayon marks out of fabric, use an iron and waxed paper. Place the fabric flat on an ironing board, cover the crayon stain with waxed paper (wax side down), then place a damp rag on top of the waxed paper. Iron with high heat (but not too hot with certain fabrics); the crayon marks should stick to the waxed paper. You may have to repeat the process a few times, but it usually works like a charm. I even used this waxed-paper method to remove unwanted crayon marks from the backseat of our new car. *Mary Esbin, Long Beach, New York*

REMOVING INK FROM CHILDREN'S CLOTH-ING ✦ When your children get ink on their clothing, spray it with hairspray, let it soak, and then wash it. *Ruth Joachim, Omaha, Nebraska*

DIRTY SHOES AND INK ✦ Use a commercial baby wipe to clean dirty leather shoes, especially athletic shoes. Baby wipes also work well at removing ink from a child's skin. *Jan Green, Fremont, California*

REMOVING BLOODSTAINS ✦ As often as children get hurt, it is good to know that hydrogen peroxide removes bloodstains from clothes. *Carolyn Watson, Fremont, California*

MY WASHER EATS SOCKS ✦ I fasten the toes of socks together with safety pins so I don't lose one in the wash. When I take them out of the drawer to wear, I either close the pin and put it back in the drawer or I fasten dirty socks together and throw them in the laundry bag. I close all Velcro ends (bibs and diaper wraps) before putting them in the wash. *P.H., Albany, California*

READY-MADE BED ◆ When I make my children's beds I always put on two sets of sheets and pillow cases. If I'm in a hurry, I just remove the top sheet and pillow case and presto — the bed is already made. *Fran Friedman, New City, New York*

8

HEALTH AND SAFETY

◆

My mother had a great deal of trouble with me,
but I think she enjoyed it.

— MARK TWAIN

Parents are faced with countless questions every day pertaining to the health and safety of their children: Should I call the doctor about that tiny rash on my daughter's stomach? Should I let my daughter walk to school by herself? As parents, we strive to react to these questions in the appropriate manner. We don't want to overreact, nor do we want to ignore a potential hazard. For example, I want my daughter to be safe, but I don't want to be overprotective. Some situations are clear-cut and decisions come easy; others are not. With experience, we learn to trust our instincts. And we seek counsel from each other.

Parents from across the land have shared some of their ingenious health and safety tips with us in this chapter—ones you won't find in a medical book. Two of my favorites can be found in the first section, titled Boo-boos and Owies. One is to use a bag of frozen peas instead of a dripping ice bag to soothe a bruise (p. 121). The other is to always keep a red washcloth handy for a bloody injury (p. 123). By diminishing the sight of blood, this will hopefully lessen the fear for the child. I can personally vouch for both tips—they really work!

Over the years my children have established a wonderful relationship with their pediatrician and his staff. Since learning about Tracy LaVelle's tip ("A Prescription for Ice Cream," p. 127), my children love their doctor even more. Similar tips can be found in the section Visits to the Doctor. Five other sections can also be found in this chapter: Time to Take Your Medicine, Colicky Babies, Teeth Care, Miscellaneous Health Tips, and Safety at Home and Away. Don't miss Alice Jordon's "Parking Lot Safety" tip (p. 139). It's a clever way to keep your children safe in a busy parking lot.

BOO-BOOS AND OWIES

BETTER THAN ICE ◆ Instead of using ice cubes to soothe a bruise, I use a small bag of frozen peas (just as they come from the grocery store). Since it's more pliable than ice cubes, it conforms to the bruise better and kids can hold it themselves. *Lyla Fries, Fremont, California*

 Ice chips or cubes in a small plastic bag of water work well too—the water gets cold and the Baggie wraps around the area nicely. I highly recommend a general first-aid and CPR course for all parents. It could save your life and others'.

FROZEN SPONGE FOR BOO-BOOS ◆ Instead of using ice cubes to soothe bumps and bruises, wet a small sponge and store it in a small freezer bag. Place the bag in the freezer for quick (and dripless) first-aid for bruises. *Sandie Fujimoto, Lihue, Hawaii*

A BAGGIE FOR BRUISES ◆ I always like to keep a Ziploc Baggie with about three-fourths cup water in the refrigerator for bumps and bruises. It forms easily to the injury and is not so cold that it hurts. *Jennifer Bystrzak, Tonawanda, New York*

COCKTAIL ICE CUBES FOR BOO-BOOS ◆ To soothe children's boo-boos, use the little plastic colored ice cubes that you can buy to put in drinks. They are refreezable and they don't leak and make messes. Children like them because they are colorful and come in a variety of shapes. Before long, the child's attention is focused on the ice cubes—not the boo-boo. *Angela Klouser, St. Thomas, Pennsylvania*

FROZEN BOTTLE FOR BRUISES ◆ I would save empty plastic medicine bottles, fill them with water, and freeze them. When someone got hurt, I would pull one out of the freezer and hold that on a scraped knee, etc. It is easier to use than a cube of ice. *Kym Gordon, Omaha, Nebraska*

SMILE, YOUR OWIE IS ON CANDID CAMERA ◆ When my child hurts himself and is crying out of control, I get a camera and say, "Let's take a picture of this one!" In the excitement of getting the camera out and discussing whether or not this owie is worse than the previous owie, it takes his mind off the pain and calms him down. *Ann Hersey, Vista, California*

OINTMENT ON BAND-AID ◆ When a skin bruise requires a first-aid ointment or other type of cream, I put a liberal amount of the ointment on the Band-Aid pad before applying the Band-Aid to the skin. This keeps the ointment on the bruise instead of the clothes. *Patty Radley, Fremont, California*

THROW THAT BOO-BOO AWAY ◆ When my daughter gets a boo-boo, we rub it out together, then we take that boo-boo in our fists real tight, and we throw it away as far as we can. It has worked every time; she stops crying instantly. It gives her the power to take that boo-boo and throw it away. *Bonnie Kushner, Cooper City, Florida*

THE MAGIC OF "SANNA SANNA" ◆ This magical intonation and touch soothes the hurt away and is great for bumps and bruises. If your child won't allow you to touch the hurt area, rotate your hand above the area while saying "Sanna Sanna." *Stacey Lopez, Fremont, California*

IF YOU STAY CALM, SO WILL YOUR CHILD ◆ Do not act overly startled or worried when a youngster gets hurt. A child will react the way you react. If the child looks and sees worry or fear on your face, he too will react with fear and cry. If the child looks at you after a fall and you react with a smile and talk happily to him while coming to his aid, the child will not have fear and will not cry. Obviously if he is hurt badly, he will cry, but it will still help the child if you appear to have it under control. *Scott Hill, Newark, California*

POPSICLES FOR BRUISED LIPS ◆ When a child falls and hurts his lip, give him a Popsicle instead of trying to put an ice cube on the bruise. The Popsicle is a more familiar thing, and he will be more likely to keep it on his lip so that the bruising is stopped. *Ruthann Struble, Raleigh, North Carolina*

RED WASHCLOTHS ◆ I always keep a red washcloth on hand for those occasions when one of my boys gets a bloody injury. Children often panic when they see blood on a light-colored washcloth, so I use a red one that hides the blood. It helps to dispel their fears. *S. Alexander, Pleasanton, California*

A BAND-AID—INSIDE AND OUT ◆ So everyone (especially playmates) know where that sore-spot site is, I put a Band-Aid on the outside of the clothing over the sore spot. *Donnelle Macho, Fremont, California*

TIME TO TAKE YOUR MEDICINE

NO-MESS LIQUID MEDICATION ◆ The eyedroppers that are provided with liquid medication are helpful with measuring, but are often messy when the child sucks out the medication. To avoid spills and messy stains, first measure the medication using the eyedropper. Put medication into a nipple, hold the baby as if to feed him or her,

and baby will take the medication much easier. No mess!
Brenda Kiba, Milpitas, California

LIQUID MEDICINE FOR BABY ◆ Rather than squirting liquid medicine into the baby's mouth, I hold the dropper and let him open his mouth and suck on it. I only have to squeeze gently, at the end. *Peg Hartley, San Bernardino, California*

It's best to point the dropper to the side of the mouth, so that the liquid medicine doesn't squirt to the back of the mouth and throat and choke the child.

PAINLESS MEDICATION ◆ If your child refuses to take a liquid medication, put it into a small amount of juice. *Dawn Robinson, Offutt Air Force Base, Nebraska*

There are many medicines that don't taste great to children, but can be mixed with a very small amount of a flavorful ingredient (fruit juice, chocolate, jams, concentrated orange juice, or maple syrup) at home to make them easier to take. Check with your doctor to make sure it's OK to mix ingredients with specific medicines.

APPLESAUCE HIDES THE BAD TASTE OF MEDICINES ◆ Many oral medicines can be mixed with a small amount (a half to a spoonful) of applesauce. The applesauce disguises the bad taste of the medicine. Always confer with your doctor or pharmacist to see if a particular medicine can be mixed with another ingredient. *Jim Stuka, Escondido, California*

ICE NUMBS THE TASTE OF MEDICINE ◆ If your child doesn't like the taste of medicine, give her an ice cube to suck on. This will temporarily numb her tongue and will make the medicine easier to swallow. *Jill Nelson-Johnson, Urbandale, Iowa*

DADDY TAKES THE MEDICINE, TOO ◆ My son didn't like the taste of his medicine, but he said he would take it if Daddy did too. His medicine was purple, so I filled up Daddy's medicine dropper with grape juice and my son's dropper with his medicine. They both took their "medicine" with little complaint. *Shelley Holland, Melbourne, Florida*

CHEWABLES ARE EASIEST ◆ If your infant or toddler fusses over liquid medication, ask your pediatrician if he could prescribe chewables. Chewables or other pills can also be ground into powder. *Gina Horne Bernbaum, Encino, California*

 Some medications can be safely mixed with food items. Ask your doctor or pharmacist.

EASY-TO-SWALLOW PILLS ◆ If your child cannot take a tablet medication, smash it up and put it into a teaspoon of applesauce or other baby food. My child is a liver-transplant recipient, and when I have to give her her blood-pressure medication, I put it in banana baby food and she loves it. *Dawn Robinson, Offutt Air Force Base, Nebraska*

PILLS DISSOLVED IN SODA POP ◆ Our six-year-old daughter had trouble swallowing bitter pills for medication. We put each pill into a medicine spoon and added a teaspoon of soda pop, which dissolved the pill. She was then able to swallow the pill easily, and she followed the pill with a soda-pop wash. *V.P., San Clemente, California*

 Check with your doctor or pharmacist to make sure the medicine is safe to dissolve. Some medicines can be "deactivated" by food or other things.

XXX

VISITS TO THE DOCTOR

XXXXXXXXXXXXXXXXXXXXXXXXXXXXXXXXXXXXXXXXXXXXXXXXX

DOCTOR'S KIT CAN PREPARE FOR REAL THING ⬦ When my son was eighteen months old he was afraid to go to the doctor. I bought him a play doctor's kit, which he loved to play with. I especially encouraged him to play with it before we went to the doctor's office. We took it with us for his appointment and the doctor gave himself a quick exam with the play kit. My son was less fearful of doctor appointments after that; he even seemed to enjoy the visits. *Debra Randall, East Haven, Connecticut*

 Ask your doctor to put a few tongue blades and Band-Aids in your child's doctor kit at the time of the visit. Your child will feel even more like a real doctor's helper.

QUALITY TIME AT THE DOCTOR'S OFFICE ⬦ If your pediatrician's office is as busy as our doctor's, then you may find yourself sitting in the waiting room a considerable time for your scheduled appointment. I try to make this quality time for my children by planning ahead. I pack into the diaper bag picture books, crayons, and coloring books. We read and draw while waiting for the doctor and very often amuse the other kids who are also waiting. It

---

KIDS SAY THE FUNNIEST THINGS

My three-and-a-half-year-old daughter refused to open her mouth for the doctor to check her throat. Later in the day when I asked her why, she said, "I didn't want him to see my private words!" *Barbara Mechlowitz-Krieger, Jericho, New York*

certainly passes the time and keeps the children from getting restless and bored. *Patricia A. McMahon, San Diego, California*

A "PRESCRIPTION" FOR ICE CREAM ◆ Our pediatrician makes an uncomfortable or painful procedure a little bit more bearable for our children by writing a "prescription" for ice cream following the visit. *Tracy LaVelle, Fremont, California*

PRACTICE SHOT ◆ My children hate to get inoculations or have blood drawn. I reassure them by promising them that it won't hurt more than a strong pinch. I demonstrate how much pain they will feel by getting them to volunteer to let me pinch them. I promise them it won't hurt more than that. Once they know the small extent of the pain, they realize it isn't so bad. I also tell them to squeeze two fingers together, as if they were squirting a watermelon seed, when the needle pinch is felt (pinch fingers of the hand opposite the arm getting jabbed, however). *Ron Burda, San Jose, California*

It's important to be honest about a medical procedure the child will experience.

IMMUNIZATIONS ◆ When taking a baby in for immunization, I try to give him a dose of baby Tylenol in the doctor's office a half hour before the shot. *P.H., Albany, California*

Always check with your doctor first.

ANTICIPATING A REACTION ✦ Our son often has a bad reaction during the first twenty-four hours following an immunization, so we try to schedule his immunizations on Fridays. If he fusses during the evening, we can sleep in the next morning. If he's ill the next day, we don't have to miss a day at work. *Patty and Ray Gustas, Fremont, California*

OUCH-A-BINGO ✦ When I was a child a nurse suggested saying "OUCH-A-BINGO" repeatedly when I got a shot. The injection still hurt, but the diversion of saying "OUCH-A-BINGO" took my mind off the pain for an instant. If kids believe it helps—it will. *T.M., Fremont, California*

✖✦✦✦✦✦✦✦✦✦✦✦✦✦✦✦✦✦✦✦✦✦✦✦✦✦✦✦✦✦✦✦✦✦✦✦✦✦✦✦✖

COLICKY BABIES

✖✦✦✦✦✦✦✦✦✦✦✦✦✦✦✦✦✦✦✦✦✦✦✦✦✦✦✦✦✦✦✦✦✦✦✦✦✦✦✦✖

BURPING IS IMPORTANT ✦ Burping the baby for at least ten to fifteen minutes following a feeding helps to make sure that most of the air bubbles in a baby's stomach are released. If the baby has eaten, burped, and is not wet, but still continues to cry—try placing her on your lap face-down and gently patting her back. Also, a warm bath seems to relax a colicky baby. *Linda Valencia Martinez, Albuquerque, New Mexico*

DISPOSABLE BOTTLES ✦ When my second child had colic, I switched to disposable bottles. These bottle liners collapse as liquid flows out, preventing air bubbles from forming and ending up in baby's stomach. Excess gas may be the cause of some colic, so whatever parents can do to prevent extra gas might be helpful in battling colic. *Beverly Morneault, New Britain, Connecticut*

SENSITIVITY TO SPECIFIC FOODS ✦ Sometimes fussy behavior can be caused by a baby's sensitivity to a specific food. Breast-feeding mothers can cut out certain foods (including milk products) in her diet and bottle-fed babies can be changed to a different formula. It may take some experimentation with various foods to see if certain items are causing a problem for baby's tummy. Always consult with your pediatrician before changing your baby's diet. *Maureen Nelson, Tampa, Florida*

FRONT PACK ◆ My infant was very colicky and fretful. Instead of just carrying him around in my arms, I used one of the front baby packs. It soothed him to be close to me and freed my hands to do other things. *Debra Carangelo, East Haven, Connecticut*

"FOOTBALL HOLD" ◆ My first child was quite cranky almost from the day he was born. Everything checked out physically so the doctors called it "colic." Nothing seemed to help until my sister-in-law from New York visited us when he was about a month old. She suggested using the "football hold." She held his head in her hand and the length of his body on her arm with his stomach resting on her arm and one leg dangling on each side of her arm by her elbow. In this position, the baby's stomach was facing the floor instead of the ceiling. You can also

use two arms by letting his head rest on one arm while the length of his body rests on your other arm up to your elbow and his legs dangle straddling your arm. His stomach will be resting on your arm. It worked for us. *Lori Percoco, Fremont, California*

THE VACUUM TAPE RECORDING ◆ The one thing that helped my colicky baby was the sound of the vacuum cleaner. I used to record it on a tape recorder and play it at night in his room. He would listen to it and fall asleep. *Debra Randall, East Haven, Connecticut*

Any repetitive noise may work. One parent in my practice recorded crickets on a summer evening and it worked to calm the child.

RUNNING WATER SOOTHES COLICKY BABIES ◆ I have had five babies and presently have a two-month-old newborn. We seem to have colicky babies, and I have found that holding a fussy baby in the bathroom while slowly running the tub water with the lights dim or off soothes the baby. Our children usually fell asleep in there. *Kathy Kelly, Salt Lake City, Utah*

A "WINDUP" SWING ◆ A must for a colicky baby is a windup (or automatic) swing. This ingenious device keeps the infant in a sitting position that can be very relaxing to a baby who has colic. It also provides some relaxation time for the parents. *Linda Valencia Martinez, Albuquerque, New Mexico*

A SOOTHING SOLUTION TO COLIC ◆ When my baby was colicky I would lay him down so his tummy was resting on top of a warm hot-water bottle wrapped in a clean towel. This often seemed to relieve him of his colicky symptoms. *K.B., Aurora, Colorado*

THE FOOT FIXER—FOR COLIC ◆ I discovered that my foot-massaging machine (The Foot Fixer by Dr. Scholl) does more than massage my feet. It's soothing for colicky babies, too. I put water in the foot massager and place my feet in, then I laid my baby across my knees. The vibrations traveled from my feet to the baby, who was wonderfully soothed. In addition, the new parents got a foot massage and a little rest. *Brenda Capone, Stamford, Connecticut*

WARM VIBRATIONS ◆ To soothe a cranky baby, place her on a thick towel on top of the clothes dryer and turn it on. The heat and vibrations are very comforting. *Always stay with the baby and hold her. Jeff LaVelle, Fremont, California*

Please keep safety in mind at all times. Make sure babies are secure and will not fall off. Never leave baby alone.

A CHANGE OF SCENERY HELPS A FUSSY BABY
◆ If a baby is crying for no apparent reason, take him to a different room or outdoors. Sometimes a change of scenery will calm a fussy baby. *N.S., San Jose, California*

"SPECIAL SONG FOR BABY"
◆ My tip is to have a special song that you sing early on and continue with for your baby. I have found that by doing this when the baby is fussy (or even in a good mood sometimes), she perks up and smiles. It seems to make everything okay again. It doesn't matter if it's an old song or one you make up, as long as they know it as their special song. *Janice Brogden, Fremont, California*

FUNNY NOISES QUIET A SCREAMING BABY
◆ When my baby screams I occasionally tap my hand gently over his mouth, which causes a kind of whooping sound. This either soothes him or amuses him, because he usually stops screaming. *J.E.F., Lansdale, Pennsylvania*

XXXXXXXXXXXXXXXXXXXXXXXXXXXXXXXXXXXXXXXXXXXXX

TEETH CARE

XXXXXXXXXXXXXXXXXXXXXXXXXXXXXXXXXXXXXXXXXXXXX

A PREVIEW OF THEIR OWN VISIT TO THE DENTIST
◆ I am a registered dental hygienist who has a lot of three-year-old patients. I usually like to have the parent bring their child in when the parent has his or her teeth cleaned so that the child can see all the equipment and get used to the sounds. I usually let the child handle the mouth mirror and my "tooth counter." Also, I show

the child my special "electric" toothbrush (polisher) and maybe polish a fingernail so the child will know what it feels like. It's important to establish a relationship with the dentist and hygienist before the child comes in for their first appointment. *Julie Reneer, Palmdale, California*

A BRAVE VISIT TO THE DENTIST ◆ My daughter had difficulty going to the dentist; she got very nervous and upset. Finally, I told her I was going to take pictures of her being brave at the dentist, and that I would make a book out of the pictures. After I got the pictures developed, I put them on card stock, wrote text underneath them, and had them laminated and then bound into a small book. She took it to share with the dentist on her next visit and has had wonderful visits since then. *Lisa Dame, Murray, Utah*

STICKY TOOTHBRUSHES ◆ Refresh children's sticky toothbrushes by running them through the dishwasher. *Jeff LaVelle, Fremont, California*

Toothbrushes are like good old friends—we hate to get rid of them. But the truth is we should replace them every three months. Buy them in the large variety packs, and don't be afraid to throw your old toothbrushes out when the bristles become soft or ineffective at cleaning.

AFTER STREP THROAT, GET A NEW TOOTH-BRUSH ◆ Recently our nephew had strep throat four times before his parents figured out that he was reinfecting himself with his toothbrush. *Kelly Hobbs, Pueblo, Colorado*

Toothbrushes have the tendency to collect germs as they sit on the bathroom sink. It's just one more reason to replace them regularly.

BRUSH YOUR TEETH, UPSTAIRS AND DOWN-STAIRS ◆ To get my two-to-four-year-olds to brush their teeth thoroughly, I describe their teeth as having upstairs and downstairs and tell them to be sure to brush every room. We describe the rooms as we brush (e.g. upstairs bedrooms and bathrooms as we brush upper teeth and the kitchen, the bathroom, living room, patio, and garage as we brush the lower teeth). I can keep children brushing for five minutes with this method. *Leslie Meyer, Redondo Beach, California*

A BRUSHING GAME ✦ To make brushing teeth more interesting for a child, discuss the various food items the child ate that day while you brush their teeth. Say, "Oh, I see some broccoli over here, and here's some bananas up there." This gives you time to get all of the teeth brushed well, and occasionally the child will remind you of a certain food he ate that day that you forgot about. *Linda Yazzolino, Newark, California*

TOOTHPASTE ON BRUSHES ✦ With three toddlers, it is sometimes difficult to know who has and has not brushed teeth. In the morning, we put the toothpaste on all the toothbrushes. That way, we know who has brushed and who hasn't. If I go into the bathroom and there is still toothpaste on a brush, I know who still needs to brush teeth that day. *Linda Skocypec, Albuquerque, New Mexico*

FLAVORED TOOTHPASTE ✦ My toddler battled getting his teeth brushed until someone suggested using a flavored toothpaste. I bought some bubble-gum flavored toothpaste and he loved it. Now, when he sees me pick up his toothbrush, he opens his mouth immediately. After I finish brushing his teeth, he demands to take over for a few swipes of his own. I guess the important thing is to make brushing as pleasant as possible for the child so he will enjoy it and eventually establish good habits himself. *Karen Lewis, Kingwood, Texas*

BABIES LOVE TO HAVE THEIR TEETH BRUSHED ✦ My baby loves to have her teeth (gums) brushed or wiped with a clean washcloth. She loves the taste and it feels good on her gums—and it's good for her. *Erin M., Fremont, California*

EARLY HABITS PAY OFF ✦ Start brushing and flossing when the first tooth appears. My daughter did this, and her four-and-a-half-year-old son never complains about brushing his teeth twice a day. He loves it and tells us we have to do it too. He is not crazy about flossing (who is?) but he lets his mother help him floss regularly. *Patricia R. Hersom, Walnut Creek, California*

TOOTH-FAIRY MAGIC ENVELOPES ◆ Whenever one of our children lost a tooth, we made a big deal of putting the tooth in a sealed envelope and then secretly switched that envelope for one with money in it while the child was sleeping. Our children were always surprised to find the envelope, still sealed, with the tooth "magically" transformed! They (now ages twenty-three, twenty-one, and sixteen) only figured out our trick a few years ago. *Richard Hall, Mesa, Arizona*

TOOTH-FAIRY SPARKLES ◆ One fun idea is to wrap the coins you will leave under your child's pillow with that clear, iridescent wrapping paper and festive ribbons. Then, sprinkle glitter on the pillowcase. In the morning, you can show your child that the fairy left some "fairy dust"! *Carol Palmer McPherson, Woodbury, Minnesota*

A TREASURE HUNT REPLACED THE TOOTH FAIRY ◆ I decided to choose a different approach when my kids lost their teeth. Instead of telling them about the tooth fairy, I sent them on treasure hunts. I would place a treasure map with clues under their pillows and hide coins around the house and yard for them to find. When they awoke, they found the maps and had a ball hunting for their treasures of coins. *Connie J. Donahoo, Independence, Missouri*

"CAN I SAVE MY TOOTH?" ◆ Many children (and some parents) want to save those precious baby teeth for posterity. If so, they should be left in bleach overnight to kill any bacteria. Then, coat them with hobby glaze (available in the paint section of hobby stores). It goes on like paint and will help preserve the teeth. *Lana J. Jarvis, Colchester, Vermont*

MISCELLANEOUS HEALTH TIPS

PAINT YOUR OWN CHICKEN POX ✦ When children have chicken pox, put calamine lotion in a little plastic cup and give them a small, clean paintbrush. They can have a marvelous time painting themselves with calamine lotion. It will keep them busy for a time, while reducing their itching. *Jane Arfa, Englewood, Colorado*

$$ OATMEAL BATH FOR CHICKEN POX ✦ My pediatrician advised cool baths to soothe my daughter's chicken pox. Instead of paying the high price of over-the-counter oatmeal baths, I blended regular oatmeal and a little water in my kitchen blender and mixed it in the bath water. My daughter reported positive results. *Laurie Stroupe, Marietta, Georgia*

STUFFY NOSE AND CONGESTION ✦ When a baby has a stuffy nose, try putting a pillow under the head of the mattress of the crib. This will help his/her nose drain while the baby sleeps. *Brenda Kiba, Milpitas, California*

 Don't put the pillow on *top* of the mattress.

CAR SEAT KEEPS HEAD ELEVATED ✦ Doctors often advise parents to elevate a child's head while he's sleeping if he is congested. For an infant, we had good luck using our car seat with adjustable positions. *D.L. Stelle, Fremont, California*

VARIATION OF TOOTH FAIRY ✦ A visit (and a little surprise gift) from the "Cast Fairy" or "Stitches Fairy" brings joy to a youngster who is home recuperating from an injury or operation. *Stacey Ann Morgan, Oakland, California*

CLEAN PILLOWCASES ✦ As a mother of five and a grandmother of ten, I cannot overemphasize the importance of changing pillowcases and bedding when you're fighting sore throats, the flu, or even adolescent acne. Put a fresh pillowcase on daily and it will help with this problem. Experience has borne that out for me many times. *Mary Krull, Indianapolis, Indiana*

TREATING "CRADLE CAP" ✦ If your child has cradle cap on her scalp, liberally apply baby oil on the crusty patches. Leave the oil on the scalp for a few hours, then shampoo. While it is still wet, gently remove the crusty cradle cap with a fine-tooth comb. *Barbara McMahon, San Diego, California*

A SPIDER A DAY SPARKS A HOSPITAL STAY ✦ When our five-year-old son was to have surgery, we wondered how we could prepare him for his stay and lessen his anxiety. We decided to go shopping; he picked out a toy for each of the four or five days he would be spending in the hospital. When we arrived at the hospital each morning with the day's toy, he was excited and waiting with anticipation. We also bought a few rubber spiders to put under the covers to scare the nurses, which brought about some real excitement for him as well as the hospital staff. *Mrs. Gordon L. Schmidt, Henderson, Nebraska*

A CHEERFUL PRESENT FOR A HOSPITAL STAY ✦ One of the children in our preschool had to be hospitalized recently, so her school friends made two presents for her. According to her parents, her favorite present was an audio recording of greetings and comments from her preschool friends. She loved it and listened to it over and over in the hospital. We also sent her a poster board containing colorful handprints of all her preschool friends. *Stacey Lopez, Fremont, California*

HOW SORE IS YOUR THROAT? ✦ When my daughter was little, she would often have sore throats. It was difficult to tell how ill she was as she seldom complained. I came upon the idea of holding one of my hands a foot or so above the other one, explaining that the top hand was the worst sore throat she had ever had while the bottom one meant no sore throat. I would then ask her to put her hand between mine at the level of pain she was experiencing. This helped me determine how uncomfortable she was and how sick she might actually be. *Jean Bodlak, Emerson, Nebraska*

POPSICLES FOR HEALTH ✦ I kept fruit-flavored Popsicles in the freezer, and if I had a child who was sick and needed fluids, I could give them one. *Christian Benschop, Raleigh, North Carolina*

"DON'T SIT TOO CLOSE TO THE TV" ✦ If you don't want your child to sit too close to the TV (Nintendo, etc.), draw a line. We use masking tape on the carpet. If your floor has patterns or tiles, you can point out an imaginary line that he must sit behind. *Pat Remmes, Walnut Creek, California*

The experts recommend that children sit at least six feet from the TV. The exposure to any electric/magnetic fields is much less at that distance.

MIDDLE-OF-THE-NIGHT HEALTH INFORMATION ✦ When my babies were little and had a medical problem in the middle of the night, I would call the nursery nursing station at the local hospital for information. They're available twenty-four hours a day. Even if you have an emergency number for your doctor, you may not get to talk to the doctor in the middle of the night or you may hesitate to call at that hour. Some things are not such emergencies or so urgent and just talking to a nurse at the nurses' station helps. *Madeline Dunn, Albuquerque, New Mexico*

Discuss this with your doctor first to be sure that the personnel giving you information are appropriately trained and competent.

SAFETY AT HOME AND AWAY

PARKING-LOT SAFETY ◆ While locking or unlocking your car in a parking lot, have the children touch the back

door of the car so they won't venture out into traffic. I had forgotten I made this rule when my daughter was little until I noticed her and two of her friends (they're now eleven) with their hands on the back door waiting for me to unlock it. *Alice O. Jordon, Stockbridge, Georgia*

"STAY IN THE CAR UNTIL I'M READY" ♦ When I have a preschooler and an infant in the car, and no other adult is present, I always take the baby out first, fasten her into the stroller, set up my diaper bag, and get ready to go BEFORE I open the older child's seat belt. This prevents the older child from being in a busy parking lot while waiting for me and the baby. *Gina Horne Bernbaum, Encino, California*

MOMMY NEEDS HELP CROSSING THE STREET ♦ When small children are out with their parents, they often want to be independent. To get my children to hold my hand while crossing the street, I would tell them as we approached an intersection, "Mother needs help crossing the street. Take my hand and help me cross the street. Tell me when it is safe to cross." The child would take my hand and very willingly tell me, "Okay Mom, it's safe to cross now." The two of us would cross safely, and the child would continue to hold my hand until we got across the street. *Ruth Loch, Cincinnati, Ohio*

DAD DOESN'T WANT TO GET LOST ♦ My four-year-old daughter wasn't very cooperative when I asked her to remain close to me so she wouldn't get lost in a crowded place. One day I used a different approach that really worked. I asked her to hold my hand so I wouldn't get lost. She liked to do that. *Doug Gregory, Stettler, Alberta*

SAFE PLAY IN THE DRIVEWAY ♦ When my kids are outside playing in the driveway, I pull my van up across the driveway where it meets the street. The van prevents balls, bikes, and other things from rolling into the street, and kids from running out into the street. Also, the van prevents cars from pulling into the driveway. *Laura Justice, New Lenox, Illinois*

"YOU'RE SPEEDING, DAD! THAT WILL COST YOU A NICKEL" ♦ When I was a child, I was able to fine my dad (who was a traffic-court judge) a nickel anytime I caught him going at least five miles per hour over the speed limit. This is a great way to teach children about traffic safety and good driving habits. *Julia Kiely, Irvine, California*

BUCKLE UP FOR SAFETY ✦ To ensure seat-belt safety in our cars, we told our daughters that the car would not start without everyone buckled up. *Anonymous, California*

VERBAL CHECKING ON CHILDREN ✦ I have a six-year-old daughter and a baby. Often when you call a child who is out of sight, she doesn't answer. To let my daughter know when she must answer, I call out, "Julie check." She always calls back "Mommy check." I started her out with this when she was about two years old and we still use this system. *C.A., Torrence, California*

SAFETY "BELLS" FOR TODDLERS ✦ Toddlers are sometimes hard to keep track of, especially at amusement parks, camping, or shopping at a busy mall. Before we leave for one of these activities, I clip on three little bells to his clothing. Now, when I look up and can't see him, I can always hear him. *Donna Bishop, Stanton, California*

Make sure bells or any other ornament is tied securely to clothing and is too big to be put into a child's mouth.

$$ RUBBER-BAND LATCHES ✦ To keep your cabinets off-limits to your children, attach one or more heavy rubber bands to the cabinet knobs in a figure-eight pattern. The children will be able to pull the doors slightly open, but not enough to get at the contents. *Anonymous, San Jose, California*

SCALDING HOT ✦ Never carry your child and anything hot at the same time. Pediatricians report treating a lot of babies in the emergency room who knocked Mom's scalding coffee out of her hand and onto themselves. *Margaret Healy, Albany, California*

Also, children are frequently burned by hot tap water. Make sure your water heater is not set too high.

RESTAURANT SAFETY ✦ The safety standards at some restaurants are not quite as high as they are in our own kitchens or dining rooms. For instance, some waiters and waitresses will put hot drinks, steak knives, and other dangerous objects right in front of a baby or small child. Occasionally, they will also place a high chair in the aisle where servers weave by carrying hot coffee and sizzling food directly over the baby's head. As soon as we sit down at a restaurant we scope it out for baby safety, including moving things (flowers, sugar, jam pots, cream, etc.) out of her reach. *Donna Mattingly, Thousand Oaks, California*

SAFETY FROM A CRAWLER'S PERSPECTIVE ✦ To keep our house safe from small objects that our baby can find and swallow, my husband and I get on our hands and knees to see things from our daughter's perspective. We remove any item that can harm her and place protective devices over things like electrical outlets. It's an eye-opening experience to view the house from a crawler's perspective. *S.L.C., Lititz, Pennsylvania*

LEARNING PHONE NUMBERS ✦ We make up a rhyming poem to help our children remember their phone number. For example, "359-0829—call my number and I'll be fine." *Tracy Bauch, Milwaukee, Wisconsin*

BEDTIME STORIES TEACH PHONE NUMBER AND ADDRESS ✦ My three-year-old is able to recite our phone number and address because I make up bedtime stories for him starting with this information. For example: Once upon a time there was a little boy named Roger and he lived at (insert your address here) and his phone number was (insert your phone number here). His grandmother was amazed when he could recite his phone number. *Maryann Landreth, Edwardsville, Illinois*

911 FOR EMERGENCIES ✦ Put nail polish on the numbers 9 and 1 on your push-button phone so children will remember what numbers to dial for an emergency. *Debra Kassarjian, Fremont, California*

KIDS SAY THE FUNNIEST THINGS

I had just finished reading "Goldilocks and the Three Bears" to my six-year-old daughter. She looked up at me with a serious face and wanted to know why the three bears didn't call 911 when they saw someone had been in their house. How times have changed!
Nancy Lagano, Farmington, Connecticut

SAFE ANT SPRAY ✦ If you have ants in your house (and who doesn't), use vinegar in a spray bottle. Ants hate it, it eliminates their paths, and (most important) it's safe for baby and the environment. *Erin M., Fremont, California*

"HAND STAMP" HELPS FIND LOST CHILDREN ✦ Before taking my young children to a place that will be crowded with people (a shopping mall, concert, flea market, etc.) I stamp each of their hands with a stamp that includes our name, address, and telephone number. If the child gets lost, your name can be announced over a loudspeaker or the information can be used to contact you or another family member at home. *Robin Elgin, Fremont, California*

HUG A TREE—SAFETY AT THE CAMPSITE ✦ Many children get lost in a forested area each year by wandering away from their campgrounds. The Mountain Rescue Association recommends teaching children to hug a tree the moment they realize that they are lost. They should pick a tree as their friend and stay with that tree. Trees offer protection from rain and wind, and it is easier for searchers to find a stationary child. *Scott Highton, San Carlos, California*

BEWARE—OPEN WINDOWS UPSTAIRS ◆ Many children fall out of upstairs windows by leaning or falling against the screen of an open window. Many screens will not hold a child in. If you need to open a window upstairs, use a window lock that is child proof and will only allow the window to be opened a short way. Make sure that your child's body cannot fit through the opening either when she is facing the front or sideways. Also, do not place furniture that children can climb on near an upstairs window. I hope this will save you the heartache my family has been through. My daughter, who was three years old at the time, fell out of a second-story window. She survived, but has had to endure a number of surgeries. It only takes a minute to check each window and child-proof it. *Shelly Greenwood, Boulder, Colorado*

9

SELF-ESTEEM AND RELATIONSHIPS

◆

Children have more need of models than of critics.
— JOSEPH JOUBERT

Children form many important relationships during their early years, but none are more significant than the ones formed with their immediate family, especially their parents. Parents play an influential role in the development of their child's sense of self and personality.

Self-esteem, the appreciation of one's worth as a person, is the greatest gift a parent can give to a child. It is usually given in little nudges—one at a time. A child's self-worth will be the barometer for his aspirations, as well as his limitations. It will determine his level of courage as he reaches each crossroad—the first day of preschool, a Little League at bat, a part in his high-school drama production, or the challenges of a new job.

The family plays a significant and dominant role in promoting a child's self-esteem. Virginia Satir, noted author and teacher, writes:

I am convinced that there are no genes to carry the feelings of worth. It is learned. And the family is where it is learned. You learned to feel high [self-esteem] or low [self-esteem] in the family your parents created. And your children are learning it in your family right now.

An infant coming into the world . . . must rely on the experiences he has with the people around him and the messages they give him about his worth as a person. For the first five or six years, the child's [self-esteem]

145

is formed by the family almost exclusively. After he starts to school, other influences come into play, but the family remains important all through his adolescence.*

Promoting self-esteem in others, especially our children, is best achieved by providing daily doses of it. For example, "catch" your child being good and acknowledge it; take an extra moment to "ooh and aah" one of his artistic creations (even if he colors out of the lines); and, above all, listen carefully to what he has to say—he appreciates this the most. Try to find a few moments, at least once a day, to give each child your "undivided attention." The busier you are, the more important this becomes.

I hope to be thought of by my daughters, years from now, as someone who had at least a small part in nurturing their feeling of self-worth. Occasionally, as I tuck my daughters into bed at night, I say, "How did I get so lucky? Of all the men in the world, I can't believe that God picked me to be your daddy." They usually look up glowing.

The following tips on relationships are divided into six sections: Promoting Self-esteem, Family Relationships, Time Alone with Each Child, Parents Need Time, Too, If You Need a Few Minutes of Private, and Baby-sitters and Day-care. Some of my favorite tips are located in this chapter. "A Free Secret" (p. 150) is a child-care tip that could pay dividends all the way through adolescence. The section If You Need a Few Minutes of Private can buy you ten or fifteen minutes of personal time. "Kisses to Go" (p. 161) is heart-warming (and countless people told me it really works). And finally, try "A Relaxing Baby-sitting Job" (p. 163) with another couple. My wife and I did—and it worked!

◆

---

*Excerpted from *Toward a State of Esteem,* which is the final report of the California Task Force to Promote Self-esteem and Personal and Social Responsibility, submitted to the California legislature on January 23, 1990.

XXX

PROMOTING SELF-ESTEEM

XXXXXXXXXXXXXXXXXXXXXXXXXXXXXXXXXXXXXXXXXXXXXXX

APPLAUSE APPLAUSE ✦ If your baby or toddler does even the littlest thing deserving praise, respond with loud clapping and cheers. Even babies love applause. *Vikki Hill, Newark, California*

CELEBRATE THOSE LITTLE THINGS TOO ✦ Make celebrations out of little successes like passing a test, losing a tooth, learning how to tie your shoe, or getting a job promotion. Buy a dinner plate with the words "YOU'RE SPECIAL TODAY" for that special person. Family members, even Mom and Dad, will beam when their dinner is served on the "special" plate. *Florence Grace, Fremont, California*

FLY A BANNER OR FLAG ON SPECIAL DAYS ✦ We have a simple wind sock that we fly in front of our house on special occasions (birthdays, first day of school, good report cards, special accomplishments, Little League victories, etc.). The children enjoy hooking up the wind sock and the celebrant feels extra special. *Thomas Leslie, San Diego, California*

"DEVIN'S DINNER" WITH DAD ✦ My husband works the graveyard shift, so our four-year-old doesn't see him much. We started a new tradition to make our few dinners together special. On my husband's night off, we have "Devin's Dinner,' when my son, Devin, helps decide the menu and prepare the food. We use candles and all the frills. *Karen Hidalgo, Newark, California*

"I HAVE CONFIDENCE IN YOU!" ✦ Whenever my children need a confidence booster or encouragement I say, "I have confidence in you!" These simple words really cheer them up. *M.B.B., San Antonio, Texas*

THAT'S A NO-NO ✦ One thing I have found to be helpful with my five children and fourteen grandchildren is to say, "That's a no-no," instead of, "No no." The former clearly prohibits the act rather than condemns the child. *Anonymous, Broken Bow, Nebraska*

IT'S AN HONOR TO WEAR THIS PIN ✦ I still have my Brownie Elf pin from when I was young. I reward my children's good deeds by giving them the honor of wearing my pin for the day or week. This is particularly special because they have a solid symbol of Mom as a role model. I believe this can really help their self-esteem and self-confidence! *Sabra Jiwa, Marietta, Georgia*

"CHEERS" AT DINNER ✦ At dinnertime, we all clink glasses, then each person at the table tells about something that makes them happy. The kids almost always talk about the family or activities we've shared. This really seems to give them the feeling that they and their family are special. *Donna Terman, Menlo Park, California*

SMALL IS BEAUTIFUL ✦ My little boy is short for his age and concerned about being smaller than his friends. I recently told him, "You may be short, but you're BIG inside where it counts." He returned a big smile. *Vicki Wynne, Fremont, California*

SHORT LIKE MOMMY ✦ When my daughter started school, she felt bad about being the shortest child in her class. But she seemed less concerned after learning that Mommy had always been one of the shortest children in her class, too. It seemed to help to share some of my feelings and experiences. *Nancy Knowlton, Wilmette, Illinois*

"I'M GOING TO WRITE THAT IN YOUR BABY BOOK" ✦ To reinforce positive behavior the first time it occurs, I take out my child's baby book and write it down, making sure that the child understands what a wonderful thing she just did. My children are eleven and twelve years old now, and they still love to look at their baby books. *Maureen Compton, Fremont, California*

THE YOUNG CHILDREN HAVE A DAILY SCHEDULE, TOO ✦ When my oldest son first went to school and every day came home to tell us what he had done, it left my second oldest feeling as if he had done nothing that day and had nothing to say. So I made a calendar for my youngest son: Monday—Art, Tuesday—Gym, Wednesday—Music, Thursday—Library, and Friday—Science. Each day we did what was on the calendar. Now when we're eating dinner, each child has something to add to the conversation which is just as exciting. This will also help teach days of the week. *Marilyn Horning, Fulton, New York*

PLAN OUTSIDE ACTIVITIES FOR THE LITTLE ONES, TOO ✦ I've found that my preschooler doesn't like driving around to all of my older child's activities. At a friend's suggestion, I have added at least one activity for the preschooler that the older child has to fit into her schedule. Now, we are not always going somewhere only for the older child. *Pat Wolak, Annapolis, Maryland*

Sometimes we adults think that we are the only ones with important jobs and activities to accomplish.

BIRTHDAY-PARTY VIDEO ✦ At times when your children may be feeling bad about themselves or having friendship problems, slip on a video recording of their last birthday party with all their friends or another home video showing happier times. Children love watching themselves in home videos. *Anonymous, Newark, California*

TEACHING "I CAN DO IT" ✦ Praise is appreciated by all children. It is particularly important for children who are reluctant to do schoolwork. Praise can have an enormous impact on building self-esteem and on helping them develop appropriate behavior concerning responsibilities. With your continual positive support, children can be motivated to develop a positive self-image and to approach schoolwork with a confident "I can do it" attitude. *Bill Senning, Milpitas, California*

BE SPECIFIC WITH PRAISE ✦ The more precise the praise that is given, the better able your child will be to understand exactly what pleased you, and the more likely that that precise behavior will be reinforced. For example, instead of saying "Good job," say "You did a great job cleaning your room. You made your bed, put away your toys, and hung up your clothes." *Sharyn Carroll, Oakland, California*

✕✦✕

FAMILY RELATIONSHIPS

✕✦✕

A FREE SECRET ✦ When my children were old enough to understand, I made the following contract with each of them: The child can come to the parent at any time or at any age and say "I need a free secret." Then that child can tell the parent anything, *absolutely anything* that he is worried about or that he has done and the parent will listen calmly and not criticize. Then the two of us will work on the solution to that particular problem. It really works to keep an open line of communication. *Rose Senier, Fort Collins, Colorado*

LISTEN TO YOUR CHILD ✦ We are often so busy with our daily routines that when our children need to talk to us we respond, "Not now, I'm busy, maybe later." If parents don't communicate and share feelings with their children when they're young, the communication will probably not be good years later, when their children are teens. The childhood years are the time to develop good communication with your children. At night, when I put my children to bed, I try to ask at least a couple of nights of the week, "How are you feeling, honey? Are there any neat things that you'd like to share with me that we haven't had time to talk about?" *Audrey Swanton, Brewer, Maine*

" 'SCUSE ME, 'SCUSE ME" ✦ A way for children to politely get your attention when you're talking to someone else is to have them place a hand on your leg or knee. You get their signal and say "excuse me" to whomever you're talking to and then acknowledge the child. *Tracy LaVelle, Fremont, California*

WORRY BOX ✦ Children can have a lot of worries. I would have my child write a worry down (or a parent can do it for a younger child) and put it into a little box. We do not look at the worry for the rest of the week. At the end of the week, she can open the box and see if the worry has gone away; most of them do. *Hetty Christensen, Santa Cruz, California*

FAMILY NIGHT ✦ Set aside one evening a week, an hour or more, for family time. Leave this time open for talking, playing a game, reading a story, etc. Each member of the family could take a turn each week to suggest what they would like to do for together time. *Nancy Painter, LaVista, Nebraska*

KIDS SAY THE FUNNIEST THINGS

All of the children in church were gathered around one of the most respected members of our congregation as he presented the children's lesson during the service. He told them that God loved all people: short, tall, thin, fat, with braces or glasses, etc. In a clear, loud voice, my four-year-old said, "He must have learned that from Mr. Rogers!" The whole congregation cracked up. *Roxana Stitt, Peck, Kansas*

FAMILY HUGS ✦ One day my daughter said she felt left out when my husband and I hugged. So we started having "family hugs" where we all have a group hug and spread kisses around. It brightens the most dismal of days. It can be done standing, sitting, or lying in bed. (We still maintain the right to have "couple hugs"—just me and my husband.) *Stacey Lopez, Fremont, California*

"DON'T KISS ME, MOM" ✦ Young boys often don't like to have their moms kiss them; my boys are no exception. Occasionally, I have to kiss them, and they say, "Look Mom, I wiped off your kiss." I reply with a smile, "Yes, but not before it went to your heart." *Liane Faulder, Edmonton, Alberta*

FAMILY COUNCILS ✦ With older children it's fun to have a "family council," a time when the whole family gets together to express feelings, grievances, joys, or special requests. It's fun to discuss vacation plans and make it a decision for the whole family. Children feel special when they're included in family decisions. *Florence Moorman, Buffalo, New York*

FLOOR TALK ✦ When someone in our family has something important to talk about, we call for a "floor talk." Everyone sits in a circle on the floor and holds hands while we discuss important family matters. *Tracy Bauch, Milwaukee, Wisconsin*

THE CHALKBOARD IS THE MEDIUM ✦ A great communication tool for our family has been large chalkboards, which we placed in each of our children's bedrooms. Our children use them to express their feelings (especially between each other), and we frequently use them to leave messages to each other. The chalkboards also provide good training in reading and writing skills. *M.R. Kelly, Rawlins, Wyoming*

FAMILY ROLE-PLAYING ✦ I would often gather my children together to form a circle, sit on the floor, and prepare to change our roles. The children would pretend to be Mom and Dad and talk to us in a manner in which they see and hear us. It certainly was an enlightenment. The children in turn could listen to us taking the role of the child again. I must admit this didn't always lead to total seriousness, but it did help. *Joan Lyboult, Syracuse, New York*

A GROUP FOR DADS ✦ When my son was born, I wanted to be the best father and learn as much as possible about fathering. I looked for a program for fathers and found that nothing was available. When I met the director of a local parents' organization, I asked why there were so many programs for mothers, but nothing for fathers. As a result, I was challenged to start an ongoing program just for fathers.

I set up two programs. In one program, dads played with their children in a nursery, talked with the other dads about fathering and "men's" issues, and shared experiences and parenting tips. The other program had a workshop format. Fathers would suggest topics to discuss and experts would occasionally speak.

At these meetings, we fathers learned that many of our fears and issues were commonplace. Our self-esteem grew from these shared stories, and a more confident father emerged from each experience. Fathers' groups can be started through parenting organizations, a men's group, a hospital educational program, or a church setting. It's been a great experience for me. *John Lopuszanski, North Wales, Pennsylvania*

"MOMMY, I DON'T LOVE YOU" ✦ When your kids tell you they don't love you anymore, it's merely a ploy to raise your temper. So just tell them "It's okay, but Mommy still loves you very much." Then smile. They probably won't know what to say. *Marilyn Horning, Fulton, New York*

"MOM LIKES YOU BEST" ✦ If a child is jealous of a sibling, explain that you love each child in the same way you like your fingers. Hold up your fingers and show them that you love and need each finger, and that you don't have a favorite. When I use this analogy, my children usually laugh—but they understand what I'm saying. *Jean Bird, Coco, Florida*

LONG-DISTANCE RELATIVES AND FRIENDS ✦ To ease your child's stranger anxieties when meeting new people or people you don't see frequently (long-distance relatives and friends, baby-sitters, etc.), fill an inexpensive mini-photo album with pictures of them. Let the child flip through the pages as he wants and tell him about the people he'll be meeting. Do this nightly as visiting day approaches. *D.L. Tarsa, Michigan*

A GENTLE BREEZE IS A KISS FROM GRAND-MA ✦ Since the day my grandson was born, I have told him at least once a day (when he is visiting) that I love him very much; that I will always love him no matter what; and that if I am not there to hug and kiss him, he should remember that every time he feels a soft, gentle breeze on his cheek, that is his grandmother giving him a kiss. *Patricia R. Hersom, Walnut Creek, California*

"THERE'S GRANDPA'S STAR" ✦ My daughter lost a grandparent when she was two years old. Coming home one evening, the stars were shining. She pointed to the first star she saw and said, "Mommy, there's Grandpa's star." Several of my uncles died a few years later, and she found a star for each of them. It seemed to give her comfort to know that when she was missing one of her dead relatives she could look up to the evening sky and associate a star with him. *Susan Wehle, Hilton, New York*

A PERSONALIZED STORY FOR AN UNFAMILIAR EVENT ✦ We created an illustrated story of "Cassy and the Court," which helped explain an upcoming court appearance my young daughter would be involved in. Because it was a story about her, my daughter loved the book and it helped take the fear away before the court appearance. *Lyla Fries, Fremont, California*

NEW OR UNCERTAIN EXPERIENCES ✦ Describing and talking about a new experience before it happens is the best way to prevent a potential fear in young children. For example, a positive yet realistic explanation before a child's first plane trip will help him understand and anticipate what will be happening. This approach can be used for a variety of situations: doctor visits, medical procedures, visiting relatives and friends, first day of preschool, etc. *Wanda Nevin, Walnut Creek, California*

TIME ALONE WITH EACH CHILD

ONE ON ONE ✦ One way to make a child feel special is for each parent to spend time alone with him. A fun activity is always nice, but make sure it's an opportunity where you can talk and especially listen to the child. *Florence Moorman, Buffalo, New York*

SPECIAL DAY FOR EACH CHILD ✦ When we were expecting our fourth child, we started what we call "Special Day." It is an opportunity for each of our children to have a couple of hours with both parents. We set a time to go out (e.g., Sunday brunch) with each child to a place where he or she would like to go. We take a couple of hours, hire a baby-sitter for the other kids, and give one child an opportunity to be the center of our attention. *Gregg Dart and Debra McLean, Salem, Oregon*

A DAILY DOSE OF DAD ✦ Five minutes of being held while sitting on Dad's lap on a once-a-day basis works wonders with a "problem child." No words are spoken unless the child initiates conversation. The younger children looked forward to "Dad's five minutes" so much that the older kids asked for it too. Perhaps it is the body contact or just the reassurance of being with Dad that works. Eventually, Mom asked for her turn at five minutes too. *Ron Burda, San Jose, California*

A PARENT-CHILD DATE ✦ Take your child out to breakfast or lunch, go out for a Coke after school, or go to the park. This lets him know that he is important to you and that you are accessible to him. *Nancy Painter, LaVista, Nebraska*

✖✦✦✦✦✦✦✦✦✦✦✦✦✦✦✦✦✦✦✦✦✦✦✦✦✦✦✦✦✦✦✦✦✦✦✦✦✦✦✖

PARENTS NEED TIME, TOO

✖✦✦✦✦✦✦✦✦✦✦✦✦✦✦✦✦✦✦✦✦✦✦✦✦✦✦✦✦✦✦✦✦✦✦✦✦✦✦✖

MY TURN TO SLEEP IN ✦ This survival tip is a must for all parents with small children: On weekends, only one parent gets up with the kids on Saturday morning while the other parent enjoys the luxury of sleeping in! Then on Sunday morning, the roles are reversed. *Kathy Tubbs, San Jose, California*

QUIET TIMES FOR SATURDAY MORNING ✦ When our kids were younger, my husband frequently took them out for breakfast on Saturday morning while I slept or just took my time getting up and having some quiet time. After breakfast they usually stopped at one of the parks so I could have at least one to two hours to myself. *Jane Gustafson, Devils Lake, North Dakota*

EXERCISE WITH BABY ✦ When my daughter was an infant, we could always calm her down by having her ride in a front pack while my husband exercised on his stationary bicycle. She liked being close and warm next to him. *Kristine Gustason, Shrewsbury, Massachusetts*

A child seat on an adult's bike also works great. Now that my older daughter can ride her own bike, she rides along as I jog. It's a fun activity for both of us—and I get my exercise.

FRIDAY-NIGHT DATE NIGHT ✦ As far as juggling work and home, my husband and I always have Friday-night date night. When we go out, like in the old days before marriage, we don't discuss work, kids, or bills, and it seems to keep the romance in our marriage. *Kimberly Carew, North Haven, Connecticut*

IF YOU NEED A FEW MINUTES OF PRIVATE

TAPE THEIR FAVORITE SHOWS ✦ I tape my child's favorite TV show and let him watch it when I need time to get things done. *Paula Greene, Virginia Beach, Virginia*

CRIB MOBILES ✦ These are a wonderful distraction for infants when you really need to get something done—like dinner. *D. Martinez, Fremont, California*

Check crib mobiles for approved safety; some have small parts that can come off or break and pose a safety threat if put into an infant's mouth. Always keep mobiles at a safe distance to keep infants from grabbing them and pulling them into their cribs.

A "QUIET BAG" BUYS A FEW MINUTES ✦ When you need a few minutes during a phone call or for bathroom privacy, give your child a "quiet bag." Keep a small bag with toys that your child doesn't otherwise have access to. Rotate toys to keep it fresh and interesting. Flea markets, garage sales, and swap meets keep us in supply of inexpensive "treasures." *Stacey Lopez, Fremont, California*

QUIET PHONE TIME ✦ I keep a stack of coloring books and crayons by our telephone. I can color with my child and talk on the phone at the same time. It's really terrific because I can interact with my child. Otherwise she would feel put off, and she would whine or try to get my attention by getting into mischief. *Sabra Jiwa, Marietta, Georgia*

"MOM ON RECESS" ✦ On occasion, I have declared "Mom on Recess," which was a short time that the children couldn't bother me. Every parent needs a few minutes of quiet time each day, even if it's for a quick cup of coffee. I suggest setting a timer; children don't seem to argue with timers. *E.S., Albuquerque, New Mexico*

A LOVING RECORDING KEEPS A CHILD OCCUPIED ✦ One of my fondest childhood memories is an idea which my mother had to occupy me when she needed a few minutes (she was a physically handicapped

single parent). She would read my favorite stories into a tape recorder using her wonderful voices for each of the characters. She used a bell to indicate when it was time to turn the page. I have fond memories of listening to these tapes as a child while my mother was getting ready for work in the morning, while I was at the baby-sitter, and especially the long lonely times when she was in the hospital. I would listen to these tapes for what seemed like hours. They are a wonderful thing to save; my mom has passed away and I would dearly love to have those now for me and my daughter. *Stacey Ann Morgan, Oakland, California*

✖✧✧✧✧✧✧✧✧✧✧✧✧✧✧✧✧✧✧✧✧✧✧✧✧✧✧✧✧✧✧✧✧✧✖

BABY-SITTERS AND DAY CARE

✖✧✧✧✧✧✧✧✧✧✧✧✧✧✧✧✧✧✧✧✧✧✧✧✧✧✧✧✧✧✧✧✧✧✖

GETTING USED TO A NEW BABY-SITTER ✦ I invite a new baby-sitter over to play with the children while I am home a week before she or he will be sitting. That way the children get use to the baby-sitter while I am still there and the baby-sitter can become familiar with our house before baby-sitting for the first time. *Kathy Howland, Springfield, Missouri*

This is a good idea, especially if the child will be watched at the sitter's home. A strange house *and* sitter may be a bit too much for a child to handle at one time.

PREPARING FOR DAY CARE ✦ To eliminate or at least reduce fear for my three-year-old son and heighten anticipation of his first experience at day care (I had gotten a job and had to work full-time), I took him on a short visit to the center on Friday, before he was to attend the following Monday. Very briefly I showed him all the neat stuff he could do and all the wonderful things he could play with there. Just as he would get into one new adventure, I'd drag him on to the next. Then I said we had to go. He almost cried. But I assured him he could come back on Monday and spend the whole day playing with everything. When I dropped him off Monday, he almost jumped from the car and the only person left crying because of the separation was me. *Linda Helser, Phoenix, Arizona*

FIRST VISIT TO DAY CARE ✦ If your child is apprehensive to go to a new day care, take your child for his first visit when no other (or few) children are present. Early morning or early evening is usually best, depending on the hours of the day-care center. By visiting at this time of day only the fun toys and activities will be highlighted for your child, not all the children. Chances are your child will be eager to return to the day-care center and play with all those wonderful toys. *Anonymous, San Diego, California*

EMERGENCY INFORMATION FOR THE BABY-SITTER ✦ When a baby-sitter comes, I leave medical release forms prewritten and signed by me by the telephone as well as written authorization for my baby-sitter to seek treatment. You just never know. Also, on the notepad where our emergency phone numbers are, I have written the two major cross streets to our home. In an emergency or even for the baby-sitter, this could be an aid when talking to emergency personnel. *Vicki Schrimmer, Irvine, California*

BABY-SITTER'S MEMO ✦ I have written my husband's and my own work telephone numbers, our pediatrician's and dentist's names and numbers, and other emergency information on a piece of paper for the baby-sitter. I covered both sides with clear contact paper, which made a permanent memo which I can send with my child when she goes to her day-care provider or to a friend's home to play. I also leave it by our telephone for handy reference for ourselves and in-home sitters. *Elizabeth Leonard-Iso, Fremont, California*

"MOMMY BE BACK" ✦ As soon as she could talk, I taught my daughter to say "Mommy be back" (in a sing-song way). Anytime I leave her with a sitter, I say it and get the sitter to say it. It calms and reassures her much better than just saying, "You're OK." *Karen Lynch, Los Altos Hills, California*

One of the ways to teach children to be comfortable with change is to give familiar cues (verbal, action, etc.) that they can rely on. "Mommy be back" is one good cue. Use it when leaving and when returning to complete the connection.

SPECIAL TOYS FOR BABY-SITTER EVENINGS ✦ I keep toys aside in a special drawer for when a baby-sitter comes. *Nancy Plymale, Ft. Pierce, Florida*

If baby-sitters bring their own "play kits," be sure to look over the items for safety and appropriateness for your child.

HUGGING CALMS A SCREAMING CHILD ✦ Hugging is very important! I had a screaming child at my house; I was a stranger to this two-year-old and he was in a strange house. I allowed him to cry a while, then I picked him up and held him in my arms on my lap. Holding him closely in a loving embrace, I told him, "I'll let you down when you stop crying." He stopped almost immediately and was even reluctant to get down. I sang to him and talked quietly and he didn't cry again. I tried this on a three-year-old in his own house and he responded in the same way. Then after a while he turned to me and said, "Are we friends now?" What a thrill! *Florence Grace, Fremont, California*

KISSES TO GO ✦ My young son was very reluctant to let me leave his day care each morning. One day I kissed him good-bye, then gave him extra kisses in his hand. I folded up his hand and told him these kisses could be used later if he should need them. These kisses became very comforting to him. He's nine years old now, and he occasionally says, "I wish I could still have kisses in my hand." *Charlotte Bonnette, Panama City, Florida*

EXTRA KISSES IF I NEED THEM ✦ When I was a child my parents told me to frequently wash my hands, so instead of putting the extra kisses in my hands, my mother put them on the back of my ears; I could pull them out whenever I needed them. *Patricia R. Hersom, Walnut Creek, California*

KISSES ON POST-IT NOTES ✦ My young daughter would get upset with me if I left the house before she woke up in the morning. Now I get Post-it notes and before I leave, I put on lots of lipstick, kiss the notes, and stick them all over my daughter's room and the bathroom so she can have lots of kisses from Mom and keep them while I'm gone. *Lyla Fries, Fremont, California*

WHEN MOM WAS IN THE HOSPITAL ✦ I was in the hospital seven days when my second child was born. My first child was with a few different caretakers during this time. Prior to the time I was hospitalized, I bought small gifts, wrapped them in tissue paper with ribbons, and put the dates on them. I instructed the caretakers that if my daughter was cooperative during that day, that evening she could unwrap one of these gifts from Mommy. I would call her before bed and she could open one of the gifts. It made the seven days go by quickly and the reports I got from her caretakers were excellent. *Susan Wehle, Hilton, New York*

A DAILY PROGRESS REPORT ✦ My nine-month-old daughter has been in day care since she was one month old. I really appreciated receiving a daily "report card" from one day-care provider where my daughter stayed. The report showed how much my baby ate and drank, the time she napped, and when she wet or had a bowel movement. The information was listed on a small Xeroxed form that the provider filled in. There was a space at the bottom where she would write anything special that happened that day. As a working mom, I really liked this because it made me feel that I didn't miss out completely on my baby's day. *Cathy Vandivort, Glendale, Arizona*

PARENTS ON TAPE ✦ My son is very attached to my husband and, when my husband is at work, asks for him often. I recorded the sounds of my husband and son playing together. When my husband is away, my son listens to the tape and remembers the fun they had together. This idea is also good for parents who bring their children to baby-sitters or who have to go away on overnight trips. *Mary Anne Pagliaro, New York, New York*

TAPE A STORY ✦ When our children were very young, the bedtime story became an evening ritual. My wife and I taped a number of their favorite stories to be played for them by the baby-sitter when we went out for the evening. *Neil McCallum, Fremont, California*

THE "MOMMY TAPE" ✦ When we are out of town and leave our two boys (ages two and four) with some family member, I tape-record a personalized talk to them just as if I were putting them to bed. I even include their prayers. They call it the "Mommy Tape" and ask for it often. *Nancy Plymale, Fort Pierce, Florida*

HOME-AWAY-FROM-HOME BAG ✦ When my husband and I leave our preschooler for a weekend or longer, I pack a special "home bag." It contains a picture of the whole family, a special new book, and a tape for the tape recorder. The tape has two favorite stories, one read by Mom, the other read by Dad. The tape and picture can really soothe a child who wants or misses Mom or Dad. *Sue Sponsel, Fremont, California*

A PIECE OF MOM IS ALWAYS WITH ME ✦ When my daughter has to go somewhere for a while, I always give her a piece of my jewelry or a picture of me so she will have a "piece of me" with her. It seems to be very comforting to her. *Lyla Fries, Fremont, California*

MOM LEFT A SECURITY BLANKET OF HER OWN ✦ If a young child is anxious about staying with a baby-sitter, bring an article of your clothing to leave with him in your absence. He will derive some comfort from holding a piece of your clothing while you are away. *Karen Cutter and Stephen Robison, Belmont, California*

"THERE'S YOUR MOMMY, SHE'S ON TV" ✦ When my friend's child missed her mother while at day care, I suggested that my friend videotape a couple of little encouraging comments for her daughter and give them to the day-care provider. When the child missed her mom, the day-care provider sat her down in front of the TV, turned on the video, and there was Mom talking to her, saying things like "Hi sweetie, I can't wait to get home today, we are going to have a great time doing such and such a project. Now you know you can call me if it's an emergency." After the little girl saw that, she felt better and went on playing with her friends. *Andria Turner, Norfolk, Virginia*

$$ RELAXING BABY-SITTING JOB ✦ We began a baby-sitting exchange with our neighbor that has saved our

sanity! Here's how it works: On a weekend night, once my neighbor's children are in bed, my neighbor gives me a call and I go over to baby-sit until 11:30 P.M., while my husband stays with my children. Then, on the following weekend, I call my neighbor once my kids are down for the night, and she comes over to baby-sit for us until 11:30 P.M. The advantages of this exchange are innumerable, but here are the top five: 1) Our kids keep their normal bedtime routines, 2) No payment is made for baby-sitting, 3) There is security knowing that another mom is baby-sitting my kids, 4) Each couple enjoys some alone time and a romantic dinner out twice a month, and 5) Even the mom doing the baby-sitting has several hours of *total* relaxation! *K.T. Hom, San Jose, California*

$$ STARTING YOUR OWN BABY-SITTING CO-OP ✦ I am a member of a very successful baby-sitting co-op that provides no-cost, high-quality child care. Our rules are simple, but important: both parent and sitter must report their hours to the coordinator; time is rounded off to the nearest fifteen minutes; parents provide all meals and snacks needed; the time-out method of discipline is used when necessary; sick children are not to be left at a sitter's house, nor are you allowed to watch other children if your child is ill; we do not discuss problems with co-op children with anyone but their own parents; and we report children's behavior honestly to their parents. Parents can choose the sitter who will watch their child (if convenient for the sitter). We are not required to use the co-op member who is behind in hours. *Kaylynn Stacy, Ft. Worth, Texas*

$$ FORM YOUR OWN "PLAY SCHOOL" ✦ When my twins were two, I thought I would go crazy if I didn't get some time to myself, but I couldn't afford preschool or baby-sitters. I found two friends who were in the same boat and we formed our own "play school." We each volunteered to host the "school" in our home one morning a week (M-W-F). This meant that two mornings each week I had time to myself and one morning a week I was the "teacher." We played games, sang songs, made crafts, and had snack and story time—with only three or four little ones it was a snap! The kids quickly became buddies and so did the moms. The best part—it was free—and so was I! *Donna Schutt, Concord, California*

$$ THE "YANKEE HILL GANG" ◆ is an informal baby-sitting cooperative among three families with six children who live on Yankee Hill. Each Saturday night, all six children go to one home where they have a party, eat dinner, and are put to bed. We rotate homes each week, so parents get two Saturday nights out in three. I don't think the children, who are close friends, have ever realized the tradition was originally started for the parents' benefit. They look forward to it each week. *Han Wingate, Sonora, California*

10

ON THE GO
(with Children)

◆

Travel is glamorous only in retrospect.
— PAUL THEROUX, *The Observer*, 1979

Although family vacations are something we look forward to, getting there is the challenge, especially with children. Careful planning and packing are the key to success. Children are usually great travelers—for the first hour. After that, their happiness will be directly correlated to the amount of food and toys you have packed. If these items are in short supply, especially on a lengthy trip, your journey will become what seasoned travelers politely call an "adventure."

Car travel is not easy on children; they get bored quickly and need to move around. Over the years I have learned the importance of traveling on the children's schedule, whenever possible. This means frequent rest stops, instead of marathon driving, and stopping to enjoy the playground at the fast-food restaurant instead of rushing through the take-out window. Such trips may take a little longer, but both parents and children arrive at their destination feeling more relaxed.

My family takes an annual trek to Disneyland each March, before the crowds arrive. The seven-hour drive from the Bay Area is usually enjoyable, but we do have our moments. For fun, my wife chronicled the first hour on the road (which was quite typical of our car travels) during our trip last year:

6:40 A.M.	Left home (only 10 minutes behind schedule). Kids still in pj's, hoping they will sleep. (Who are we trying to kid?)
6:43	Returned home. Retrieved the diaper wipes.

6:48   First argument over a toy.
6:51   Juice served.
6:55   First spill. It was Mom.
7:06   Mom and Dad sing along with kids' tape, songs about a fire-breathing dragon and Little Bunny Foo Foo. Kids aren't interested in the songs.
7:15   First tears. Our older daughter realizes she will lose her turn to be a leader at school.
7:36   First rest stop. Use potty and change diapers.

On our return trip, a great thing happened—the kids fell asleep before we drove out of the Disneyland parking lot. So we drove—and drove—until we got sleepy ourselves, around midnight, and retired to a roadside motel. We had driven halfway home without hearing one request from the backseat. The next day was a quick and painless three-hour drive home. Now, when we travel by car or plane, we often choose to travel in the evening. The kids travel in their pj's and, sooner or later, fall asleep, making the trip more relaxing for all.

Traveling by plane with children is even more intense than car travel, but luckily it's over sooner. I'm the poor guy you see inching through the airport—the daddy Sherpa—carrying two car seats, one child, a day pack, toy bag, stuffed bunny, and blankie. After boarding, there are new concerns. *I immediately begin to hope:*

1) . . . *that no one will sit in the vacant seat next to us*—especially if we didn't buy a seat for our youngest daughter when she was under two years of age. No amount of savings on airfare can compensate for a four-hour flight with an active baby on your lap. We learned the hard way. A few years ago, as we were waiting to take off on a four-hour flight, I winked at my wife as the attendant started to close the cabin door. We had gambled and won. The vacant seat was ours—we thought. Just then, a huge woman, three hundred pounds or more, pushed open the cabin door the attendants were trying to secure. I quickly surveyed the plane; there were three vacant seats. I put a hex on her as she ambled up the aisle, but she stopped at our row.

"I believe this is my seat," she said sweetly, pointing to our infant, who was already strapped in. We moved the baby. She sat down in her seat, and part of mine. We never gambled again.

2) . . . *that I will not have to change a dirty diaper during the flight.* This is only my concern, not my wife's. My wife can change diapers anywhere, anytime. I need a fully equipped changing table: ointments, abundant diaper wipes, room deodorants, etc.

3) . . . *that our baby will not cry during the majority of the flight.* I hate it when other passengers give you "THE LOOK," which usually translates into, "Can't you take care of that child? You're ruining my flight." I know this "look" because I used to give it myself, before having children, of course.

No matter what the mode of transportation, the recipe for a successful trip with children includes the following ingredients: two calm adults; children who maintain their regular schedule (as closely as possible); lots of yummy food (for nutrition AND DISTRACTION); plenty of proven activities, and a few new inexpensive toys you can bring out when none of the above work.

The following travel tips were collected from seasoned family travelers. The first section, Are We There Yet? (Car Travel), is followed by Airplane Travel, Vacations, and Errands and Shopping. For suggestions on how to turn a boring trip of errands into a lively learning session, refer to Chapter 4 and the section titled Learning in the Car.

◆

XXX

ARE WE THERE YET? (CAR TRAVEL)

XXXXXXXXXXXXXXXXXXXXXXXXXXXXXXXXXXXXXXXXXXXXX

TRAVEL BOX ⬥ On long car trips I always include a special "travel box" for my four-year-old. It is a shoe box that I have covered with bright paper (cover the lid and box separately). In it, I have placed coloring books, new crayons, sticker books, markers, and a few favorite toys. I also prepare a grab bag of new items which I keep with me and bring out only when my daughter gets restless. The flea market and garage sales are a great place to pick up items in good condition for a fraction of the cost. *Stacey Lopez, Fremont, California*

GRAB-BAG TOY TIME ⬥ Before setting off on a trip, I purchase one toy per child for each day we will be on the road. I wrap each toy in used Christmas paper. The new toys keep the children quiet or amused until we arrive at our destination. *Mrs. Jane R. Kruger, East Greenwich, Rhode Island*

ACTIVITIES TO GO ⬥ My children keep a small carrying case that has separate compartments (or you could use a small fishing-tackle box) filled with travel games, notepads, crayons and markers, pencils, and other small toys. They take it in the car for travel activities and on camping trips. Small stocking stuffers each Christmas replenish their supplies. *Sharon Heimiller, Baltimore, Maryland*

AN APRON OF TOYS ⬥ Recently, we took a trip by car that took twelve hours. A friend made me an apron that hooked over the headrest of the front seat to hang down into the backseat. She put pockets of several sizes on it. We filled them with coloring books, crayons, travel-size games, snacks, wet wipes, books, etc. It gave plenty of things for the kids to do on such a long trip, yet it wasn't all over the seat and floor and stayed within easy reach. *Sheryl Saxton, Tekamah, Nebraska*

THE BACK OF THE FRONT SEAT IS BORING ✦ If possible, adjust the child's car seat so that it's high enough for the child to see out the window. The back of the front seat is bound to get old fast. *Fred Schroeder, Denison, Texas*

Always follow the safety guidelines for the child-care products you purchase.

TOY CHAIN LINKS FOR THE CAR ✦ To make traveling easier for our family, I hang plastic toy chain links from the hand strap or hooks above the side window in the backseat. Then I attach a bottle of water so my son can have a drink whenever he wants. Now that he is two and no longer uses a baby bottle, I use a bicycle water bottle for him. Toys or a pacifier can also hang from the links and will keep them from getting lost in the car. *Erica Agesen, Omaha, Nebraska*
Toy chain links are also great for use on strollers, playpens, and cribs (see Chapter 1 — Toys).

Be careful of the miniature toy chain links that could be swallowed.

$$ COOKIE SHEET BECOMES A PORTABLE MAGNET BOARD ✦ A cookie sheet can be used for many different activities in the car, especially for long-distance driving: a magnet board (five to ten small magnets offer hours of creative fun), a raceway for small cars and trucks, or a platform to hold Legos or blocks. *Arlene Stocking, Fremont, California*

TRAVEL TOYS ✦ A deck of cards or flash cards with pictures, etc., make wonderful travel toys and are easy to carry in a purse or pocket. *Pat Remmes, Walnut Creek, California*

POST-ITS ON THE CAR WINDOW ✦ One of the things I have found to be most useful when taking a trip is packages of Post-it removable stickers. A child can spend quite a bit of time sticking the Post-its against the car window. *Janet Romanchyk, Fulton, New York*

A PINWHEEL FOR THE CAR ✦ To easily and inexpensively entertain an infant while driving, clip a shiny pinwheel to your visor and direct your car's air vents towards it to make it spin. Young babies will be fascinated by the movement. Older children can hold the pinwheel themselves. *Susan Lowther, Glendale, Arizona*

WE'RE IN FLAGSTAFF, TIME FOR A PRESENT ✦ I made a cross-country trip at Christmastime with four children ages eleven, six, three, and eleven months. We packed a suitcase full of sandwiches and planned to stop as little as possible in order to get to my parents' place before Christmas. The lifesaver for the long haul was another suitcase full of wrapped surprises each labeled with the name of the town (e.g., Flagstaff, Arizona) or landmark where it was to be opened. The gifts were small—a coloring book and crayons, play dough, a new story, a small puzzle, or origami paper for folding, for example. The anticipation of the next opening point increased the children's interest in moving ahead and minimized their desire for rest stops. Watching the map for progress between unwrapping points promoted geographical knowledge and map-reading skills. It also helped that each child had specific responsibilities—the eleven-year-old passed out sandwiches and snacks and fed the baby. The six-year-old was the tire checker at every stop (got some wiggles out that way, too). The three-year-old was the special watcher for various things along the way and he and the six-year-old took turns opening the packages and disposing of wrappings. *Marge West, Lakewood, Colorado*

"BOOKS ON TAPE" FOR CAR TRIPS ✦ In our family, each child has a Walkman to bring along for lengthy car trips. The library offers children's "books on tape" to borrow or you can purchase them as well. It keeps the kids occupied for hours. *Vanetta Hayhurst, Farmington, Connecticut*

A RECORDED ACTIVITY FOR TRAVELING ✦ My son learned how to operate a child's tape recorder when he was between two and two and a half years old. I would prerecord activities and stories for long car trips. I stacked a pile of books and his tape recorder next to his car seat. The recorder would begin by saying, "Find the book with three kittens on it. Stop the tape until you find it. Now, turn to page one. Do you see the baby black kitty?" Then I read the words for that page. I rang a bell and said, "Now turn to page two." I frequently asked questions as I read the story such as, "What color mittens is the kitty wearing?" It's a wonderful activity that also teaches them early reading skills. *N.S., San Jose, California*

A TRAVEL DIARY FOR CHILDREN ✦ Older children love to keep a travel diary, which includes their favorite activities, time of food stops, gas amounts, mileage, etc. It's enjoyable to them, it keeps them busy, and it's good writing and calculating practice. *Rita Wilson, Fremont, California*

BACKSEAT ENTERTAINMENT ✦ We have two young children (five and two) whom we occasionally take on a ten-hour driving trip to visit family. When the girls get tired of the drive, I move to the backseat, sit between them, and read stories, sing, and play games with them. Even though I'm continuing activities which I was doing with them from the front seat, my moving closer to them stretches their patience and the general level of peace in the car a long while. This works best as a last resort. *Nancy Lee, Pasadena, California*

CAR TRAVEL GAMES ✦ There are two games that keep our children occupied when we travel by car. One is to have the children keep a list of all the different state license plates they see go by. The other is to have them find all the letters of the alphabet on road signs. *William and Sandra McNiff, Dracut, Massachusetts*

A CAR VIDEO ✦ We have a small video cassette player than can hook up to the cigarette lighter in our car. We place the screen between the two front seats in our mini-van, facing the backseat. The children are entertained for long periods of time. *Beverly Killion, Anaheim, California*

A TWO-BIT QUESTION ✦ We love to travel by car, although long days of driving are not always our eight- and six-year-old children's dream trip. At the beginning of each long driving day, we determine how many times each kid can ask, "Are we almost there?" or any form of that question. Generally, we decide each child can ask twice, after which it costs them twenty-five cents of their allowance. We make sure that they know, throughout the day, exactly where we are, what time we expect to arrive, how many more hours until our next stop, etc. We've found this has eliminated the annoying asking completely. *Stacy Krimetz, Livermore, California*

THAT QUESTION WILL COST YOU A NICKEL ✦ For older children who appreciate money and are traveling on a long trip, get each child a roll of nickels. For every time they ask "Are we there yet?" or "How much further do we have to go?" you take a nickel from their pack. Therefore, the less they ask how much longer it will be, the more money they will have to spend when they get there. *Karen Peters, Garden Grove, California*

Remember to regularly update the children as to your location and estimated time of arrival. Keep in mind the child's need for exercise, regular bathroom stops, anxiousness, boredom, cramped car seat, etc.

A CAR-TRAVELING SYSTEM FOR KIDS ✦ Make a stop every hour and a half. In the morning, before starting off, have the children pick out four or five toys for the day, then give them one or not more than two toys for a one-and-a-half hour spell. At the end of the hour and a half, stop for a quick snack and stretch the legs. At that time, put away the earlier toys, and get out another one. At the end of three hours of traveling, it is time to stop for lunch, or at least a place to go to the bathroom for all, and another leg stretch. After lunch, try to encourage a nap. You might take along a portable tape recorder if your car doesn't have a tape deck and play some quiet-time music. If naps don't work, and the traffic situation is such that you can devote some time and attention, play a game such as Animal, Vegetable, Mineral or Twenty Questions. Or you might have a sing-along. *Mrs. Jane R. Kruger, East Greenwich, Rhode Island*

STOP AND HAVE A PICNIC ✦ We try to drive three to four hours before stopping on a long trip. If the weather permits, drop the kids and one parent off at a local park while the other parent finds a café with take-out food. Kids play hard, eat good, and can't wait to get to another park for supper three to four hours down the road. *Jane and Bob Gustafson, Devils Lake, North Dakota*

RACING OFF EXCESS ENERGY ◆ During lengthy car trips I would periodically stop at a park or grassy area and have the kids run foot races. It helped to stretch their legs and burn off excess energy after sitting in the cramped car. *Char Janzen, Hays, Kansas*

> This works for air travel, too. Before boarding a lengthy flight or between connecting flights, I find a deserted area at the airport (inside or outside) and start foot races with my children. Afterwards we are all better able to endure our cramped seats during a four- or five-hour flight.

SNACKS ON THE GO ◆ Cheerios, raisins, crackers, and boxed juices make wonderful traveling companions. *Patricia R. Hersom, Walnut Creek, California*

ALPHABET CAR GAME ◆ A fun game to play with kids on a long car ride is what my family calls the "Alphabet Game." First, we start looking for the letter "A" on a license plate or sign along the freeway. When we find an "A," we start looking for a "B," then a "C," etc., until we reach the end of the alphabet. It's fun and it makes the trip go by faster. *Dan Dubois, Gaithersburg, Maryland*

NONSPILL WATER BOTTLES ◆ Save plastic syrup bottles with the pop-up caps to use as water bottles in the car. Each child can have his own serve-yourself bottle and you don't have to worry about spills on the upholstery or clothing. *Beverly Killion, Anaheim, California*

PLASTIC LEMONS FOR ON THE GO ◆ I take the plastic lemons that you buy at the grocery store, empty the lemon juice leaving a little juice (for lemon-flavored drinks), add water, and freeze them (other flavors can be used too). When the children are thirsty in the car, they can take off the top of the lemons and squirt the juice into their mouths. This makes a good nonspill drink for children on a long trip, and it's always nice and cold. *Marilyn Walton, Oxford, Ohio*

> Be careful that the small caps are not swallowed by young children. Any item that has small pieces should be supervised by an adult.

ONLY WATER IS ALLOWED IN THE CAR ✦ To avoid messy and sticky spills of soft drinks and juices, we only allow plain water in the car for drinking. *Bonnie Lowe, Fremont, California*

PACIFIER "LEASH" ✦ To prevent our baby from losing his pacifier while riding in the car, we attach the pacifier on a "leash" to the car-seat shoulder strap. *Peg Hartley, San Bernardino, California*

Make sure the "leash" is short, and not long enough to wrap around any part of the infant.

PIDDLE JARS FOR LONG TRIPS ✦ On long car trips with young boys, bring along a plastic bottle with a cap for emergency potty needs. The bottle can be emptied at a rest room when you stop for a break. *Anonymous, Winnipeg, Manitoba*

WHEN NO BATHROOMS ARE IN SIGHT ✦ We have four little boys with two still in diapers. When we are out and can't find a bathroom for the older ones, we just use a diaper from one of the little ones and throw it out when we find a trash can. *Gloria Kam, Orange, California*

"QUIET DOWN OR I'M PULLING OVER" ✦ When we would go on a long trip and our six sons would get tired and noisy, their dad would say, "I'm going to pull over to the side of the road and sit there until you all quiet down, and then we can go again." This worked for us. *Vera Bates, Wharton, New Jersey*

FOR ARGUMENTS IN THE CAR ✦ When little people can't stop bickering on a long car trip, I turn up the volume on a radio station playing music which I like, but I know they don't. After a few minutes of grand opera drowning them out, they usually assure me that they can get along. I hope as a side benefit they'll learn to like opera because it's familiar. *Peggy Gilbreth Nipper, Omaha, Nebraska*

COMPOSE A SONG ABOUT YOUR TRIP ✦ You and your children will remember that special trip together forever if you will write (and sing together) a song about it, composing it as you go. All it takes is two couplets of rhyming lines per verse. It is important to have the children help you with the composition, changing and improving as you go. It's best to write new words to the tune of a song they know and like. *Mr. and Mrs. Roland Giduz, Chapel Hill, North Carolina*

BEFORE YOU LEAVE AT 3 A.M., READ THIS ✦ One authority suggested that a parent or parents should get an early start on a trip—say 3 A.M.—while the children are still asleep. I thoroughly disagree! Just about the time the children are awake and raring to go, the parents are dead tired. *Mrs. Jane R. Kruger, East Greenwich, Rhode Island*

✖◆◆◆✖

AIRPLANE TRAVEL

✖◆◆◆✖

MAKING RESERVATIONS ✦ To get room for your child to move around on an airplane, and if your child is young enough to sit on your lap, try the following: Ask for the row which has the most leg room. This is generally a bulkhead row. Reserve a window seat for one adult and an aisle seat for the other adult. Unless the flight is full, the airlines will not fill a center seat if there are any other seats available. This will increase your chances of having the center seat vacant and thus more room for your child to move about without having to pay for the seat. If the flight is full, you will need to ask the person who has the center seat to change with one of yours. I am sure you will not have any problems in getting them to change, as who in their right mind would sit in the middle of a family that is holding a child? *Vikki Hill, Newark, California*

REQUEST A CHILD'S MEAL ✦ When making airline reservations, make sure to order a special "child's meal" if your flight includes any meal. It's free, it makes the child feel special, and it usually includes food items that children will eat and enjoy. *Bob Ingrum, Granada Hills, California*

ASK FOR SEATS IN THE BACK ✦ Ask for seats in the back of the plane when traveling with children. Unless the fight is full, the empty seats will usually be in the back so your kids will have some additional space to stretch out or roam without disturbing other passengers. It's noisier in the back, so any disturbance is more likely to go unnoticed. Plus, the engine actually tends to have a calming effect on the little ones. *Patricia Wilson, Dallas, Texas*

DON'T DRESS THE CHILDREN IN OVER-ALLS ✦ The metal hooks and snaps in my young daughter's overalls activated the metal detector at the airport. It was a very scary experience for both of us. *Nancy S. Jamison, Newtown Square, Pennsylvania*

Overalls are also difficult to take off and put on again in cramped airplane bathrooms. Also, airport security requests that toy guns be checked in at the ticket counter prior to entering the airport security checkpoint.

CAR SEATS ON FLIGHTS ARE MORE THAN JUST "SAFE" ✦ Using a car seat is ideal on an airplane. This gives the child a familiar place to sit and prevents him from running around. Children are more likely to fall and stay asleep in their car seat than in your lap or the airplane's seat. If you do use the car seat, you will have to pay for the airline's seat even if the child can sit on your lap. *Scott Hill, Newark, California*

PACKING FOR THE PLANE ✦ I work for an airline and we fly on a regular basis with our two children (ages one and four). A friend of mine advised me early on to provide toys and food nonstop throughout, and it works! We always pack a snack bag of fruit, crackers, cheese, and anything else we can think of besides junk food. I also stop by the discount store and get new coloring books, new storybooks, magic eraser boards, Silly Putty, and anything else that is inexpensive and lightweight. We pack a small backpack for the kids with their stuff. *Patricia Wilson, Dallas, Texas*

SURPRISE BAGS ✦ My tips relate to air travel with two daughters aged two and five. Pack a "surprise bag" with small, inexpensive, and entertaining items. Be sure to GIFT-WRAP each item, and space them out to forestall the next "antsy" period. *Anna P. Smith, Pensacola, Florida*

WALKMAN AND LEGOS ARE GOOD TRAVELING COMPANIONS ✦ When traveling with my six-year-old son on a twenty-eight hour flight to East Africa, we tried every kind of diversion. By far, the most popular were the following two: First, a new Walkman with earphones and a supply of new kids' tapes purchased for the trip. This has also become a very successful car travel activity. Second, Legos, because they could be played with on the airplane's fold-out table and empty food trays. *Han Wingate, Sonora, California*

COLOR-FORM SETS FOR HIGH-ALTITUDE FUN ✦ A small or medium-size color-form set is a great activity for children on an airplane. The plastic pieces stick like magic to the special board and can be used over and over to create different scenes. *Linda Marshall, Haslett, Michigan*

NON-SPILL CUPS ✦ We always bring a non-spill cup, such as a Tommie Tippee Cup, on board a plane for our children (even our six-year-old) to drink from. It avoids inevitable spills from those tippy plastic cups that the airlines serve drinks in. *Anonymous, San Diego, California*

MAGIC BOOKS FOR FLYING ✦ We started flying when my oldest was four years old. I took gum for her to chew and munchables to eat. We also brought "magic books" (the color is already on the page so a colorless marker magically brings out colors!). If the plane is not full, the flight attendants are usually pretty nice folks, and you can ask to get a full row of seats. This provides squirming room for the little ones, who can also lie down and sleep. We took a cheap stroller and sent it through baggage, and every time we got off the plane an airline employee had it opened and waiting for us! *Nancy S. Jamison, Newtown Square, Pennsylvania*

TRAVEL GAMES ✦ Pocket versions of some of the most popular games (checkers, chess, Connect-Four, etc.) are now available in most toy stores. The Magna Doodle and Etch-A-Sketch also make wonderful traveling companions. Color-form stickers (which peel off and are reusable) will adhere to the airplane windows and are especially beautiful in the sunlight. *Anna P. Smith, Pensacola, Florida*

HIGH-FLYING PLAY DOUGH ✦ Play dough is a great activity during an airplane flight. Pull down the seat tray and you have a perfect place to make creations. *Robin Bunton, Fremont, California*

CHEERIO NECKLACE ✦ Making a Cheerio necklace is a fun activity during an airplane flight. Give your child an eighteen-inch piece of string or yarn and a container of Cheerios. He will keep himself entertained for a long time by stringing and eating the Cheerios. *Janice Fonteno, Union City, California*

As a variation, try Froot Loops. By alternating certain colors, the child can make beautiful designs.

PAINTING ON A PLANE ✦ A "paint with water" book (where the muted colors become vivid when the kids paint them with water) and brushes, with water from the flight attendant, will keep children busy for long stretches of time during a plane trip. Bring along extra "neat" snacks for waiting times and delays. Be sure to carry wipes and a plastic bag for throwaways. *Anna P. Smith, Pensacola, Florida*

STRING KEEPS KIDS BUSY ✦ For cars and airplanes, keep a small amount of string (about two yards long) in your pocket or purse. Children of almost any age can spend hours trying to figure out what to do with it. You might give some hints. It takes up so little space and provides quite a lot of entertainment. *Gail Lynch, Washington, D.C.*

Always supervise with younger children.

RELIEVING EAR PRESSURE ✦ My daughter was careful to plan the time of the flight so that her baby would be ready to take a bottle during take off. Since he can't chew gum, this was the way he was relieved of painful ear pressure. *Grannie Bobbie, Newark, California*

This works on landings too.

WET RAG RELIEVES EAR PRESSURE ✦ To help your infant's ears pop during an airplane flight, give him a wet rag to suck on. *D.L. Tarsa, Michigan*

PACK SOME EXTRA FOOD ✦ To relieve ear pressure during takeoff and landing, pack chewing gum or juice boxes. Keep in mind that although there is food on the plane, the flight attendants can't serve before the plane takes off or just before landing, and they may be busy with other passengers, so better to have your own stash. When all else fails, walk the aisles. Unless the carts are in the aisle, or the seat-belt sign is on, it usually isn't a problem. *Patricia Wilson, Dallas, Texas*

Gum is not advised for young children.

COLDS AND DECONGESTANTS ✦ On a recent air flight, I had a cold. When the plane descended, I had excruciating pain that shot from both ears, down both sides of my neck. I looked around the plane, and everyone else looked fine. A few months later, I read a newspaper article in the travel section of my local paper that described exactly what I had felt. It advised taking a decongestant prior to flying when one has a cold. The article attributed the screaming of babies during descent to this problem. Parents might want to pick up a children's decongestant to take with you on the chance one of your kids picks up a cold during your trip. Gum chewing did not relieve my problem. *Gail W. Hinson, Harbor City, California*

Check with child's physician—doses and medication may vary according to the child's age and needs.

AIRPORT CAR RENTALS ✦ Before making a reservation for a car rental, ask the rental company if they are located at the airport, and if not, how far away are they. Sometimes they're as far as two miles away, and you don't need *another* long wait and ride with little ones in tow! *Grannie Bobbie, Newark, California*

VACATIONS

MAILING FOR TRAVEL INFORMATION ✦ Help your child write a note to the chamber of commerce or tourism office of your travel destinations. If you request travel and vacation information, they will send colorful brochures and maps that your child will love to look at and play with. Don't be surprised if he finds some great attractions that you may have missed. Children can also learn about the local geography by looking at the maps they receive in the mail. *Robyn Pappas, Peoria, Arizona*

MEMORABLE-EXPERIENCE BOOK ✦ As a personal memento of a special experience or excursion with the child, keep receipts, tickets, postcards, menus, photos, even your own crude drawings or anything tangible the child will associate with the experience, and make up a special scrapbook with penciled explanations about that experience—if only on stapled sheets of paper—and titled with the child's name on the cover. *Mr. and Mrs. Roland Giduz, Chapel Hill, North Carolina*

$$ MARK THESE ITEMS BEFORE EMBARK-ING ✦ Sew or mark your child's name on jackets, sweatshirts, and shoes. These are the items most likely to be separated from the child on a trip. *P.H., Albany, California*

"JOY BAG" FOR VACATIONS ♦ Before we embark on a vacation, each family member contributes at least one item for our "joy bag." It is a large zipper bag containing items (cards, checkers, books, Legos, etc.) that can provide joy for the whole family and that encourages group participation. A joy bag provides great entertainment at the motel, by the pool, or in the car. *Char Janzen, Hays, Kansas*

LATE-NIGHT READING AT THE MOTEL ♦ I enjoy reading after the children go to bed, but when the whole family is staying in a one room motel, the reading light

keeps the children awake. I retreat to the bathroom, close the door, and sit on the toilet-seat lid while I read. Now, not only do I look for a motel that has a playground or grassy area, but I take a peek in the bathroom to make sure the toilet has a lid on it. *Anonymous, East Greenwich, Rhode Island*

A book light or a small flashlight attached to a headband (available in sporting-goods stores) allows you to read in your motel bed while your children are in the same room.

ERRANDS AND SHOPPING

INVOLVE THE CHILDREN IN ERRANDS ✦ Tell the children before you leave exactly where you're going, what you're going to do there, and about how long it will take at each place. Involve the children as much as possible. For example, let them put the orange juice in the grocery cart, hand them a coupon and ask them to help you find that particular item, etc. Don't try to do too much in one trip. One short errand every day is easier on kids than trying to do all the errands in one "fell swoop." *Elizabeth S. Pagel, Fresno, California*

YOU CAN'T LEAVE WITHOUT THEM ✦ You will *never* leave behind an important baby item when you visit someone's home if you put your car keys in or with that important item (such as a diaper bag, medicine in the refrigerator, etc.). *K.T. Hom, San Jose, California*

TOYS FOR THE CAR ✦ I have toys that can only be played with in the car. They aren't allowed in the house. They include a Magna Doodle, some special "touchy feelie books" and some colored pads of paper. It's always a treat to ride in the car now. *Greg and Cindy Marchant, Indianapolis, Indiana*

HANDY WIPE FOR ON THE GO ✦ Carry a wet, folded washcloth in a sandwich bag in the car or in your purse. It's handy for wiping dirty hands or faces when you're away from a bathroom. *Doris Pansius, Phoenix, Arizona*

COLORED PIPE CLEANERS ✦ One of the things that helps me keep my three children occupied is keeping a package of colored pipe cleaners in my purse. When we are stuck waiting at a doctor's office or in traffic, I pull out a couple of pipe cleaners and the kids are happy for a while. *Christian Benschop, Raleigh, North Carolina*

BALLOONS TO GO ✦ I always kept a few balloons and a few short pieces of string in my purse for use on shopping trips and errands. If my children got fussy in a store, I would take out a balloon, blow it up, attach a string, and hook it on the stroller or shopping cart. It would distract them while I shopped. Always be cautious when a small child has a balloon; it can be swallowed after it pops and cause a choking hazard. *Bonnie Lowe, Fremont, California*

GAME SHOW IN THE CAR ✦ Driving around town doing errands has become more fun for my two young children since we started playing "THE GAME SHOW." The minute my children get in the car they say, "Ask us questions." The game-show host (that's me) alternates asking questions to each of the girls, making sure that the questions are geared to their age level. To liven up the show, I make a buzzer noise if they get the question wrong, and I cheer for a correct answer. I ask our two-year-old questions such as: "What's the color of our house?" or "What are the names of our next-door neighbors?" I quiz my five-year-old on things she is learning at school or home. It makes the driving go by fast and the children learn new things. *Thomas Leslie, San Diego, California*

LEARNING TOWN GEOGRAPHY ✦ When my step-kids and I are in the car, I help them learn their way around the city. I have them tell me what direction we're going and how to get someplace and how to get home— *specifically*. It makes driving more enjoyable, the time passes fast, and the children learn geography to boot. *Deb Skillstad-Rost, Omaha, Nebraska*

JUNIOR NAVIGATORS ✦ As the children get older, take a map along in the car. Have them find their location and track their route through town. Before you know it, they will be mapping out your route for your next vacation. *Anonymous, California*

SHOPPING WITH A TODDLER ✦ Since boredom and hunger can cause cranky behavior, I now take along a toy and a snack for my toddler when I go shopping. He doesn't jump around as much while he's in the shopping cart and his attention span is much longer. *Debra Randall, East Haven, Connecticut*

KIDS SAY THE FUNNIEST THINGS

When my son was around four or five, I invited him to go run some errands with me. With a big "Whoopee," he jumped in the car. He began chattering away, "Is it far away? Will there be toys? When will we get there?" "Where?" I asked him. "At Erin's! Who is Erin anyway, Mom?" *Janet Francom, Napa, California*

"HOLD ME UP TO THE DRINKING FOUNTAIN" ✦ Children love drinking fountains, but they usually get wet in the process of drinking and the parent strains muscles to hold them up to the fountain. Here's a solution: bend your leg so your thigh is horizontal to the ground and let them stand on your knee so they can reach the fountain and turn on the faucet themselves. *Anonymous, Milwaukee, Wisconsin*

MEASURE THAT TABLE ✦ I carry a small tape measure in my pocket in case my children get bored when we go out. I tell them to measure things, which keeps them occupied. *Beth Weis, Buffalo Grove, Illinois*

A SHOPPING PUZZLE KEEPS TODDLERS BUSY ✦ Here's a grocery-store survival tip for ages one or two. I would poke a hole in the plastic wrapping around paper towels or toilet paper, and my son would amuse himself in the cart by putting a penny through the hole. The penny would drop through the cardboard roll and he'd shake it around and then try to remove it. It kept him busy while I shopped. *Carolyn Mosser, York, Pennsylvania*

Be careful he doesn't put the penny in his mouth. Better yet, use a safe-sized object.

SAFETY "BELT" FOR THE SHOPPING CART ✦ Use a belt to secure a child into a shopping cart so she won't climb out and hurt herself. *Debra Kassarjian, Fremont, California*

LOOK DAY, BUY DAY ✦ Our child used to beg for a toy, book, or candy every time we went shopping, so my husband and I decided that before we left the house to go shopping we would decide whether this was a buying day or a looking day. When we make that decision at home, my son knows that he need not beg for something. If it is a buying day, he takes his money that he has to spend and he spends that. Now we have less fussing and tantrums on our shopping trips, especially as we cruise through the toy section. *Sue Hamilton, Grand Island, Nebraska*

"DON'T TOUCH THAT, HOLD YOUR THUMB" ✦ If you don't want your children to touch delicate things in a store, ask them to hold their thumbs while you're shopping. It avoids those "accidental" purchases. *Too Ying Joe, San Jose, California*

NO HANDS FREE FOR SHOPPING SPREE ✦ When you are going shopping and don't want your child touching anything in the store, make sure he takes his stuffed animal or favorite toy along. If he has something in both hands, he can't pick up anything in the store. *Linda Williams, Highland Heights, Kentucky*

FOOD-SHOPPING GAME ✦ The children and I would clip magazine or newspaper coupons and/or pictures of items needed from the grocery store. The pictures would be pasted to index cards, with the word for that item printed next to it. Then, I'd give each child a card or coupon for them to match at the store. I'd make sure that the item was on the aisle we were on, so they wouldn't be too disruptive. When they returned with the items, I'd trade them another coupon or card. This game is geared for a child two to three years and up. Each child received a small prize at the end. As the children became older (usually school-aged), I adapted the game into a scavenger hunt. Each child was given a list of items to find. The first child back received a prize and the privilege of sitting up front on the way home. The other children also received a prize. *Elaine Strickland, Brandon, Mississippi*

HELPING MOM SHOP ✦ Children love to help you shop for groceries. I allow my children to cross off items as we find each one. If your children can read, it helps them learn letter sounds and correct pronunciations. *Rita Wilson, Fremont, California*

CONSUMERISM BEGINS EARLY ✦ Every now and then I've taken the kids to the grocery store and had them buy groceries, including writing and recording the check (I sign though). All I do is walk alongside and help decide how many or what size. I don't help them find anything. They think it's fun and grocery prices are a real eye-opener for them. *Deb Skillstad-Rost, Omaha, Nebraska*

"LET'S MAKE A DEAL" SHOPPING TRIP ✦ I make a deal with my children before going shopping. I tell them if they're good on my shopping errands, they can go to their favorite store or arcade (for older children) after I finish my shopping. I'm usually able to finish my shopping faster without listening to them complain about having to shop. The kids know they have something fun for them at the end. *Lorrie Rubio, Fremont, California*

MATH AT THE GROCERY STORE ✦ To keep my children occupied at the grocery store, we make shopping a game requiring a pad and pencil or calculator. We use weights and measures to determine which item is the best buy. One child determines the best buy, one child keeps a total of the items to be purchased, and the third child makes sure we buy all the items on the list. Sometimes we use exact amounts, other times rounded-off amounts. At the end, we calculate the tax and check to see if our totals correspond with the checkout amount. *Elaine Strickland, Brandon, Mississippi*

This is a great tip for older kids, too—right before they go to college.

II

NIGHTY NIGHT

◆

There never was a child so lovely, but his mother was glad to get him asleep.

— EMERSON, *Journals*, 1836

The Nightly Mission: Get the children to bed on time, keep them in bed through the night, and hope they awake refreshed and in good humor the next morning. Bedtime can be a challenge to parents because most children at least occasionally experience problems with bedtime or sleeping. This is often the case because different developmental stages in a child's growth require different amounts and patterns of sleep.

Child-care experts strongly recommend that parents create a "bedtime ritual," a predictable sequence of events each evening that help a child calm down and prepare for bedtime. Such a ritual might include putting on pj's, brushing teeth, reading stories, singing soothing songs, or getting comforting words and hugs from Mom or Dad (or both).

Such rituals can really help children relax and ease into sleep, but there can also be an occasional snag. For instance, my wife established such a set regimen for our daughters every night that it was difficult for anyone—including me—to take her place. I vividly remember one dreadful evening when my older daughter was a toddler. My wife was away, and at bedtime my daughter demanded I sing a song called "Hush Little Rooster." When she discovered I didn't know the words, she broke into tears, wailed for over an hour, and finally cried herself to sleep.

Some friends of ours had a similar experience. Returning one evening, they were met by their frazzled baby-sitter. "What," she asked, "*is* 'dum-de-dum'? The kids asked for it over and over and went bananas when I couldn't find it."

"Oh," said the wife sheepishly, "I should have told you. Every night, just before bed, my husband waltzes the girls around their bedroom—singing 'dum-de-dum' to the tune of 'Tea for Two.' "

The tips that follow in this chapter are an arsenal of ideas for coping with bedtime. Find out how your clothes dryer, fish aquarium, and even "Jell-O" can help your child go to sleep; how "noise" calms babies; and how crib climbers can be stopped with some alterations to their pj's. Also, a special section titled "Things that Go Bump in the Night" offers many creative solutions for shooing monsters out of bed-rooms.

Pleasant dreams!

◆

NAP TIME

"IT'S HAPPY NAPPY TIME" ◆ My adult children have told me that they liked nap time when they were little because I called it, "Happy Nappy Time." I did not say that they *had* to take a nap. I simply said, "It's Happy Nappy Time." It was a positive approach that worked well. *Joy Merkley, Siren, Wisconsin*

"WHATEVER YOU DO, DON'T FALL ASLEEP!" ◆ When our sons were toddlers in need of a nap, their opposition to naps often overpowered my ability to implement this needed time to recharge. When this stage in their lives passed, and I was often called on to watch my little nieces, I learned something new. Leading these little girls to bed for naps, I would say something like, "Now, I *do not* want you to fall asleep. Just rest for only seven (or nine or thirteen . . .) minutes. I'll get you after seven minutes. But *no* sleeping. If you want to shut your eyes, okay, but *don't* sleep." If they called out, "Is it time yet?" I would answer with, "Four and a half more minutes left." Almost always, they fell asleep. (Now they are in high school and college and they still remember nap time at Aunt Louise's.) *Louise Murray, Fairport, New York*

NAP AFTER LUNCH ✦ I found that a child will be ready to nap *immediately* after lunch. People get sleepy after eating a meal, so take advantage and put him to bed right away. *Florence Moorman, Buffalo, New York*

"ALL YOU HAVE TO DO IS FALL ASLEEP" ✦ It needs to be a rule that they take a nap. Discuss this with them when it is not nap time. Then keep the nap time as constant as possible. If they still object, talk to them and remind them of the rule. Next, tell them that if they are good it can be a real short nap. All they need to do is fall asleep, and as soon as they wake up they can get up. The key words are that they need to "fall asleep." Then it is up to them how long they stay asleep. Keep telling them that all they need to do is to wake up and they can get up. *Vikki Hill, Newark, California*

NO LATE NAPS ✦ When babies get to be about four months old, try to keep them up until they're good and worn out. They will sleep better—and so will you! *D. Martinez, Fremont, California*

CHOICES AT NAP TIME DEFLECT ARGU-MENTS ✦ To get the children to take naps I would ask them "Do you want the door open or closed to take your nap?" This gave them the ability to make a decision but not the decision of whether or not to take their naps. *Roberta Dunaief, Coconut Creek, Florida*

QUIET TIME ✦ I missed the naps my daughter used to take; she didn't. I really missed that one and a half to two hours of quiet time that I had while she was napping. I decided to require "Quiet Time" every day, a time when she had to do a quiet activity in her room. It worked great; I got my work done and she enjoyed the activities in her room. I also credit this time to contributing to her interest in books, since this was usually the activity she chose to do. *Anonymous, San Diego, California*

✕✕✕

BABY'S BEDTIME

✕✕✕

NIGHT-LIGHT FOR THE NEWBORN (AND PARENTS) ✦ Newborn babies are used to lights being on twenty-four hours a day in the hospital nursery, so leave a small light on in their room for the first week or so. Most babies also love soft music. *Patti Potts Johnson, Omaha, Nebraska*

TWENTY-FIVE-WATT BULB FOR BABY'S ROOM ✦ Bright lights are annoying to children and parents alike during the middle of the night when you're changing diapers or calming fears from nightmares. A good night-light or the lowest setting on a three-way bulb twenty-five watt is perfect) gives you enough light to see and makes it easier for your child to resume sleeping. *Jep Prince, Fremont, California*

DIMMER SWITCH ✦ A dimmer switch allows you to control the amount of light you need. It's perfect for the nursery. *Susan Bony, Reno, Nevada*

It also helps keep anxious new parents from running into the furniture.

IS THE BABY MONITOR ON? ✦ I put a ticking clock next to the infant monitor in my baby's room. Hearing the ticking through the intercom tells me the monitor is working and also when I've moved out of range. *Jill Nelson-Johnson, Urbandale, Iowa*

$$ A "BABY TUB" BASSINET ✦ I didn't have a portable bassinet for my newborn, so I used a "baby tub" as an alternative. I lined it with receiving blankets and she fit perfectly. It was easy to carry it from room to room so I could keep an eye on her. A tub might not work for bigger babies, but it worked great for my five-pound, eight-ounce, eighteen-inch daughter. *Naomi Mulligan, Livermore, California*

A WOMBLIKE FEELING MAKES BETTER SLEEP-ING ◆ Newborns are used to having their heads against the walls of the mother's womb. After they are born, even a bassinet is overwhelming in size. When I put my baby down to sleep, I put his head near the bumper cushions of the crib. He sleeps better that way. *Debbie Janulis, Chicago, Illinois*

A PROVEN TRADITION ◆ New parents never get enough sleep at night because the new arrival wakes up crying. Wrapping the little one snugly in a blanket or sheet so it can't move its arms and legs seems to give it a feeling of security. We found it worked wonderfully with our five kids. For centuries newborns were wrapped tightly in "swaddling clothes." The tight wrap may make the newborn feel secure by simulating the confining womb. *Ron Burda, San Jose, California*

NURSING A BABY TO SLEEP ◆ I have nursed all three of my children to sleep. It is the best tried-and-true way to get a baby to go to sleep that I have found. *Judith Nicholson, Westborough, Massachusetts*

This works great for infants, but eventually they will need to learn to go to sleep on their own.

A TWIN BACK RUB ◆ When I got up during the night to feed my twins boys, it was difficult to get the first one fed back to sleep so that I could feed the other. I would pat the back of the first fed to reassure him and get him to fall asleep. However, neither boy wanted me to stop patting his back. I developed a technique of patting a child's back for a bit, then just resting my hand gently on his back, and finally putting a stuffed animal on his back. It wasn't too big a stuffed animal, just big enough to leave pressure on their backs to let them feel that someone was still there. Then I could feed the other twin and get some sleep for an hour before it was time to start all over again. *Sally Fennell, Loveland, Ohio*

"ROCK-A-BYE BABY" WITH A HAPPY END-ING ✦ I never liked the ending to "Rock-A-Bye Baby" ("And down will come baby, cradle and all"), so I changed the words: "Rock-a-bye-baby in the treetop, when the wind blows the cradle will rock, when the bough breaks the cradle will fall, AND MOMMY (DADDY) WILL CATCH YOU, CRADLE AND ALL." *Lorraine Kosarchuk, Fremont, California*

LINE UP THOSE PACIFIERS ✦ My child takes a pacifier to bed. During the night, he loses it and, when he realizes he can't find it, he crys and then is up for a while. Now, I take two or three pacifiers and line them up by the headboard. If he loses one, he now knows to reach over his head and there is another for him. *Debbie Janulis, Chicago, Illinois*

PACIFIER PJ'S ✦ I use a pacifier hook to attach my son's pacifier to his pj's at bedtime. It attaches easily to the flap that snaps at the top of the zipper on his "sleeper" pj's. *Annette Reynolds, Lansing, Michigan*

LEARNING TO SLEEP ✦ My best friend told me to occasionally put my newborn son down for a nap or bedtime while he was still awake, so he could learn to comfort himself to sleep. If you always hold him until he falls asleep, you may end up with a three-year-old who refuses to go to bed because he never learned to go to sleep by himself. I tried this and my children have no problem at nap time or bedtime. *Alana D. Emmet, Yonkers, New York*

✦✦

CRIBS

✦✦

CUSHIONING THE CRIB ✦ My son had problems at night sleeping because he would wake up at night, stand in the crib, and bang himself on the side of the crib when he fell back down. So we put about two inches of foam all the way around the inside of the crib with sheets around the foam held together by safety pins. Now when he falls he doesn't get hurt and is able to go back to sleep. *Richard Guziec, Omaha, Nebraska*

CRIB CLIMBER ✦ Our not-yet one-year-old decided he could climb out of his crib, which he did at 2 A.M. He threw trash all over the house, emptied drawers, etc. Our pediatrician advised us to cover the crib to prevent injury, but none of the covers we devised were safe enough. Finally, we sewed a triangular piece of knit fabric between the top of the legs of his sleepers, and that has cured the "climbing" problem. The child can walk and crawl, but he cannot spread his legs to get out of the crib. It also works in regular pants for naps. If the child figures out how to unzip and take off the sleeper, put the sleeper on backwards, so the zipper is in the back. *Michele Lastovica, Omaha, Nebraska*

FROM THE CRIB TO A BIG BED ✦ When my daughter was ready for the big change, I first removed the crib from her room and allowed her to sleep on the crib mattress on the floor (just to maintain familiarity at a time of change). Then we removed the crib mattress and placed her new twin bed mattress on the floor. She had the opportunity to adjust and there was no danger as the floor was only inches away. Then we put in the big bed, and she hasn't had any problems. *Stacey Ann Morgan, Oakland, California*

"TIME TO GO TO BED"

EGG TIMER CONTROLS BEDTIME ✦ We had a difficult time getting our toddler to bed at night so we used an egg timer. When the timer alarm went off, it was time for him to go to bed. There was no arguing as to who made the decision—he couldn't argue with the bell! *Donna Porzuc, Berlin, Massachusetts*

PREPARED IN ADVANCE FOR BEDTIME ✦ When our child is going to be out with us for the evening, we take his pajamas, toothbrush, and whatever else is needed to get him ready for bed before we leave for home. That way we won't have to wake him to undress and brush his teeth when we get home. *Maryann Landreth, Edwardsville, Illinois*

DON'T USE "BED" AS PUNISHMENT ✦ Bedtime should be a pleasant time—stories, songs, quiet conversation, etc. If the bed is seen as a place of punishment, bedtime may be a struggle. *Florence Grace, Fremont, California*

CAPTURING BEDTIME ✦ I am a single parent with two daughters, ages eleven and thirteen. Bedtime has always been a problem with us. I've always told the girls that on school nights they are to be in the house at 8 P.M. to bathe, brush teeth, get clothes ready for school the next day, etc. Bedtime was exactly at 9 P.M. It never failed—no one started their nightly ritual until around 8:50 P.M. no matter what. Then I began to "recapture" the minutes they were up past their bedtime. For every minute after 9 they were still up, that many minutes earlier they went to bed the following night. If they didn't make it to bed until 9:15, the following night they had to go to bed at 8:45. It worked! *Terri L. Pender, Duluth, Minnesota*

BEAT THE CLOCK ✦ To get our children to bed on time we played "beat the clock." We would set the timer for a certain amount of minutes (enough to change into pj's, brush their teeth, etc.) and the children would try to get in bed before the time went off. Before we instituted this "game," our children would prolong the evening bedtime ritual for as long as they could get away with. *Dick Perry, Worcester, Massachusetts*

"TIME TO GET IN YOUR TENT" ✦ Bedtime was a battle every night with my six-year-old son until I bought a "slumber tent" that sits on top of his bed. They come in a variety of styles with imprints of children's favorite characters. Bedtime is more fun now. Climbing into a "tent" is much more fun than going to bed. *Jeanne Gopez, Fremont, California*

$$ MAKE YOUR OWN SLUMBER TENT ✦ A homemade slumber tent (a tent that sits on the bed mattress) can be constructed quickly and inexpensively by using PVC pipe. Construct a frame using the pipes and connectors so that a sheet or blanket can lie over the frame as it rests on the mattress—creating a tent. This lightweight frame can be easily moved anywhere to create a simple, but fun, child's tent. *Jim Stuka, Escondido, California*

"I'M TOO TIRED TO GET OUT OF BED" ✦ If any of my three children balked at getting up in the morning, I would say, "Oh, oh, that means you didn't get enough sleep. Guess you'll have to go to bed a half hour earlier tonight." They jump right out of bed! *Carolyn Catell Mongillo, North Haven, Connecticut*

✖✦✦✦✦✦✦✦✦✦✦✦✦✦✦✦✦✦✦✦✦✦✦✦✦✦✦✦✦✦✦✦✦✦✦✦✦✦✖

BEDTIME RITUALS

✖✦✦✦✦✦✦✦✦✦✦✦✦✦✦✦✦✦✦✦✦✦✦✦✦✦✦✦✦✦✦✦✦✦✦✦✦✦✦✖

ROUTINES ARE IMPORTANT ✦ I find that having a bedtime ritual (bath, story time, etc.) every night really helps my children calm down for bedtime. We follow this routine and they go to bed happily and sleep through the night. *J.S., Richmond Hill, New York*

TALK TIME/STORY TIME BEDTIME ROU-TINE ◆ Once the kids are in their pj's and have brushed and flossed their teeth, one child goes with Mom for talk time and one child goes with Dad for story time. After fifteen minutes, we switch. During talk time, we play games, talk about what happened during the day and what will happen tomorrow. The child can pick what he wants to do with Mom. During story time Dad reads to them or they read to Dad. This is one-on-one time with each parent every night and has become a very special time for both parents and children. Children truly value this undivided attention and time with their parents. This routine can be modified to ten-minute intervals if you have more than two children. *K.T. Hom, San Jose, California*

A STORY OF FAMILY VALUES ◆ We have used our young children's love of bedtime stories to teach our family values, ethics, relationship lessons, etc. to our children by making up our own short stories. We insure that part of the story always is the same, such as the main character (Tiny Bug) and where he or she lives (in an old oak tree) and that the child is included in the story. Parents' sound effects and large gestures make the story more interesting. Stories are kept short, about five minutes, because children's attention spans are short. Favorite plot lines or more important lessons are repeated. *Ron Burda, San Jose, California*

BEDTIME ROUTINE—THE SHORTENED VER-SION ◆ Our bedtime routine consists of one or two stories and a song—about fifteen minutes. On nights when we are running late, I cut the routine short by replacing books with "baby stories." I share a quick story about things that happened when our son was a baby—like how he chewed on his toes, or when he first sat up, nicknames we called him, etc. This always causes giggles and hugs and we follow this with our good-night song. The whole routine is only five minutes and he doesn't feel deprived of the bedtime routine. *Sue Sponsel, Fremont, California*

ROOM TIME ◆ Our two-and-half-year-old son NEVER wanted to go to bed. He'd be up until 2 A.M. every night if we allowed it. As a result, my husband and I never had any time alone together. Our pediatrician suggested "Room Time." At a time we designated, our son had to go to his room. He could do whatever he wanted to do, but he had to stay in his room. After six months of doing this we modified room time to be a time when he had to go to his room and quietly read books. It surely made the transition to bedtime a lot easier. *Donna Ireland, Fremont, California*

BEDTIME STORIES WITH A FAMILIAR VOICE ✦ Buying cassette tapes for my boys to listen to at bedtime was becoming very costly until I discovered a wonderful source of outstanding and inexpensive cassettes: Try giving Grandma and Grandpa several of your kids' favorite books to read and record on a cassette player. They can also include their own original stories about the good ol' days when they were growing up. *K.T. Hom, San Jose, California*

SOOTHING A CHILD TO SLEEP

A CLOCK IS MESMERIZING ✦ Buy a lighted alarm clock with a large face for your child's bedroom. If the child has a difficult time going to sleep, ask him to watch the hands of the clock. Tell him that you will come back to check on him when the hands on the clock are in a certain position. Staring at the hands of the clock helps children to drift off to sleep. *Doris Pansius, Phoenix, Arizona*

WARM PJ'S ✦ To get a reluctant child changed for bed on a chilly night—warm pajamas a few minutes in the dryer before putting them on the child. *Anonymous*

WARM BLANKET FROM THE DRYER ✦ When your infant is fussy, take a receiving blanket and warm it in the dryer. Then wrap the baby up nice and tight in the warm blanket. Generally, that will calm him down. *Karen Wilmes, Omaha, Nebraska*

HEATING PAD WARMS SHEETS ✦ As the mother of two small children ages two and three and a half months,

I found the following tip to be very useful, especially with a winter baby. Take a regular-size heating pad, turn it on low or medium heat, and place it on the crib sheet. When the baby is ready for bed, remove the pad—*please remember to turn it off and take it out of the crib*—and put the baby on the warm sheet. This keeps the baby from being startled by the cold sheet. *Melanie Jones, Brewton, Alabama*

HOT-WATER BOTTLE MAKES COZY SHEETS ✦ Use a hot-water bottle wrapped in a towel to warm up those cold sheets before placing your baby in her crib. *Carmen Shier, Edmonton, Alberta*

Be sure to remove the hot water bottle from the crib before placing baby in.

IMAGINE BEING AS LOOSE AS JELL-O ✦ To help my children relax at bedtime, I asked them to try to relax so their bodies felt like Jell-O (spineless, boneless, etc.). They could relate to this analogy, and they were able to transform themselves into Jell-O—which was really "relaxation" in disguise. *Cindy Barwacz, Fremont, California*

LOVE DUST AT BEDTIME ✦ I am a single mother who usually works night shifts. When my daughter was small and I had to leave her with a sitter, she would have trouble falling asleep. So I would give her "Love Dust." I would twinkle my fingers over her body and give her an extra kiss and she always said that it helped her sleep better and have good dreams. She is nine years old now and still wants Love Dust when she goes to bed. *Cheryl Grabowski, North Lauderdale, Florida*

SIMON SAYS "GO TO SLEEP" ✦ Often my two-and-a-half-year-old son is not ready to go to sleep at bedtime, so my husband decided to play the Simon Says game. "Simon says touch your eyes. Simon says touch your nose. Simon says touch your feet." In the end, he would say, "Simon says use the bathroom and Simon says go to sleep in your bed." We got him to go to sleep and he also learned his body parts. If the child is old enough, try to trick him by asking him to do something without saying "Simon says." This also helps keep his attention. *Neeta Sanghvi, Fremont, California*

"TELL ME ABOUT THE BEST PART OF YOUR DAY" ✦ I am the mother of four children, three school age. At night, as part of their bedtime routine after they have said their prayers and are back in bed, I say to each one individually, "Tell me the best part of your day." They have to repeat back to me something positive about their day and then I repeat back to them something positive that I have observed about their behavior that day. The last thing on their mind before going to sleep is reviewing their day and the positive things that happened during it. We call it the "best part of the day." *Nancy Dalton, Fullerton, California*

"SPEEDY SLEEPER" COUPON ✦ Bedtime at our house was turning into bedlam every night after my children were in their beds and all tucked in for the night. Two of them were in the same room and as soon as my husband and I left the room they would start to talk, giggle, get toys, pillow-fight, etc. It seemed we were putting them to bed ten or fifteen times a night. In order to solve this dilemma, we began to issue a "Speedy Sleeper" coupon to the first child asleep. We would place it under the pillow of the first child asleep or under both pillows if they were both asleep when we checked on them. They redeemed their coupons at the end of the week for a specified amount of money or a special treat. This has worked wonders and has turned bedlam into bliss. *Jodi V. Wilding, Centerville, Utah*

PILLOW TALK ✦ My child had a difficult time going to bed at night until I recorded my voice on a cassette tape singing a favorite lullaby or telling a favorite story. My child loves to listen to the tape at bedtime. *Diane T. Johnson, Morgan Hill, California*

RELAXATION TAPES ✦ My brother-in-law sent my husband some relaxation tapes. My daughter wanted to hear the tapes and put them on when she went to bed. "How were the tapes?" I asked the next morning. "Lousy," she said, "I fell right asleep." My theory is that she learned to drift off peacefully rather than fighting sleep. *Anonymous, Pennsylvania*

SOOTHING BACK RUBS ✦ Everyone loves a back rub, especially children. I used to rub my sons' backs at bedtime to help them relax and get sleepy. *Evelyn LaTorre, Fremont, California*

KEEP THE ROOM DARK DURING DAYLIGHT SAVING TIME ✦ During daylight saving time, the children would wake up very early in the morning because of the sunlight coming through the miniblinds. Instead of installing permanent dark curtains, we took large sheets and sewed Velcro to one end and put the opposite part of the Velcro above the windowsill. We put the sheets up over and covering the miniblinds, and the room stayed nice and dark in the morning. When the children did wake up, we took down the sheets and folded them up until we were ready to put them up the next night. *Karen Platt-Clark, Rochester, New York*

SWEET-DREAMS PILL ✦ I have two small boys, ages five and three. After many nights of having them crawl out of bed and telling me that they were afraid to sleep because they would have bad dreams, I decided to devise a way to ease their fears. I took a large old prescription bottle (washed out carefully), made a label that says "Sweet Dreams," and applied it to the outside of the bottle. I emptied "Smarties" candies into the bottle. Now every night before they brush their teeth, they take their vitamin and a "sweet dreams" pill. It works like a charm—neither has complained about bad dreams since! *Roxanne McCurdy, Bellevue, Nebraska*

Make sure that as parents we don't fall into a generally accepted practice of using a "pill" or "substance" that reinforces the idea that we need to "take something" to feel good or safe.

FOOD-AND-WATER SEDATIVES ✦ Water is a great sedative! Try a quick, warm shower or bath right before bedtime. Make sure he's got his favorite pillow, blanket, etc., and sing his favorite lullaby or say his favorite prayer. Consistency is the key, and remember always lots of affection! *Jennifer Orozco, Sunnyvale, California*

"HERE'S SOMETHING FOR YOU TO DREAM ABOUT" ✦ One trick I used when I put my children to bed at night (especially if they were upset or afraid about something) was to tell them, "Here's something for you to dream about." Then I would start a story about something I knew they liked. I would go far enough into the story to involve them, and then tell them to dream the ending. Sometimes this actually did give them a real dream, but other times it just gave them something pleasant to think about long enough to drop off to sleep. Not long ago, my twenty-five-year-old asked me what she should dream about. (I think it was a time when she was worried about something.) I know it works, because I can remember my mother doing the same for me. *Carol Case, Lafayette, Colorado*

THE ANGELS WILL HELP YOU SLEEP ✦ I used to tell my three little pumpkins, "You don't need to sleep, but just keep your eyes closed, and the angels will watch over you." By the time I finished a long prayer of asking God to bless everyone and everything they would be drifting toward sleep. *Ms. Jean Nielsen, Cut Bank, Montana*

This idea or a similar one can work wonders for the child who "tries too hard" to fall asleep.

KIDS SAY THE FUNNIEST THINGS

Last night my four-year-old daughter was looking very pensive. She turned to me thoughtfully and said, "Mom, when Scooter (our cat) goes to heaven, will he break our ceiling?" *Wendy Mueller, Fullerton, California*

WHEN INSOMNIA STRIKES A CHILD ◆ My nine-year-old granddaughter has a father who is seriously ill with a life-threatening disease and has been in and out of the hospital for many months. It is sometimes difficult for her to fall asleep due to separation anxiety as well as fear. It is also difficult for her to fall asleep at night if there has been a problem at school or some other emotional or psychological reason. We have worked out a system that works out well for me as an adult and works very well for her. When she goes to bed at night after she has said her prayers, she takes the alphabet and chooses a category such as girl's names and works her way through the alphabet. For example, A is for Ann, B is for Betty, C is for Carol, etc. Sometimes the topic is boy's names or fruits or vegetables. Usually she is asleep before she gets to the middle of the alphabet. Incidentally, this works very well for me and I have used tropical fish, song titles, etc. It is amazing! It focuses on something other than your problems and causes you to go to sleep in a relaxed manner. This should work for children from the age of seven. *Mary Carol Burdett, Los Altos, California*

"I CAN'T SLEEP" ◆ If my seven-year-old has gone to bed, then comes out to tell me, "I can't sleep," I let him have fifteen to twenty minutes of Reading-to-Himself-Time. This solution has worked better than anything I've tried (and I've tried numerous ideas). It does help to set a timer and be firm about the time limit set. *Kathy Tubbs, San Jose, California*

A CAR RIDE LULLS A BABY TO SLEEP ◆ This tip is used by many people. If your child won't go to sleep, put him in the car seat and drive around the block a few times. If he is tired, he will fall right asleep. *Denise Fulford, Southlake, Texas*

PUT THE CAR SEAT ON TOP OF THE DRYER ✦ A friend of mine had a child who couldn't go to sleep—unless he was in his car seat. Since we were living in northern Canada at the time, it wasn't practical to bundle up the baby and go driving. Instead, this couple bought an extra car seat and bolted it onto the top of the dryer, which simulated the movement of the car. The baby fell asleep quite nicely on top of the dryer each night and was then placed back in his crib. *Mary Lea McAnally, Stanford, California*

Don't leave the baby on the dryer too long or the buzzer will wake him up. *Phil Stenstrum, Suffolk, Virginia*

 Please keep safety in mind at all times. Make sure babies are secure and will not fall off. Never leave baby alone.

There is also a commercial product (available in many baby stores) that attaches to a baby's crib and is claimed to simulate the motion and sound of a car. Another product emits audio "womb" sounds.

MUSIC TO SLEEP BY ✦ My little girl is now three months old. When we first brought her home, she refused to sleep in her own crib. After a week of my sleeping either on the couch or with a baby in the bed, I put a radio under her bassinet, tuned it to a local soft-rock station, and turned it down so only she could hear it. She slept peacefully and alone. Now she sleeps in a crib and we have miniature speakers hooked to one end (by her feet), and she sleeps through the night. *Kris McGlothlin, Verdi, Nevada*

MUSIC BOX ◆ I tied a music box on the side of my daughter's crib and turned it on every night. It was very relaxing and helped her to go to sleep each night. *Ronda Bachtell, Sparks, Nevada*

Be careful with anything tied to cribs, especially with string. A child could get caught in or strangled with string.

MUSIC CASSETTES ◆ After reading to my two little girls at bedtime, I put on one of their favorite music cassettes. Before one side has played through, they are usually fast asleep. Music can soothe the savage beast and little kids too. *A.C., Flushing, New York*

LULLABIES ◆ Singing the same soothing lullaby to infants every night will eventually help them to feel sleepy when they hear the song. My preschooler still gets sleepy the instant she hears my lullaby. Tape recordings of lullabies also work well. *Marie Levie, St. Paul, Minnesota*

NOISE CAN BE SOOTHING—REALLY!

VACUUM DOES MORE THAN CLEAN ◆ My youngest of five children was born with an allergy and she cried all the time. We finally discovered that when I was running the vacuum, she would stop crying and fall asleep. I wore out an old canister vacuum by putting it under her bed and turning it on when it was time for her to go to sleep. It worked every time. *Helen Quinn, Omaha, Nebraska*

To save wear and tear on your vacuum cleaner, tape the noise onto a cassette tape. *Lori Albertson, Benicia, California*

CLOCK TICKING IS SOOTHING ✦ To make bedtime easier, I use a windup alarm clock that ticks loudly. For some reason, the sound of that ticking, maybe because it reminds the baby of the mother's heartbeat while still in the womb, seems to comfort my children when it is time for bed. *Maureen Reilly, Holland, Massachusetts*

SOOTHING SOUNDS FROM THE DISH-WASHER ✦ Many years agao, a good friend of mine discovered that her youngest child could go to sleep easier if he could hear the electric dishwasher running. It really worked. *N.J., Warwick, Rhode Island*

BUZZING SOUNDS WORKS LIKE A CHARM ✦ At nap and bedtime, I use a Norelco air freshener in the baby's room. We call it the noise maker because it muffles out background noises while the little one is sleeping. You could also use an electric fan. *Kathy Howland, Springfield, Missouri*

BLOW-DRYER TAPE CALMS BABIES ✦ When our infant gets upset and can't settle down, we get out the vacuum or the blow dryer. The noise really soothes him. We taped a forty-five-minute segment of these sounds and play it when he is upset. It calms him right down. *Julie Swanson, Omaha, Nebraska*

RANGE FAN HUMS A CHILD TO SLEEP ✦ The humming sound of our hood range fan in the kitchen has a calming effect on our baby. It actually lulls our baby to sleep. *H.P., San Jose, California*

SOOTHING SHOWER SOUNDS ✦ My husband had our baby in an infant seat one morning in the bathroom as he took his shower. When he got out, he noticed she was asleep. It didn't take us too long to realize that if we taped a few showers, we'd have sixty minutes of soothing shower sounds. That's what we did, and every time it played, she slept. *Greg and Cindy Marchant, Indianapolis, Indiana*

FISH AQUARIUM ✦ The soothing bubbling noise from a fish-aquarium pump is calming to children and the light provides a perfect night-light. *Anonymous, California*

THE 3 A.M. BLUES

SOOTHING A CRANKY CHILD ✦ If the child awakens from a night's sleep or a nap and is ornery and out of sorts, pick him up and hold him firmly, close to your chest, all the while telling him a favorite story in a low, steady voice. The child feels secure because you are holding him and quiets down because he wants to hear the story. It helps to keep his cheek next to yours as you speak quietly into (or near) his ear. *Dorine Braun, Teaneck, New Jersey*

DON'T REINFORCE BAD SLEEPING HABITS ✦ Trying to get children to sleep through the night has always made parents pull their hair out. Try to put the child down at the same time every night. If the child wakes up during the middle of the night, keep the lights off. Move over to the child and touch him softly as you assure him that everything is okay. Let the child know that you are there. Do not take the child out of the crib. Do not turn on the lights. If you do either of these, you will contribute to waking the child even further. If the child does not settle down, tell the child again that everything is okay and move to your bedroom. Wait there at first for about two minutes; if the child still does not settle down, go back and repeat. Do this every night that the child wakes. Within a week, the child will be sleeping on his own. It sure worked for us. *Scott Hill, Newark, California*

A SLEEPING BAG IN THE PARENTS' ROOM ◆ When our kids were younger, they would go through stages of waking in the middle of the night from fears or nightmares. I did not want them to start sleeping in our bed or to expect us to frequently comfort them in their rooms. So we placed a sleeping bag next to our bed. They knew they could come and crawl into it whenever they felt the need, and we encouraged them to do it quietly so as not to wake us. This seemed to comfort them and our sleep was minimally disrupted, if at all. The sleeping bag was also handy to use when they were ill. *Karen Cutter and Stephen Robison, Belmont, California*

MOM'S KIND OF BORING LATE AT NIGHT ◆ After getting up in the middle of the night with my first child for the first seven months of his life, I decided there had to be a better way. When we brought our second child home from the hospital, I let him know from the very beginning that "nighttime" was not "playtime." From the start, I let my actions show that we were not having fun. I would first change him and then feed and burp him. I would not talk to him, smile at him, or play with him. I did not turn on a bright light; in fact everything was done in the dark. By the time my son was two weeks old, he was sleeping through the night. I was never mean to him; he just found out at an early age that Mom was kind of boring at nighttime. *LeAnn Melloway, Sparks, Nevada*

A HAPPY ENDING FOR NIGHTMARES ◆ Whenever my son wakes up with a nightmare, I ask him to tell me the nightmare, then I finish it with a happy ending. Now, he is able to think of a happy ending for his own nightmares, then fall right back to sleep. *Ann Kremer, East Lansing, Michigan*

A "STAR" FOR STAYING IN BED ◆ We had problems with our children getting into bed with us in the middle of the night and disrupting everyone's sleep. With time and patience, we solved the problem in a positive way. First we bought our son a special sleeping tent of his choice, then we made up a chart. For each night that he did not enter our bedroom, he received a star. When he had accumulated thirty stars, he was allowed to pick out a special toy. If he came into the room, he was not scolded, simply reminded that he needed to stay in his own bed.

Within a month, he was remaining in his own room. *Audrey Swanton, Brewer, Maine*

PARENTS LOCKED THEIR BEDROOM DOOR ✦ When our youngest was four years old, she began waking during the night. The more I comforted her, the more she woke up, until the problem had escalated into five or six nightly battles with me screaming and her crying and both of us miserable. The books suggested locking her in her room, but I couldn't do that. Finally, a psychologist suggested that my husband and I lock *our* door. So I explained to her that all this fighting was not good, that I had to sleep, and that our bedroom door would be locked. For the next three nights, off and on, she pounded on our door and cried and carried on while I put a pillow over my head and gritted my teeth and held out. After the third night, all was peaceful. *M. J. Stern, Gary, Indiana*

✕✦✦✦✦✦✦✦✦✦✦✦✦✦✦✦✦✦✦✦✦✦✦✦✦✦✦✦✦✦✦✦✦✦✦✦✦✦✦✦✕

THINGS THAT GO BUMP
IN THE NIGHT

✕✦✦✦✦✦✦✦✦✦✦✦✦✦✦✦✦✦✦✦✦✦✦✦✦✦✦✦✦✦✦✦✦✦✦✦✦✦✦✦✕

"MONSTER SPRAY" KEEPS THE MONSTERS AT BAY ✦ When both my children were about five years old, they had very scary nightmares about monsters being in their room. A friend of mine gave me the tip of putting water in a spray bottle with just a dash of perfume to give it a scent. When the child goes to bed at night I spray this around their doorway and tell them that "monster spray" will not allow monsters in their room. This worked effectively for both of my children. *Kathy Berntson, Spring Lake Park, Minnesota*

MONSTERS HATE PLEASANT SCENTS ✦ Add a few drops of food coloring and almond extract to the water in the spray bottle for a pleasant scent (monsters hate

pleasant scents). Spray wherever monsters are found. Guaranteed to rid your home of monsters forever. *Nancy H. Blakey, Bainbridge Island, Washington*

"MAGIC RING" WARDS OFF MONSTERS ◆ We gave our three-year-old a "magic ring," which she would put on and wear only at night to ward off monsters that lurked in her bedroom. *Tracy LaVelle, Fremont, California*

"SCARE THE MONSTERS OUT OF THE BED-ROOM" ◆ My young daughter couldn't sleep on occasion because she thought there were monsters in her bedroom. My son, who was in high school, put on his football uniform and told my daughter that he was going to get rid of all the monsters in her room. He went into her room, shut the door, made a lot of noise, came out, and told her that the monsters were gone and would never return. Sure enough, we have never had a problem with monsters since that day. *Pat Johnston, Vista, California*

GHOSTS DON'T LIKE GREEN CURTAINS ◆ My grandson was frightened of ghosts until I told him that ghosts don't like green curtains. Of course, there were green curtains in the room where he slept when he visited my house. This worked so well when he visited me that his mother eventually put green curtains in his room at home. *Genie Gross, Lansing, Michigan*

"THERE'S A MONSTER IN MY CLOSET" ◆ Whenever my children were afraid of monsters in their room at bedtime, I would inspect every nook, cranny, and closet gathering up the monsters (like I would be gathering people to me). At the same time I would be saying: "It's time to go now, come on!" When the monsters were all "gathered up" (not to make *too* big an issue of it—ten to fifteen seconds), I then opened the door, put them outside, and told them not to come back. Then I closed the door. This worked for all three of my children. *Sue Bronner, St. Paul, Minnesota*

MONSTERS ARE SCARED OF MY MOM'S PER-FUME ◆ When my son was three years old, he was convinced there was a monster in his closet. My husband and I would have to stay with him until he fell asleep. One night I told him that monsters would never come into a room if a mom or dad was there. I explained that monsters can't see in the dark, but they can smell. Our solution was to sprinkle some of my perfume in the closet so the monster would think I was still in the room. It was a simple solution, but it really worked. Occasionally, my son would get my perfume and put a drop or two in the closet himself. *Jeanne Lawrence, Lansing, Michigan*

A NIGHTTIME PROTECTOR ◆ My children and I picked a ferocious-looking toy or stuffed animal to protect them at nighttime. *Cindy Barwacz, Fremont, California*

LOVE POWDER CHASES MONSTERS AWAY ◆ To help children go to sleep, take a small empty medicine bottle with the label off and a childproof cap, put salt or sugar in it, and cap it securely. Put it under their mattress and show it to them and explain that it is special love powder and will make the bad things go away. This will make them feel secure and they will have no trouble going to sleep. *Patty Reafsnyder, Garden Grove, California*

WITCH'S SWITCH FOR PROTECTION ◆ Give a child a "witch's switch" if they have fears when they go to bed at night. The witch's switch is usually a flyswatter. *Christine Bodeau, Fuquay-Varina, North Carolina*

BEAR SPRAY ◆ We moved from the city to a more rural area, surrounded by trees, and my daughter, then age three and a half, was afraid of bears. Although she couldn't read, she easily grasped the international symbols and their interpretations. So our "Monster Spray" consisted of colored water (a drop or two of food coloring added) with a picture of a bear on it with a big X from corner to corner. At night, we would go around the room and "flick" the drops in all directions to ban the dreaded bears. Where all reasoning failed, our concoction brought a peaceful night's sleep. *Penny Vaughan, Chesapeake, Virginia*

A BEDSIDE FLASHLIGHT ◆ If a child is afraid of the dark, keep a small flashlight next to his bed. It works wonders to calm fears. *N.S., San Jose, California*

SESAME STREET MONSTERS PROTECT CHILDREN ◆ My son was frightened of monsters being in his room until I told him that his Sesame Street monsters (stuffed animals) would protect him. My son also believed that Grover and Cookie Monster would make friends with the other monsters. He never worried after that. *M. Ring, New Hampshire*

12

CELEBRATIONS

◆

The illusions of childhood are necessary experiences. A child should not be denied a balloon because an adult knows that sooner or later it will burst.

— MARCELENE COX, *Ladies' Home Journal, 1948*

Everyone loves a celebration, whether a spur-of-the-moment recognition of a family member, a birthday, or a formal holiday. But no one enjoys a celebration with the same magical zeal as does a child. Parents can get caught up in their children's excitement too. In fact, one of the best fringe benefits of parenting is being able to again experience a holiday through the eyes of a child. For example, it's not clear who has the most fun on Easter at our house: my wife arranging the baskets, me hiding the eggs, or my children hunting for their goodies.

Birthday parties can rival holidays in the way children look forward to the big day. Our children begin to anticipate their own birthday parties as early as six months before the actual day. Last year our three-year-old hosted so many imaginary birthday parties for herself by lining up her dolls and singing "Happy Birthday" to herself that we decided to celebrate the half-year mark for each daughter. We have a small family celebration that usually includes cupcakes for dessert with half a candle on the cupcake of the celebrant. It has helped break up the long year between real birthdays.

This chapter is divided into five sections: Gift Ideas, Thank-You Notes, Party Time, Holidays, and Family Memories. For a great tip about a wonderful gift that grandparents can give grandchildren, see "Grandparent's Bedtime Tapes Are a Hit" (p. 216). A gift idea that works every time for our children is described by Neil McCallum in "Walnut Surprises (p. 216)." And if you want a tip on how to get your

214

children to write thank-you notes, read "You Can't Play with Your Gift until You Write a Thank-You Note" (p. 218). For an exciting birthday cake that will get the attention of even the hard-to-please child, check out the tip "Volcano Birthday Cake" (p. 222).

◆

GIFT IDEAS

A SHOWER GIFT SHE WILL CHERISH ✦ When you have a relative or close friend who's just had a new baby, include in the baby-shower gift a ticket that's redeemable for a night or two of free baby-sitting. New parents often get overwhelmed at what they've gotten into, and knowing in those first few weeks or months that they have a baby-sitter who's dependable and experienced waiting in the wings is the best mental-health medicine around. *Sue Mac-Donald, Cincinnati, Ohio*

THE BEST GIFTS FOR A NEW MOTHER ✦ I worked in the baby nursery at a local hospital. Instead of sending flowers or candy to the new parents, give them diaper service for a month, a meal for their freezer, some baby-sitting time, or pitch in with others and give them one big gift such as a high chair. Don't bring fancy little bonnets, frilly clothes, or clothes with a lot of buttons and bows for the newborn. The baby will be much happier if you bring a soft little nightgown and a knit cap. Wait a couple of days before you visit. The mother is tired and so is the baby and just getting home is enough for one day! *Patti Potts Johnson, Omaha, Nebraska*

BEFORE YOU BUY A STROLLER ✦ When you go shopping for a stroller, be sure to take the floor model out to your car and try to fit it into your trunk, because many of the strollers are too large to fit in trunks. That way you have the perfect stroller for your car and life-style. *Suzanne Green, Corona, California*

A MINT OF A BABY GIFT ✦ A baby gift that will be treasured for years is a silver proof coin set for the year in which the baby was born. The United States Mint sells the set in an attractive display case. The set includes the half dollar, quarter, dime, nickel, and penny. The cost is approximately $20. Contact the U.S. Mint, 10001 Aerospace Road, Lanham, MD 20706. *N.M., Tahoe City, California*

GRANDPARENTS' BEDTIME TAPES ARE A HIT ✦ Instead of purchasing prerecorded stories and songs on cassette tapes, have grandparents or other relatives record their own tapes. These tapes will be more special at bedtime and can be passed down through the generations. *Jill Nelson-Johnson, Urbandale, Iowa*

HANDPRINTS TO GO ✦ A child's footprints and handprints on a T-shirt or sweatshirt make a fun, inexpensive gift for the grandparent who has everything. And making these shirts is a fun activity for the children. Spread shirt-decorating paints on your child's hand or foot and then firmly place it on the material. If using a shirt, place newspapers between the two sides of cloth so the paint doesn't soak through. Add a name or message. *Stacey Lopez, Fremont, California*

WALNUT SURPRISES ✦ Most children love surprise packages. I carefully split open English walnuts, remove the meat, and replace it with some small gift (coin, stamp, sticker, jewelry, toy, etc.) and then use white glue to put the halves back together. After the glue dries, I spread out a large towel or sheet, and the children begin opening the walnuts with a small hammer on a cutting board. Six to ten walnuts, plus a couple that still have the meat, provide an enjoyable activity for children—and adult observers. Since young children may swallow the small objects hidden in the walnuts, this activity is only recommended for older children. *Neil McCallum, Fremont, California*

A NEWSPAPER HISTORY ✦ From the time my children were born and until they were eighteen years old, I saved a copy of the newspaper that was printed on each of their birthdays. It was fun for them to look back at their own "history" and remember what was playing at the movies, the top news stories, and the prices of various products. *Marsha Meckler, Honolulu, Hawaii*

HOMEMADE "OFFICE KIT" IS ALWAYS A HIT ◆ A great birthday or anytime gift is an assortment of real office supplies neatly arranged in a medium-size shipping box. The possibilities to include in the kit are endless, but all kids seem to enjoy an assortment of envelopes and stationery, tape, glue sticks, stickers (especially the little stars that come in a small box and a few sheets of colored dots), pens and pencils, little notebooks, stamp sets (especially real date stampers or the child's address stamp), jumbo colored paper clips, play money, hole-reinforcement stickers, small notepads, receipt books, index cards, small Post-its, etc. A "post office" kit would also be a fun gift. All of these items can be purchased at a stationery store. *Stacey Ann Morgan, Oakland, California*

A similar-style "craft box" also makes a great gift. See p. 14 ("Craft Box").

THANK-YOU NOTES

A PHOTO THANK-YOU ◆ A fun and much-appreciated way to send a thank-you note from a young child is to take a snapshot of the child wearing or holding the gift he or she received with a simple note attached. *Tracy Bauch, Milwaukee, Wisconsin*

THANK-YOU NOTES ◆ We always felt it was important to teach our children the importance of learning social etiquette/skills, and one of the things we were always adamant about was thank-you notes for gifts received. Before they are able to write, have them sit down with you and dictate to you what they would like to say in their own words in their thank-you notes. Once they are able to write themselves, the tradition continues. *Lois Ulrich, Fremont, California*

EVEN PRESCHOOLERS CAN SEND THANK-YOU NOTES ✦ Even children as young as two or three years old can send thank-you notes to friends and relatives. Have them color a page out of their coloring book and send it with a quick note attached from you. The receiving person will appreciate posting your child's masterpiece on his or her refrigerator. *Julie Cochran, Lakewood, Colorado*

"HANDPRINT" THANK YOU NOTES ✦ Before my son could start writing his own thank-you notes, I discovered a way to make a set of thank-you notes that our friends and relatives really enjoyed receiving. I photocopied my son's handprints with the right and left hands on each side of the page. In the middle of that original copy I wrote (attempting to make it look like child's handwriting) the following verse: "I can't yet write my own thank-you note, and I have a few years left before I can vote, But making these handprints is one thing I can do to say 'Thank you' for the great gift from you!" It made an inexpensive and original thank-you note that can be copied over and over again. *Kathy Tubbs, San Jose, California*

"YOU CAN'T PLAY WITH YOUR GIFT UNTIL YOU WRITE A THANK-YOU NOTE" ✦ The best way to insure that a thank-you note will get written is to have a rule that the child cannot play with that gift (or cash the check) until the note gets written and mailed. You'll be surprised at how quickly the note will get written. *Julia Kiely, Irvine, California*

A THANK-YOU NOTE TO THE HOST ✦ My four children detested writing thank-you notes to the host family where we had stayed during a recent visit. So I began a new rule: the thank-you notes must be written before we leave the home we are staying at and the note must include at least one specific thing that the child has especially appreciated (a game, activity, food, etc.). The children hide their notes somewhere (refrigerator, bed, etc.) where the host will find it after our family has left. This has worked great and we don't have to constantly remind the children to do this good deed when we return home. *Judith Schmidt, Crawfordsville, Indiana*

PREADDRESSED THANK-YOU NOTES ✦ To save time sending out thank-you notes after a large party (such as a baby or bridal shower), have each guest fill out her mailing address on an envelope, which she places in a large raffle jar. At the end of the party, pick one envelope to identify the winner of a prize. The winner is thrilled, but the real winner is you—you don't have to address one mailing envelope for your thank-yous. *Teresa Dodson, Forestville, Maryland*

PARTY TIME

BIRTHDAY-PARTY TIPS ✦ Let the children enjoy decorating their own cupcake with icing, M & M's, etc. Also, birthday parties come alive with an opportunity for face painting. I had an instant camera and took pictures of each child so he or she could take a picture home as a souvenir. *Debra Carangelo, East Haven, Connecticut*

SAFER (AND MORE FUN) PINATAS . . . ✦ I have always worried about children being hit by the stick or bat swung at a piñata and have also noticed that the blindfolded child who breaks the piñata with the bat usually doesn't have a fair chance at the goodies which fall out. So, I make piñatas with strings hanging from the bottom. Only one of the strings has a knot on the end inside the piñata. The children take turns pulling the strings out until one child pulls the string with the knot. Pulling the knotted string opens the bottom side of the piñata and all of the treats fall out. The child who opened the piñata can immediately join the scramble, and no one is at risk of being hit by the bat. To make this kind of piñata, find a flat-bottomed piñata and cut the entire bottom into two flaps. Then poke holes all over both flaps and, using an embroidery or upholstery needle, thread a piece of string or yarn through each hole. The knotted string should be placed somewhere near the center of the piñata's underside. Make sure the knot is large enough so that it will not pull through the hole when tugged hard. Fill the piñata with treats and seal the flaps closed with tape. The piñata is reusable! *Mrs. Vigil, Newark, California*

PING-PONG BALL PARTY GAME ✦ Place one Ping-Pong ball in the center of a table with two teams of kids on each side. The object of the game is to blow the ball off the other team's side of the table. You can't touch the ball with your hands and you can't blow so hard that your face turns blue. (One eight-year-old child almost hyperventilated from blowing too hard.) A parent should always monitor this game and enforce the rules. *Deborah M. Beason, Duluth, Minnesota*

HAPPY UNBIRTHDAY TO YOU ✦ Whenever I send a birthday gift to a grandchild, I also include a modest "unbirthday gift" (usually money) for the other children in the family. This makes the unbirthday child feel happy, too, and everyone looks forward to everyone else's birthday. Of course, the main emphasis is still on the birthday person, but it always adds a little something extra, especially when the children are young, and it seems forever before a birthday comes around again. *H.L. Nipper, Jacksonville, Florida*

DRESS-UP PARTY ✦ Invite your party guests to come dressed up in Mom or Dad's old clothes. Or, if you have a large dress-up box or trunk, this could be a fun activity during the party. Either way, you will have the opportunity to get some great group photos. *Arlene Stocking, Fremont, California*

Certain toy chests or similar containers have been associated with strangulation hazards, resulting from the lids falling on a child's head or neck. Avoid containers with a hinged lid that could fall freely.

SHOE SCRAMBLE (party game) ✦ Have each child remove one shoe. Then pile the shoes together some distance from the children and give a signal. The child who runs to the pile, finds and puts on his or her shoe, and runs back to the starting line first wins! Have older children remove both shoes if desired. *Linda DeVito, Titusville, Florida*

AHOY, MATIES, IT'S A PIRATE PARTY ✦ Children love pirate parties. Have the guests come in costume or have an old chest at the door full of costume jewelry, newspaper hats, bright scarves, etc. Our main event was a treasure hunt, but we had a different game at each landmark where the treasure map (a map in a bottle) led us. A few of the favorite games were walk the plank, pin the hook on the pirate (draw a pirate on posterboard), and fishing (construction-paper fish with paper clip and dowel rods with magnet at end of string to catch fish). The treasure (seashells, gold chocolate coins, keys, toy rings, etc.) can be buried in a sand box. Instead of a cake we had cupcakes with skeleton flags attached to toothpicks. *Gloria Adamov, Uniontown, Ohio*

POP AND DARE GAME ✦ A popular birthday party game is called "Pop and Dare." First, write out a dare (such as singing a song, hopping on one foot, etc.) for each party guest to do, a consequence for not doing the dare, and a prize if she does it. Place each slip of paper inside a balloon before filling it with air. Give each child a balloon and ask her (children love this part) to pop the balloon and read the dare. You can make the dares as silly as you like. Then, sit back and watch the entertainment. *Sonia Lleras, Bronx, New York*

Supervise all dares so that they remain safe, fun, age-appropriate, and do not get out of hand.

VOLCANO BIRTHDAY CAKE ✦ Bake a cake in a large metal bowl. After baking, turn it upside down so it resembles a mountain. Make a cavity in the middle of the cake, large enough to place a small juice glass inside. For a realistic effect, place a few small pieces of dry ice inside the glass and place the glass inside the cavity of the cake. Use chocolate frosting to resemble the lava flowing out of the top of the cake, and place a few small toy dinosaurs at the base of the cake. Children love it! Keep young hands away from dry ice. *Michael Kassarjian, Fremont, California*

BREAD-DOUGH PARTY ACTIVITY ✦ A fun, easy-to-do, and inexpensive party activity is called ''bread dough creations.'' I prepare and let the dough rise once before the guests arrive. I give an apron to each guest and then let them make their own shapes of bread on a floured table. Then I let the dough rise again before I bake it. Each child gets to take his creation home with them. They love it! *Deborah M. Beason, Duluth, Minnesota*

HIS "FIRST" POOL PARTY ✦ I bought a small wading pool for my son's one-year-old birthday party. When it was time to serve the cake, I stripped my son down to his diapers, placed him in the middle of the pool, and served him his cake and ice cream. He had a grand time eating and smearing it around. After he finished, we took him out of the pool, hosed the pool off, and filled it halfway with water. He and his birthday friends spent the rest of the party skinny-dipping in his new pool. *Shelley Holland, Melbourne, Florida*

PENNY SCRAMBLE (party game) ✦ I got five dollars' worth of pennies and lined them up across the end of the driveway horizontally. I lined up the children horizontally about twenty feet away. When I gave the signal, they all ran with paper bags and the child who collected the most pennies won. *Linda DeVito, Titusville, Florida*

CRAFT PARTY ✦ Each child attending the craft party is to bring one item (enough for all the children) that can be used in the craft project. Children especially enjoy gluing items to large colored pieces of paper—making masterpieces that can be taken home. *Patricia R. Shamshoian, Fremont, California*

$$ RECYCLE PARTY SUPPLIES FOR A DOLL PARTY ◆ My daughter enjoys giving parties for her stuffed animals and dolls. I let her have leftover party goods (plates, hats, napkins), gift wrap, and small boxes. She wraps her own toys in the boxes as gifts for her guests. *Nancy Knowlton, Wilmette, Illinois*

"WHOSE PICTURE IS THAT" BABY-SHOWER GAME ◆ Ask each guest to bring a baby picture of him or herself. Number each picture, then tape or tack each picture to a poster or cork board. Give each guest a blank sheet of paper and tell them to "guess" the name of a person for each numbered picture. Everyone enjoys this game. It's a real ice breaker. *Keri Brittingham, St. Charles, Missouri*

"WHAT WILL SHE SAY IN THE DELIVERY ROOM" BABY-SHOWER GAME ◆ For a hilarious time at a baby shower, have one guest secretly write down all the comments the mother-to-be says during the party, especially her remarks as she open her gifts. Towards the end of the party the scribe says, "This is what (name) is going to say to her doctor in the delivery room." Then, she reads off the funniest comments, such as "Who gave me this?" and "Thanks so much. Come here so I can give you a kiss." The guests and the mother-to-be will be rolling in the aisles. *Andrea Robinson, Huntsville, Alabama*

HOLIDAYS

CHILDREN GET THEIR OWN CHRISTMAS TREE ◆ Children are naturally attracted to a Christmas tree with beautiful ornaments, bright lights, and colorful packages. To protect the family Christmas tree from being dismantled by little hands, I buy my smaller children a little tree that they can decorate and play with. They have their own little ornaments and enjoy taking them off and putting them back on all through the month. *Marcia Harward, Fountain Valley, California*

Make sure the ornaments and decorations are not made of glass or other material that could break. Artificial trees are also good for this; have the children make all the ornaments for their tree. Obviously, don't use any electrical decorations.

A PLAYPEN FOR THE CHRISTMAS TREE ✦ All of our children were at the crawling stage at Christmastime. After several accidents and picking the Christmas tree up off its side and putting the baby in the playpen, I reversed it. I put the Christmas tree and gifts in the playpen and let the baby free to crawl around safely. *Sheryl Saxton, Tekamah, Nebraska*

Keep an alert eye out that your infant doesn't try to climb over or fall into the playpen. Some playpen designs have been associated with injury.

SPECIAL WRAPPING PAPER FOR EACH CHILD ♦ We have five children and at Christmastime have had difficulty with lost gift tags. Now, we (Santa) assign different-colored paper for each child and for Mom and Dad (this obviously doesn't include gifts from other people). We don't have any gift tags at all. From the time they are about two years old they know what color paper is theirs. I keep a chart with each child's name and a sample of their wrapping paper so we don't get mixed up. *Vicki Surges, Carson City, Nevada*

"THIS PRESENT IS FOR PRANCER, THIS ONE IS FOR DOPEY" ♦ We have nosy people at our house during the time before Christmas—always shaking and rattling the packages with their names tags—and often they actually guess what's in them. I have decided to use different names on the packages so whose is whose is a mystery on Christmas Day. For instance, this year I used the names of Santa's nine reindeer, and last year, I used the names of the seven dwarves. No one knows whose package is whose, but I keep a key so that I will know on Christmas. Numbers or letters of the alphabet can also be used. *Beverly Prizzi, Campbell, California*

PHOTO ORNAMENTS ARE LASTING MEMORIES ♦ Ever since our boys were born, we put a photo ornament on the Christmas tree every year for each child. It's fun and amazing to see how they have changed through the years. As the children get older they are now able to make their own ornaments to hold the photo for that year. *Kathy Tubbs, San Jose, California*

COUNTDOWN TO CHRISTMAS ♦ If your religion doesn't use Advent calenders to count the days before Christmas, use a chain made of construction paper. Make the chain twenty-four links long, one link for each day from December 1 to December 24. Attach it to a construction-paper Christmas tree and hang it on the wall near the child's bed. Each night before the child goes to bed, she removes one link from the bottom of the chain. As the

chain gets smaller, the child gets more and more excited, until finally the last link is removed and it is Christmas Eve. My daughter is eager to go to bed because she can remove a link. *Sharon Zanoni, Penn Valley, California*

HOW MANY CLOTHESPINS UNTIL CHRISTMAS

♦ Before Christmas, the children are always saying, "How many more days till Christmas, Mommy?" In desperation, I put up a little clothesline in the kitchen and put clothespins on the line. Each day, we take down one clothespin so the children can see at a glance how many more days until Christmas. *Hazel Woodsmall, Santa Ana, California*

PROOF THAT SANTA CLAUS WAS REALLY HERE

♦ Our child was getting to the age where he didn't believe in Santa Claus. So on Christmas Eve I put baby powder on my shoes and made footprints from my son's bed to the hallway. The next morning we said, "Look, Santa came and checked on you while you were asleep." His little eyes got real big and said, "Wow, I do believe." *Natalie Gibson, Greenville, South Carolina*

This is a great idea for younger children, but don't be afraid to acknowledge the point when your child is ready to give up those childhood fantasies and move into real-world concepts. This provides an excellent chance for you to be a loving and caring guide as your child enters this "new world."

PLACE BABY JESUS IN THE MANGER ON THE 25TH, BEFORE THE CHILDREN GET UP

♦ One of our Christmas traditions is to wait and put baby Jesus in the manger scene on Christmas morning when he is actually born. The children get very excited waiting for Christmas because they know that is when the baby Jesus goes in the manger scene. *Natalie Gibson, Greenville, South Carolina*

"MOM, CAN I OPEN A PRESENT BEFORE CHRISTMAS?"

♦ Remembering that when we were children, my brother and I used to ask my mother to let us open just one of our Christmas gifts early, I tried something different with my son. To take the edge off waiting to open Christmas gifts, I purchased twelve inexpensive gifts, wrapped them, and put them in his Christmas stocking. We called it the Twelve Days of Christmas, and he was allowed to pick out and open one each of the twelve days before Christmas. It did not matter to him what the gifts actually were (sometimes it was nuts or candy or gum). The excitement of being able to open something each day accomplished more than I hoped. He learned to count the days left by the unopened gifts. He learned patience and that grown-ups understood how he felt, and never did he beg me to open the big ones. He is a young man now and still won't let me quit the practice. *Diane Bates, Chesterton, Indiana*

A HOLIDAY TAPE FOR THE AGES ◆ We save one tape and on this same tape every year at Christmastime we videotape our boys side by side while they tell us what they would like for Christmas. It's a wonderfully compact way to see how they have grown through the years and hear about all the toys that were popular that year. *K.T. Hom, San Jose, California*

HOLIDAYS ARE MORE THAN PARADES ◆ Local, state, national, and international holidays provide an excellent opportunity to learn about heritage and the value of cultural diversity. Parades and other public events are fun for children, but they need to know the real significance and history of the celebration. A short lesson before dinner, a reading from a history book, or a personal comment from the parents can make a lasting impression on children. *Bill McMahon, Spokane, Washington*

HOLIDAY DECORATIONS ◆ We keep one drawer of holiday decorations accessible to our preschooler. He gets great pleasure out of playing with Easter bunnies, flags, paper witches, and little pilgrims out of season. Keeping them all together in one place seems to preserve their "specialness." *Donna Terman, Menlo Park, California*

FAIR EASTER-EGG HUNTS ◆ Set a limit on how many Easter eggs each child can find. This allows smaller children to get as many eggs as the older children. *Pamela Nakaso, Fremont, California*

EGGS IN YOUR POCKET ◆ When taking a preschooler for an Easter-egg hunt, it is a good idea to carry

several hard-boiled, colored eggs in your pocket (or purse) to hide especially for your child to find. This prevents disappointment when quicker, older children find all the eggs. *Sharon Zanoni, Penn Valley, California*

$$ SAVE THOSE LEGGS HOSIERY CONTAINERS ◆ Save the Leggs hosiery containers that are shaped like large eggs. They make wonderful containers for Easter-egg hunts and other Easter activities. *Jim Knowlton, San Marcos, California*

EASTER BUNNY'S HELPER ENCOURAGES GOOD BEHAVIOR ◆ We have a tradition at Easter that helps to keep the kids behaving for the week before Easter. We have a basket filled with paper grass. Within this basket we place a stuffed bunny who is the Easter Bunny's Helper. We bring this basket out one week before Easter. Then at random intervals we will place a couple of M&M's under the bunny. This is done only when the kids are not looking. The next time the kids look under the bunny, they find that it has laid some candy. *And as long as the kids stay good the bunny will continue to generate candy.* As each day passes, we add more candy and at greater intervals. Then on Easter morning you will end up with one big basket of candy and presents to be shared by the family. *Vikki Hill, Newark, California*

HALLOWEEN HAUNTED HOUSE ◆ My sons love to make a haunted house in our basement and then invite their friends to a "scary" time. Everyone wears a costume and cardboard cutout bats hang from the ceiling. The guests bob for apples and touch various items in bowls while they are blindfolded. They must guess what they are

touching. Boys especially like the feel of peeled grapes and cooked macaroni—monster eyes and guts they say. *Deborah M. Beason, Duluth, Minnesota*

HALLOWEEN FAIRY ◆ A friend of mine takes the candy her kids collect on Halloween and leaves it out on the kitchen table for the "Halloween Fairy" to come and take. In exchange, the fairy leaves each child a nice present! The kids get to trick-or-treat to their hearts' content but don't end up eating twenty pounds of candy. They get to pick out a few pieces to eat, but gladly give up the rest to the Halloween Fairy. *Ellen Steinmetz, Manhattan Beach, California*

◆◆◆◆◆◆◆◆◆◆◆◆◆◆◆◆◆◆◆◆◆◆◆◆◆◆◆◆◆◆◆◆◆◆

FAMILY MEMORIES

◆◆◆◆◆◆◆◆◆◆◆◆◆◆◆◆◆◆◆◆◆◆◆◆◆◆◆◆◆◆◆◆◆◆

MEMORY BOX ◆ Let each of your children establish a "Memory Box" to store special items they want to keep (ticket stubs, pictures, travel momentos, letters or cards, etc.). They will treasure it when they're older. *Jeff LaVelle, Fremont, California*

PHOTO ALBUMS FOR ADOPTED CHILDREN ◆ I am the mother of two boys (ages two and four), both of whom are adopted. I keep photo albums for each of the children aside from the family ones. Should they ever meet their birth parents, they can share their baby pictures and will be able to keep their own pictures and not fight over the family ones. *Nancy Plymale, Ft. Pierce, Florida*

$$ BORROW A VIDEO CAMERA ◆ We don't have a videocamera, but we have relatives who do. I take a cassette to family gatherings every few months and borrow a video camera to get fifteen minutes of the baby. Eventually

I'll edit the tape and make copies for the grandparents. *Margaret Healy, Albany, California*

PHOTO ENVELOPES ✦ Since photos are a major part of growing up, keep a stack of the photo envelopes at home. Fill them out at home—mistake free—instead of at the store with children crawling up your leg. *Jan Harvey, Fremont, California*

LABEL THOSE PHOTOS IMMEDIATELY ✦ After receiving photographs from the photo store and before sending them to family and friends, I put a small adhesive label on the back and date it. I also do this on pictures in our photo frames at home. This helps us remember just when the event was or the age of the child. *Vicki Schrimmer, Irvine, California*

THE SAME PICTURE—EACH MONTH ✦ Each month during your baby's first year, on his or her birth date, take your baby's picture. Put the infant in the same place (same chair, sofa, etc.) with the same toy or stuffed animal each month. This gives you a good reference to see how baby grows and changes during the first year. *Wendy Ericsson, Lansdale, Pennsylvania*

A PLACE FOR EXTRA PHOTOS ✦ My son has always liked to look at the photo album I keep for him. He was making a mess of it and the pictures were falling out. I bought an inexpensive bride book and put any extra pictures of him and his friends in it and wrote his name on the front. This is his very own photo album, which he likes very much. *Debra Randall, East Haven, Connecticut*

A CHRISTMAS SCRAPBOOK ✦ The first year our son was born I started a family Christmas album using a scrapbook. Each Christmas I put a picture of our family in the album and all the picture Christmas cards we had received that season. I also write a brief summary describing the activities and events our family has experienced during the past year. This family book has become a beloved custom and treasure in our household. As the children have gotten older, they now add their own "Family Update" each year. *Kathy Tubbs, San Jose, California*

13

BABY BASICS

◆

When I approach a child, he inspires in me two sentiments: tenderness for what he is, and respect for what he may become.

— LOUIS PASTEUR

Parenthood is a daring adventure, and at no time is the adventure more challenging than during the first year after becoming a new parent. However, no matter how well prepared they are, most new parents are surprised at how immense a task it can be to care for an infant who is totally dependent on them. Not only are there new skills to learn (feeding, diapering, bathing, and all the rest), but new parents often must make drastic changes in how they use their time and energy. In our family, for instance, our life changed so much that my wife and I jokingly describe our marriage in terms of "BK" (before kids) and "AK" (after kids).

In writing this book, I received scores of letters from experienced parents who had the same message for those with new babies: RELAX! Variations included, "Don't sweat the small stuff" and "Don't try to be perfect." One mother summed it up best: "Don't worry about making mistakes. Your baby doesn't know you're a rookie, because he's a rookie too."

Another message these seasoned veterans offer is to enjoy these early years because they're some of the best—and they go by too fast. Babies are not just hours of work and sleepless nights. They also offer a magical world of unfolding wonder to anyone who is willing to pay attention. Just watch, and every day you will see new feats and accomplishments, each new behavior more exciting than the last. One day your child will discover how to sit up, soon thereafter how to stand, and before you know it, how to walk. And soon, like me, you will find yourself missing those early days. I still fondly remember, for instance, the infusion of love I felt as my daughters and I gazed into each other's face during a late-night bottle feeding.

The following tips are arranged in eight sections, covering all the baby basics from teething to weaning. If you are as frustrated as I used to get over leaky baby bottles, read the tip "No-Drip Baby Bottles." Plus, you can double your savings on baby wipes by trying the tip "Budgeting Your Baby Wipes." If you're a parent on the go with little time to write in your child's baby book, read "A Journal on Tape." For tips on how to soothe a fussy baby, refer to the section titled Colicky Babies in Chapter 8 (Health and Safety).

Happy diapering!

◆

PREPARING AN OLDER SIBLING FOR A NEW BABY

PREPARING BIG BROTHER ◆ It took our son a good six months to adjust to the arrival of his baby brother. I was not prepared for the degree to which this event would affect his behavior. My mother-in-law put the whole thing into perspective when she said, "Just think if one day out of the blue, your husband came home and told you that in two weeks he would bring home a new wife. Then when this new wife arrives, your husband tells you that he expected you to love this new wife and share everything with the new wife, including him." Well, after hearing this, I had much more patience and understanding for helping my oldest son through this monumental adjustment period. *K.T. Hom, San Jose, California*

NEWBORN BRINGS GIFT FOR BIG SISTER ◆ I wasn't sure how my daughter would react when I brought her newborn brother home from the hospital. After all, she'd gotten all the attention for the first two years and nine months of her life. So when Timmy came home for the first time, he brought with him a baby doll for his new sister. That way, she had a baby and so did I. And when I was busy with my baby, she could be busy with hers. That doll was her favorite toy for many months and it kept her occupied while I was nursing, changing, feeding, or trying to get her little brother to sleep. Helpless infant siblings bearing gifts are things to treasure. *Sue MacDonald, Cincinnati, Ohio*

PROUD OF "OUR" BABY ◆ Our two older children were very excited to have a new baby sister. While I was still pregnant, they came with me to my doctor visits and were able to listen to their sister's heartbeat. After she was born, I talked about her as "our" baby, and they took great pride in being part of her life. Good preparation and participation helps older children cope with a new sibling. *Elaine Fredianelli, Fremont, California*

PROUD TO BE THE "BIG BROTHER" ◆ One month before our second son was born, we went to a T-shirt store and had iron-on letters put on a shirt for my four-year-old son that spelled out "Big Brother." Whoever saw this shirt on him was sure to strike up a conversation with him about being a big brother. My son wore that shirt every day and night before and after the baby was born. The shirt helped him share in the spotlight too. If I had to do it all over again, I would have bought two identical shirts so I could at least get one into the washer. *Kathy Tubbs, San Jose, California*

SIBLING SHARES BEDROOM WITH BABY ◆ About two months before our third son was due, and having only two bedrooms for the children, I suggested to our second son that he rearrange his room to make a space for his new sibling. I let him decide how he wanted things placed. By allowing him to make the decisions (no matter how unaesthetic it seemed to me), he felt more like he was in charge rather than being intruded upon. Our first night home with the new baby, I put the bassinet beside me in our bedroom. Our second son, who was five years old, was upset and said, "I thought he was going to live in MY room where there are four people to watch him." When I asked him what four people, he replied, "Me, God, Jesus, and Santa Claus!" I explained that on the baby's first few nights at home, I needed to keep a close watch on him. *Memory Campbell, Charlotte, North Carolina*

BIG BROTHER NEEDS SPECIAL TIME, TOO ✦ A new baby takes so much time and concern that you must *make* time for the other children! I was able to do this by stopping all chores the minute the older ones came through the door. We would have a cookie-and-milk break—that twenty minutes was all *their* time. *Patti Potts Johnson, Omaha, Nebraska*

xxxxxxxxxxxxxxxxxxxxxxxxxxxxxxxxxxxxxxxxxxxxxx

BREAST-FEEDING

xxxxxxxxxxxxxxxxxxxxxxxxxxxxxxxxxxxxxxxxxxxxxx

"WHICH SIDE DID I USE LAST?" ✦ Breast-feeding moms are told to alternate the side you begin with each feeding. Some people suggest putting a pin on your bra to remember which side to start with, but I use a ring on my pinkie finger because it is easier for me to change the ring than the pin. *Sharon Kraynak, Lansdale, Pennsylvania*

NURSING AT THE MALL ✦ If baby gets hungry when you are at a shopping mall or at a department store, you can duck into a ladies' changing room to feed your baby. If you're at a mall and you go to a store where they lock the dressing rooms, quite often, if you ask, they will be happy to open them up and let you nurse. Just make sure you choose one that has a bench in it or a chair because some dressing rooms don't. *Linda Bennett, Centre Hall, Pennsylvania*

QUICK CLEANUP ✦ Use a commercial baby wipe to clean spit-up off your and your baby's clothes. They are always nearby, they smell good, and they do a good job. *Kim VanGorder, Cary, North Carolina*

BREAST-FEEDING IN COMFORT ✦ My neck and shoulders used to ache from holding the baby to nurse. Then I put a bed-reading backrest pillow on a bed and another pillow above it against the wall. I put a pillow (covered with a diaper for drips and urps) on my lap and the baby on that. Once the baby has latched on, I raise him and the pillow closer to my chest with my knees (with my feet on the bed), and lean my head back against the other pillows. This way I'm able to nurse completely relaxed. *P.H., Albany, California*

WARM TOWEL RELIEVES AIR BUBBLES AFTER NURSING ✦ I have a little trick I found that works wonders to relieve a baby's air bubbles after nursing or taking formula. I warm up a damp towel in the microwave—not too hot!—place it into a plastic bag and seal, then put it inside another dry towel. Then I place the towel on my lap and lay my baby gently on it (tummy side down) and pat her back until the bubble comes up. It works every time and makes the baby relax enough to fall asleep. *Joni McCartt, Melbourne, Florida*

TEA BAGS RELIEVE SORENESS ✦ To ease soreness in those first few weeks of breast-feeding, make a cup of tea, then put the warm tea bags on your nipples for fifteen to twenty minutes. The warmth is soothing and the tea helps promote healing. It really works! *Wendy Ericsson, Lansdale, Pennsylvania*

HELP FOR BREAST-FEEDING

The La Leche League offers support and information for breast-feeding mothers. Call 1-800-LALECHE or write to P. O. Box 1209, Franklin Park, IL 60131-8209 for information about local chapters in your area.

TAKE A WATER BOTTLE ALONG ✦ When I was nursing my child and had to be away from home, I would put a bottle of water for myself in the diaper-bag pocket meant for a baby bottle. A bicycle or jogging bottle works best; it's easy to handle with only one free hand to drink. *Rose Pershe, Campbell, California*

EVEN MILK PRODUCTION ✦ It is possible to even out milk production between breasts by trying harder and longer to express on the drier side. After a week or two it will produce noticeably more. *Peg Hartley, San Bernardino, California*

BREAST PUMP ✦ I was able to nurse my baby without a problem, but I had poor luck using the electric breast pump. Then, a friend suggested using the breast pump on one breast while my baby was feeding from the other. It worked well. The baby's sucking action on one breast helped the other breast let the milk flow for the breast pump, and I was able to pump a lot of milk that way. It also saved time: I could express the milk while I fed my baby. *Laura Phelps, Scotsdale, Arizona*

A SOLUTION FOR BREAST ENGORGEMENT ✦ My newborn daughter had a very difficult time breast-feeding. The more engorged I became, the harder it was for her to latch on to my nipple. After two days of trying desperately to breast-feed her, I called the nursing staff at the hospital where we had delivered. A nurse suggested that I take a regular nipple from a baby bottle and place it on top of MY nipple. It worked! For the next few days our daughter nursed by sucking on the larger baby-bottle nipple through which my own milk flowed. On about the fourth day, I gently pulled the bottle nipple off my breast as she nursed, and she took to my own nipple immediately. *Gail Rosenblum Davis, Minneapolis, Minnesota*

BOTTLE FEEDING

SWITCHING TO COW'S MILK ✦ Switching from formula or breast milk to cow's milk is often no easy task. Start by adding one ounce of cow's milk to bottles of formula or breast milk. Increase the cow's milk by an ounce every day. Within a week or so, your baby will have switched to all cow's milk. No fuss, and easier on your baby's tummy! I call it sneaking up on my baby! *Michele Robson-Bermudez, Fremont, California*

IF BABY WON'T TAKE A BOTTLE ✦ If a baby insists on Mom's nipple and will not take a bottle, have someone other than Mom offer her a bottle. Sometimes babies won't take a bottle from Mom, but will from someone else, like Dad or Grandma. Also, try different brands of bottle nipples or a medicine dropper. Some babies have a preference. *Elaine Fredianelli, Fremont, California*

$$ BOTTLE HOLDER ✦ To help your infant hold its bottle better, cut an old sock off at the ankle and slip it over the bottle. This gives the baby a better (and softer) surface to grip. *Brenda Kiba, Milpitas, California*

NO-DRIP BABY BOTTLES ✦ When you carry baby bottles around in a diaper bag, to keep the milk from spilling, just put sandwich bags over the bottle of milk before you screw on the lid. Once you have screwed on the lid you can pull the remaining plastic over the nipple, and that keeps the nipple clean and keeps the milk from spilling much better than using the plastic caps that come with the bottles. *Lisa Rodriguez, Oceanside, California*

FEEDING TWINS—AT THE SAME TIME ✦ Feeding my twin babies was a difficult task until I learned the following method: I sit on the couch or floor with one twin who leans back against my abdomen and chest and faces forward, on my lap. I hold this twin's bottle with one hand. My other twin sits upright (to prevent gagging) in an infant seat facing me on the same side as my "free" hand, which I then use to hold the bottle and feed the twin in the seat. I always keep another infant seat nearby if I'm not sitting on the floor. This enables me to quickly place the baby sitting on my lap into a seat if I need to pick up the other baby. I take turns holding each baby on my lap for equal "mommy cuddling" time during feedings. Occasionally, I will place both babies in their infant seats facing me while I hold each of their bottles. They don't get as much body contact this way, but I can sing, smile, and talk to both of them easily. *Lisa Shapiro Solomon, Rockaway, New Jersey*

THERMOS KEEPS FORMULA WARM ALL NIGHT LONG ✦ To avoid making bottles in the middle of the night, I put powdered formula in the bottle and the warm water in a thermos. Then in the middle of the night, all I have to do is add the warm water to the bottle. *Gail Lynch, Washington DC*

COLD KEYS ✦ When my children were still being bottle fed, I frequently would leave a home where we were visiting and forget the bottles and baby food in the fridge. To solve this problem, I just placed my car keys in the fridge next to the bottles. I left with cold keys, but always left with food and bottles in hand. *A.V.S., Fremont, California*

PREMEASURED FORMULA ✦ When we have to pack formula for an outing, I measure out the powdered formula, put it into the individual bottle bags (like Playtex), and tie it with a twist tie. You can always find a place to get the water. That way you can take several packs of formula and only one bottle. *Linda Skocypec, Albuquerque, New Mexico*

A WARM BOTTLE AT THE CAMPSITE ✦ Our baby prefers warm or lukewarm formula, which was difficult to arrange while camping. We solved this by boiling water at night. A little hot water in a wide-mouth thermos heated the evening bottle. The sealed thermos kept the rest of the water hot until needed to mix with a can of formula, which could be done quickly in the middle of the night. Offhand, I would strongly suggest not weaning a baby before camping! *P.H., Albany, California*

COMMAND CENTRAL
(THE CHANGING TABLE)

CHANGING DIAPERS ✦ My toddler can't stand to have her diaper changed. To distract her, I always hand her a wipe while I work on changing her. Some times she will play peek-a-boo with the wipe, but most of the time she ends up wiping her own hand. It saves time on both accounts. *Kimberly Carew, North Haven, Connecticut*

$$ CORNSTARCH INSTEAD OF BABY POWDER ✦ Cornstarch is not only cheaper than baby powder, it doesn't have any perfumes or chemicals that can irritate baby's skin. *Julia Kiely, Irvine, California*

$$ NON-CLUMPING CORNSTARCH ✦ Regular cornstarch tends to clump, but the alternative—baby powder—is expensive. To save money without compromising on quality, mix 1 container of cornstarch baby powder with 4 boxes of regular cooking cornstarch. Refill the powder container with the new mixture. It won't clump, smells good, and costs about a fifth of the price of commercial cornstarch baby powder. *Brenda Capone, Stamford, Connecticut*

PICK A TOY FOR THE CHANGING TABLE ✦ Before changing my son, I let him choose a toy or book that he can play with while he is getting his diaper changed. He squirms less and I can finish the task at hand faster. *Nancy Green, Sherman Oaks, California*

BALLOONS ON THE CEILING ✦ My daughter (now fifteen months old) loves to play with helium-filled balloons. She especially loves the Mylar balloons with cartoon characters and other fun designs. Regular balloons easily pop and burst into pieces that pose a choking hazard. The Mylar balloons rarely pop and they float for days longer than regular balloons. When the balloon deflates, I tape it on the ceiling over my baby's changing table. She has a whole collage of balloons to look at while I am changing her diaper. *Susan Lowther, Glendale, Arizona*

BABIES LOVE TO LOOK AT THEMSELVES ✦ A small mirror that the baby can hold and look into is a great distraction while on the changing table. *M. Ring, New Hampshire*

A "TALKING" STUFFED ANIMAL ✦ I kept my baby occupied on the changing table by hanging a stuffed animal over her head and out of her reach. Every time I would change her diaper, I would talk to her pretending to be the animal. The animal kept her occupied so I could change her without too much fuss. *Naomi Mulligan, Livermore, California*

TOES TO NOSE ✦ When baby is around three or four months old, start playing "toes-to-nose" with him whenever you change his diaper. Later, when the baby begins to roll over, diaper changing will be much easier because the baby will think it's fun to put his toes up to his nose. To play "toes-to-nose," gently flex the baby's legs so that the toes are nearly touching the nose, then say, "Toes to nose! Toes to nose!" in a singsong, repetitive way. Now that my baby is nine months old, if he starts to roll over during diaper changing, I just say, "Toes to nose," and he lifts his legs up and laughs. *Susan Bristol, Omaha, Nebraska*

CHANGING DIAPERS BY THE BATHROOM SINK ✦ My baby refused to be changed on the changing table, so I let him stand on the bathroom counter facing the mirror. He didn't mind being changed while standing up, and he was distracted looking in the mirror while I changed his diapers. Occasionally, I would ask him to touch his nose or ear to entertain him during the diaper change. *Khush Lodhia, Fremont, California*

THIS WET BAR SERVES DIAPERS ✦ We converted our wet bar into a changing area for our baby. The sink is handy for cleanups and the cabinets can be used to store diapers and supplies. *Anonymous, Cincinnati, Ohio*

$$ VINEGAR FOR THE DIAPER PAIL ✦ Vinegar in the bottom of the diaper pail (about ½ cup) prevents odors. Bleach and diaper-pail deodorant disks also work effectively, but they cost more and are toxic. *Liz Ruuska, Merrillville, Indiana*

OLD MacDONALD HAS A DIAPER, E-I-E-I-O ✦ My boys didn't like to take time out to have their diapers changed and would cry loudly the whole time. I found that singing to them, especially "Old MacDonald Had a Farm" with lots of weird animal sounds, distracted them, and they'd lie still and listen. This worked very well until they were toilet trained. *Peggy Gilbreth Nipper, Omaha, Nebraska*

NEVER LEAVE HOME WITHOUT THEM ✦ We keep emergency baby supplies in both of our cars. A small box holds diapers and wipes, bib, cup or bottle, baby Tylenol, and a few small toys. They sure come in handy at a restaurant or family outing. *Patty and Ray Gustas, Fremont, California*

$$ BUDGETING YOUR BABY WIPES ✦ If you use store-bought baby wipes when changing diapers, you may realize how quickly you go through one box. Periodically, I take a handful of wipes and tear each wipe into four squares and then place back into the box, so they are ready to use when I have to perform a speedy diaper change. It certainly makes the box of wipes last a lot longer. *Patricia A. McMahon, San Diego, California*

Even if you tear them only in half, you have doubled your savings.

$$ INEXPENSIVE CLEANING SOLUTION FOR DIAPER CHANGES ◆ Instead of using expensive diaper wipes, make your own. Mix an equal amount of baby oil and water in a bottle. Shake before using, then pour a small amount over soft toilet tissue and wipe baby. *Khush Lodhia, Fremont, California*

BABY OIL ON THE BOTTOM ◆ Drizzle baby oil on an infant's bottom before you use a wipe. You'll save time and effort. *Janet Johnstone, Fremont, California*

Baby oil helps dissolve and remove old diaper ointments. Follow with soap and water as a regular cleaning procedure.

$$ HOMEMADE WET WIPES ◆ Here's how I make my own baby wipes: Mix all ingredients (2½ cups water, 2 tablespoons baby oil, 1 tablespoon baby bath soap, and ½ roll of Bounty paper towels) except paper towels in a 3-quart Rubbermaid container. Cut a roll of paper towels in half (you will have what looks like two thick rolls of toilet paper). Remove the center cardboard—the wipes will spiral out from center. Add a half roll of paper towels to other ingredients in container. The paper will absorb the liquid. I keep the wet wipes in the Rubbermaid container. Tear off any length needed. For portable use in diaper bag I use a leftover blue plastic wet-wipe container and refill with my homemade ones. *Liz White, Gulf Breeze, Florida*

WARM BABY WIPES ◆ Place two or three wipes in the microwave for just a few seconds. *Test them before using on baby.* Babies hate cold wipes. *Carrie Grimaldi, Maywood, New Jersey*

DISPOSABLES FOR NIGHT ◆ We use a disposable diaper at night for our seven-month-old baby because it seems to keep him drier and more comfortable. That didn't matter until the baby started sleeping more of the night, because we used to change him each time he woke. *Margaret Healy, Albany, California*

DIAPER PINS ◆ If using cloth diapers with pins, stick the pins in a bar of soap while changing the diaper. This will help the pin go through the diaper more easily. *Brenda Kiba, Milpitas, California*

FIRST FEW DAYS ◆ The first few bowel movements a baby has are very sticky and messy. Putting petroleum jelly on the newborn's bottom when you first get your baby in the hospital makes cleanup a breeze. *D. Martinez, Fremont, California*

UMBILICAL STUMPS ◆ A trick I used many times with newborns is to cut a V in the center front of disposable diapers during the first few weeks to keep the umbilical stump from becoming wet and irritated. *D. Martinez, Fremont, California*

 Another way to keep from irritating an umbilical stump is to fold the top of the diaper downward and outward just below the umbilical stump.

IF YOUR TODDLER TAKES HIS DIAPERS OFF ◆ For those toddlers who love to pull their disposable diapers off and run around naked, turn the diapers backwards and tape front to back. If you do this a few times, they will get discouraged and stop taking their diapers off. *Jill Nelson-Johnson, Urbandale, Iowa*

DON'T ROLL OFF ◆ I put the baby crosswise on our very wide changing table, with his feet towards me and his head towards the wall. Even if he were to roll over, he wouldn't fall off. *P.H., Albany, California*

STORIES FOR THE CHANGING TABLE ◆ I have an obstinate three-year-old son who still isn't toilet trained. When I change his diapers, he is so uncooperative, it drives me crazy. He arches his back, kicks his legs, etc. To get him to cooperate during these moments, I have developed a series of "Meow Meow" stories about a little mischievous kitten who's always getting into trouble. These stories distract him into cooperation. *Audrey Swanton, Brewer, Maine*

A FAN OF DRAWSTRING BOTTOMS ◆ We used long nightgowns with drawstring bottoms for a brand-new infant instead of sleepers because it was less difficult to undress the baby to change diapers in the middle of the night. *Peg Hartley, San Bernardino, California*

WARM SOAPY WATER FOR DIAPER RASH ✦ When small children have diaper rash, I run about two inches of warm water in the tub and place them in it. I soap them up and let them play for about fifteen minutes or so. The cream and powders somehow never did the whole job. But after letting them soak in the warm soapy water, the rash clears up quickly. *Hugh Heydt, Omaha, Nebraska*

 Using soap and plenty of water for every diaper change, instead of convenience wipes, will help prevent and eliminate diaper rashes.

BAKING SODA IN BATH WATER ✦ A small amount of baking soda in the bath water will help cure and prevent diaper rash. *Julia Kiely, Irvine, California*

HAIR DRYER FOR DIAPER RASH ✦ I have found that when my baby had diaper rash, I used a hair dryer on low setting to dry my baby's bottom after changing her diaper. When used along with frequent changes, the hair dryer really helps dry and heal diaper rash. *Tracy Smedley, San Diego, California*

 Be careful not to burn your child. Test the distance and time carefully.

SUNLIGHT AND AIR FOR DIAPER RASH ✦
Sunlight and fresh air help infants to overcome blistery
diaper rashes. *D.L. Stelle, Fremont, California*

ALKALINE CLOTH DIAPERS FOR RASH ✦ If you
use cloth diapers from a diaper service company and your
baby is troubled by diaper rash, you may want to consider
trying alkaline diapers. Many companies offer these alternative diapers, which are best for babies with sensitive
skin. Consult your diaper-service representative for more
details. *Anonymous, San Diego, California*

DISPOSABLE DIAPERS—SKIN SENSITIVITY ✦ If
your baby is sensitive to diaper rash, try a variety of disposable diaper brands until you pinpoint which are the
best ones for your baby. We discovered that one of the inexpensive brands was best for our baby. *Jennifer Beasley,
Lakewood, California*

✕✦✦✦✦✦✦✦✦✦✦✦✦✦✦✦✦✦✦✦✦✦✦✦✦✦✦✦✦✦✦✦✦✦✦✦✦✕

AT ARM'S REACH OF
THE CHANGING TABLE

✕✦✦✦✦✦✦✦✦✦✦✦✦✦✦✦✦✦✦✦✦✦✦✦✦✦✦✦✦✦✦✦✦✦✦✦✦✕

KEEPING TRACK OF BABY'S PROGRESS ✦ Keep
the baby calendar on the wall by the changing table, along
with a pen. Since a lot of time is spent at this location, one
can job down a quick note on the calendar to record baby's
progress—before it leaves one's mind. *Jan Harvey, Fremont, California*

FROM CALENDAR TO BABY BOOK ✦ I used to
struggle to remember all the important "milestone
events" (first crawl, first tooth, funny things our baby did
or said, etc.) to write in our baby book until I started to jot

things down on the calendar. Later, when I had time to write in the baby book, I just had to look at the calendar to jog my memory. *Marsha Meckler, Honolulu, Hawaii*

A PHONE FOR THE NURSERY ◆ Inevitably, the phone always rings when I'm in the middle of an activity in the nursery: changing diapers, reading stories, etc. Putting an extension phone next to the changing table will save you time and hassle. Of course, I turn off the ringer during naps or bedtime. *Becky Chapman, Watsonville, California*

◆◆

PACIFYING THE TEETHER

◆◆

Never leave your infant alone when chewing on something that can be broken or chewed off and cause choking.

FROZEN BANANA PIECES ◆ Teethers love to bite on frozen banana pieces. For best results, slice rounds (approximately ¼ inch) widthwise from a fresh firm banana. Freeze in freezer bags. *Debi Carlson, Mesa, Arizona*

FROZEN WASHCLOTHS ◆ When my six-month-old child was teething, I would wet one end of a washcloth and put it in the freezer for a couple of hours, then give it to him. It would soothe his gums while the other end of the washcloth absorbed any drooling that he might have. *Jacque Marshall, Palm Bay, Florida*

CHILL A WASHCLOTH IN THE REFRIGERATOR ◆ My baby loved to gnaw on a wet washcloth that had been chilled in the refrigerator. *Stacey Lopez, Fremont, California*

HANDY TEETHING HOLDER ✦ Before placing a washcloth in refrigerator or freezer, fold it in half lengthwise, fold it in half again, and pin it together. This will create a convenient holder for the baby's hand. *Arlene Stocking, Fremont, California*

CORNCOBS FOR TEETHERS ✦ Teethers love to bite and suck on corncobs that have been stripped of the kernels. They taste good and the texture is just right to soothe sore gums. *Barbara McMahon, San Diego, California*

PINKIE FINGERS TASTE GOOD ✦ My baby loved to suck and gnaw on one of my fingers, preferable my pinkie or index finger. It's one teething item that's always available. *Joanie Stewart, Toronto, Ontario*

FROZEN BAGELS FOR TEETHERS ✦ Take the small bagels, cut them in half, and freeze them. Then give the baby a frozen bagel to teeth on. I take it away from them when it gets mushy and soft. *Ann Hersey, Vista, California*

$$ HOMEMADE TEETHING BISCUITS ✦ Make your own inexpensive and more healthful teething biscuits by baking slices of different breads in a low oven (150–200 degrees) for 15 to 20 minutes. Make sure there are no items (raisins, nuts, etc.) in the bread that a teether could choke on. *D. L. Tarsa, Michigan*

FROZEN WAFFLES FOR TEETHING ✦ Teething babies love to gnaw on frozen waffles. They taste good and feel good on sore gums. *Laura Linnell, Canmore, Alberta*

❖❖

WEANING (BOTTLES, PACIFIERS, AND BLANKIES)

❖❖

WEANING ONE FEEDING AT A TIME ❖ To wean my baby from the breast to the bottle, I gave up one of my daily feedings at a time, one week apart. Each time, I replaced the feeding with a cup of milk. *Jayme Trolle, Fremont, California*

BOTTLES WENT BYE-BYE ❖ The child is told in advance that it is time to stop drinking out of the bottle and that the day is coming when all of the bottles will be thrown away. Allow the child a few days, or a week, to adjust to the idea. Then announce to the child that it is time to throw the bottles away, since the child is a big girl or boy. Clean out all bottles from the cupboard and let child help place them in a bag. Have the child carry or help carry the bag of discarded bottles out to the trash and place it inside. Remind the child as you return to the house that there are now no more bottles. (This helped me to resist the temptation to give her one for convenience or comfort. I had the garbage can arranged so that I could easily remove the bottles to give away.) This also helped when the child asked for a bottle as she was reminded there weren't any in the house. It eliminated whining on the subject. *Marlene D. Gerber, Livermore, California*

"I GAVE IT TO THE TRASH MAN" ❖ There comes a time when every child has to let go of all that baby stuff. We found a wonderful way for our daughter to let go of The Bottle and The Blankie, etc. She knows who the trash man is, and that he takes the trash away for good. When it was time, we went out and met the trash man by his truck. Our daughter handed him her bottle or whatever she was giving up and watched him put it into the back of his truck and compact it. Later, if she asked about the item, I would remind her that she gave it to the trash man, and she wouldn't give the item another thought. *Liz Avery, Monterey, California*

KIDS SAY THE FUNNIEST THINGS

My son, Matthew, was about two years old when we
had gotten him out of the habit of using the bottle.
Well, somehow he would get his way at his grandparents' and get that bottle. So, to try and reason with
him, Grandpa said, "Matt, you're a big boy now, you
should drink milk out of a cup." With that Matthew
replied, "When I'm at home I'm a big boy, but when
I'm here, I'm a baby!" This left Grandpa at a loss for
words and he told us that he could not argue with
logic such as that. *David Oshiro, Alameda, California*

**THIS "BIG BOY" GAVE HIS BOTTLES TO A REAL
BABY** ✦ For the transition from bottles to cups, my husband and I gradually reduced the number of bottle feedings for our son. We also talked about the big day when he
would be a "big boy" and would give all his bottles to a
new baby. We allowed our son to pick out his own "big boy
cups" with his favorite characters on them. The transition
was smooth and he was proud to give his bottles to a "real
baby." *Neeta Sanghvi, Fremont, California*

"THE EASTER BUNNY TOOK YOUR BOTTLE" ✦ My daughter was three years old and didn't want to give up the bottle. Just before Easter, I told her that the Easter Bunny was going to come and take her bottle and bring her an Easter basket. On Easter morning I replaced her bottle with an Easter basket. When she awoke and asked for the bottle, I told her that the Easter Bunny took her bottle and left the Easter basket. That was it, she quit the bottle. *Maria Moore, Reno, Nevada*

Other holidays or events can be used, too (Santa Claus, the Bottle Fairy, etc.).

IT'S TIME TO BURY THE BOTTLE ✦ Several years ago I had a grandson who couldn't be broken from using his bottle. This little guy was three years old at the time and every conceivable solution was tried, but all in vain. While we were camping with him and his parents, I came up with the following solution. We had dug a garbage pit and were about to cover it when I suggested that we have him throw his bottle in the pit and help us cover it up. We gave him a large spade shovel and helped him cover it up. That was the end of the bottle problem. He never asked for his bottle again. Since then, I've seen it work three out of three times; most buried the bottle in their backyard or garden. It's important to make it into a game and always let the child help cover up the bottle. *Paul M. English, Havre, Montana*

BOTTLE WEANING WITH STRAWS ✦ When you want to wean your toddler from bottles to cups, a good intermediate step is a plastic cup with a straw through a snap-on lid. The sucking mechanism is very similar, especially if you cut the straw short the first time so it doesn't take too long to get something up to the mouth. An especially delicious drink will also give a favorable first impression of this new bottle substitute. *Peggy Gilbreth Nipper, Omaha, Nebraska*

MY BOTTLE JUST DOESN'T TASTE THE SAME ✦ Three days after my baby daughter and I had been home from the hospital, my three-and-a-half-year-old son decided he wanted a bottle again. My mother explained to him that he hadn't realized that in the year that he had stopped taking a bottle that he had grown into a big boy and that his tastes had changed. To prove her point, mother prepared a special bottle for big brother—four ounces of milk with one tablespoon of white vinegar. One sip and he handed the bottle back to his grandmother and assured her that she was right, it just didn't taste the same. Later that day, I made him a strawberry shake in a tall glass and we celebrated "Big Brother Day." *Arlene Stocking, Fremont, California*

ONLY WATER IN THE BOTTLE ✦ To encourage bottle weaning, only put water in the bottle. Offer milk in a cup. Children will quickly learn that if they want milk, they will have to use a cup. I recommend introducing this practice gradually, not all at once. *Shanon Armfield, Greensboro, North Carolina*

SPECIAL TREAT—ONLY IN BIG-GIRL CUP ✦ To interest my daughter in drinking from a cup instead of a bottle I would prepare her favorite treat only in a cup. This yummy treat (blended strawberries mixed in milk) was never available in a bottle. She loved it so much that the cup was not an issue. After a couple of days she forgot about her bottles entirely. *Margaret Rawstern, Orlando, Florida*

PACIFIER WENT BYE-BYE ✦ I inadvertently lost my child's pacifier and couldn't find it so I started giving him crackers and little cookies to gum on instead. When I did find his pacifier, I gave it to him and he spit it out. He didn't like it anymore. By giving him something to chew on, he found something he liked better than a pacifier. He's fifteen months old now and he hasn't used the pacifier since. *Charlene Busch, Salem, Oregon*

Make sure when you give crackers, cookies, etc. that the infant is old enough for them, and that they don't break into pieces that might be choked on.

SANTA CLAUS TOOK MY PACIFIER ✦ We set age two as the limit for using a pacifier. So around that age, at Christmastime, we talked to each of our two-year-old children about Santa. We put the pacifier in a box, wrapped the box, and sent it to Santa at the North Pole so that he could take the pacifier to another baby and put it under that baby's tree on Christmas morning. We had no problems, and our children never asked for a pacifier again. It worked great! *Lori Krouse, Red Lion, Pennsylvania*

AN INCONVENIENT PACIFIER ◆ To wean a child off a pacifier, tie the pacifier to a door. Let the child know that he or she can have it anytime and that it will always be

there if needed. Do not tie it in an out-of-the-way place as the child needs to remain with people while using it. This allows the child to have the comfort of the pacifier while remaining with his loved ones. It also allows the child to choose between standing next to a door and watching as others play or playing himself. Usually the child will choose the pacifier less and less. *Scott Hill, Newark, California*

Be careful not to tie it with too long a string. You don't want the child to get tangled in the string and strangle.

PACIFIER STAYS IN CRIB ◆ My son was very attached to his pacifier; he had to sleep with one in his mouth and one in his hand. When he was around eighteen months old, I told him his "nukie" had to stay in his crib. I was consistent, and it worked. When he wanted his pacifier, he would call me to put him in his crib, and he would sit in there and suck on it. When he was through, I would take him out! *D.L., Gulford, Connecticut*

THE SHRINKING PACIFIER ✦ To help our children lose interest in their pacifiers I would cut a very small piece off the end of the nipple with a razor blade every few days. Eventually the child would announce that the pacifier was "broken" and toss it in the trash. *Anonymous, Winnipeg, Manitoba*

BLANKET WEANING ✦ As a baby and toddler, my daughter took her blanket everywhere. Then we began to limit where she could take it. We discussed each new rule first. We started leaving it in the car, then she could only have it at home. I don't see any reason to pack it away. She uses it for comfort when she sleeps, is upset, or sick. Days go by when she hardly touches it but it is always there. She is allowed to take it with her for vacations or to grandma's anytime she is sleeping over. *Stacey Ann Morgan, Oakland, California*

THE SHRINKING BLANKET ✦ When a child is older and wants to take his security blanket everywhere he goes, it may be helpful to "shrink" it very gradually so it's not dragging on the ground all the time. Every few days cut an inch or so off one end until it's a manageable size. The child won't notice and it's actually easier to carry. *Peggy Gilbreth Nipper, Omaha, Nebraska*

TRADE IN THAT BLANKET ✦ When my son was five, he was offered a trade-in on his blanket. "If you ever want to trade this in, it is worth a toy." He wasn't ready at the time but six months later there was a toy he really wanted and he traded. His blanket has been stored away with no problem. *Marlene D. Gerber, Livermore, California*

LOST: ONE CHILD'S WHITE BLANKET, VERY DIRTY—REWARD ✦ My grandson had a security blanket which he didn't want to be without for any prolonged length of time, so his mother would have to wash it after he went to bed at night to keep the peace. When the second son was born, I suggested giving him two identical blankets. He always had one available while the other was in the wash or stored on a closet shelf out of sight until needed. By rotating the blankets, when laundry day arrived, they aged identically and even he could not tell them apart. The value of this idea was impressed upon me even more when I saw a classified ad in the newspaper recently that read, "Lost: One Child's White Blanket, Very Dirty—Reward!" *Irene Gilbreth, Upper Montclair, New Jersey*

$$ A "PILLOWCASE" BLANKIE ✦ By the time my third son was born, I had gotten smart about the "security blanket" issue. By starting son number three out with a plain white pillowcase as his bedtime covering, I eliminated the battle of trying to wrench away the frazzled blanket in order to wash it. Also, we did not have to experience the wails of distress if the "blanket" was forgotten on a trip—everyone has a white pillowcase. *Memory Campbell, Charlotte, North Carolina*

A "DIAPER" BLANKIE—WITH FRILLS ✦ To make a soft and cuddly blankie for your new baby, I suggest using new cloth diapers (available at department stores) and satin or silk (available at fabric stores). I took a two-inch piece of satin, folded it in half, and sewed it on each long side of the diaper so the fabric was attached to both the top and bottom edge of the diaper. I made a dozen of them. Needless to say, we never had the trauma of losing a blankie. *V. Seaborg, Fremont, California*

1 BLANKIE BECOMES 4 ✦ When our children's security blankets got tattered, I cut each up into four pieces. As each piece wore out, they got another until there were no pieces left. By this time, they had no problem with not having a security blanket. *Wendy Watson, Orange, California*

MY OWN (BLANKIE) KEY RING ✦ When a child is three-and-a-half to four years old and still insists on dragging a blanket about, let her know that her blanket is probably as important to her when she leaves the house as your house and car keys are to you. Then take the child to a store and let her pick out a key ring with a fun key fob attached. Cut a small section of her blankie and attach it to the key ring. The larger piece of blanket remains at home and the small piece attached to the key ring is for those times when the child goes out. *A.V.S., Fremont, California*

XXX

MISCELLANEOUS TIPS FOR BABY

XXXXXXXXXXXXXXXXXXXXXXXXXXXXXXXXXXXXXXXXX

WHO'S WHO OF IDENTICAL TWINS ✦ If you are having identical twins, keep their name bracelets on. When they outgrow them, buy new ones. I have identical boys, and for about the first six months of their lives, we were not always sure who was who. When you take pictures, make notes who was on what side of the photo and who was wearing what. We have hundreds of pictures and have no idea which baby is which. *Robin Nicewicz, Valencia, California*

NATIONAL ORGANIZATION OF MOTHERS OF

TWINS

For information, assistance, and the address of your local chapter, call 1-505-275-0955

RED TOENAILS DISTINGUISH TWINS ✦ Paint the toenails of one baby red to distinguish between identical twins. This practice is especially helpful when one is ill and must be given medicine. *Ruthann Hunt, Newark, California*

$$ BABY KNEE PADS PREVENT RUG BURNS ✦ Many babies get rug burns from crawling. One solution is to buy baby knee pads that are sold in baby catalogs. Another solution is to make your own out of a pair of men's athletic socks (the white ones with the stripes on top). Cut off the striped area and hem the ragged end. Presto—baby knee pads! *Marjean Rowe, Little Rock, Arkansas*

THE TODDLING WALKER ✦ When my children decided it was time to try to walk by themselves, I put a piece of heavy tape on the bottom of their hard-soled shoes to keep them from slipping on the floor. I also would put a round clothespin in each hand. This seemed to give them security and helped them to keep their balance. *Lois Ambrose, York, Pennsylvania*

When children are learning to walk, let them go barefoot as much as possible. When children do need to wear shoes, soft, flexible soles are best.

GUESS WHO'S PREGNANT? ✦ To announce the upcoming birth of our first child to their long-distance grandparents, I purchased a pair of yellow booties and sent one bootie to each set of grandparents along with a note, "Please return on or before November 14." No other explanation was necessary, and the grandparents thought it was "oh so clever!" *Donna Sanson, Fremont, California*

SCHOOL WAITING LIST ✦ Don't wait until the last minute to get your child on the waiting list for popular preschools or private schools. Some schools have long waiting lists that take years to reach the top. Get your child on that school list now. *C.P.G., Seattle, Washington*

A JOURNAL ON TAPE ✦ I have made an audiotape journal of my infant daughter's life. Each entry includes the date, age of the baby, special event, maternal feelings, or whatever is going on in her life. I will give the tapes to my daughter when she is older. It's a great way to share these early experiences. This is also a great idea for people who either don't have time to write (working moms) or don't feel comfortable writing. *Naomi Mulligan, Livermore, California*

AUDIO RECORD FOR POSTERITY ✦ As soon as my son could talk, I began recording his voice on a cassette tape player. On holidays, his birthday, and special occasions, we recorded him saying a few things, the alphabet or a song or two. Now, at age six, this is one of my son's favorite tapes (. . . and one of mine, too)! *K.T. Hom, San Jose, California*

A LETTER HELPS ME REMEMBER ✦ About every six months, I write a letter to myself describing what my child was like. It's fun to go back and read these from time to time. *Marsha Meckler, Honolulu, Hawaii*

These letters will also be fun for your children to read when they're older.

PETS NEED TO ADJUST TO A NEW BABY ✦ To help our pet dog adjust to our new baby, we put the dog in a kennel for a few days accompanied by a blanket that our baby had been wrapped in at the hospital. When we brought our dog home, he walked in the baby's room, sniffed around a little, then walked out as if it was no big deal. We believe the blanket with the baby's smell on it helped the dog adjust to this new family member before actually seeing the baby. The dog and our baby became best of friends. *Nancy Green, Sherman Oaks, California*

THE SNEAKY TOENAIL CLIPPER ✦ I always·clip my child's nails during his daytime nap. Baby-sized toenail clippers give a better cut than the blunt-ended scissors. *Peg Hartley, San Bernardino, California*

Also, try clipping nails after bathing, which can make the job easier because the skin and nails soften, and nails do not crack or break.

WHERE'S THE PACIFIER? ✦ Buy a pacifier holder (available at most large department stores) and attach one end to the pacifier and the other end to the child's clothes or favorite blanket. No more hunting for pacifiers! *Lori Krouse, Red Lion, Pennsylvania*

Make sure that any pacifier "holder" is safe, and infant or child cannot choke on the cord used.

PARENTS' BILL OF RIGHTS AND RESPONSIBILITIES

1 We, as parents, have a right to be treated with respect.

2 We have the right to say no and not feel guilty.

3 We have a right to know where our children are, who their friends are, and who they are with at any time.

4 We have the right to demonstrate we care by occasionally verifying or spot checking our children's whereabouts. We may, for example, call host parents on parties or overnight stays.

5 We have a right to set a curfew and enforce it with restrictions and loss of privileges.

6 We have a right not to condone any alcohol or drug usage and to say no to attendance at activities where alcohol or drug usage may occur.

7 We have a right to make mistakes and/or change our minds.

8 We have a right to ask questions and expect answers about all things which may affect our children.

9 We have a right to monitor all school-related activities: academic, behavioral and social.

10 We have a right to know and consult with adults who influence our children's lives, i.e., coaches, employers, teachers, youth-group leaders, ministers, and counselors.

11 We have a right to know what is happening within our own home, to set "house rules," and know the identity of guests who come into our home.

12 We have a right to assign our children chores and other family responsibilities appropriate to their ages.

13 We have a right to promote time together, as a family, which may include meals, outings, study time, and other planned activities.

14 We have a right to be authoritative when logical explanation and reason has not succeeded.

15 We have a right to have family rules and consistently enforce them with appropriate consequences.

Printed with permission of the Tri-City Substance Abuse Coalition (Fremont, Newark, Union City, California.)

INDEX

xxx

KNOW A CLEVER CHILD-CARE TIP?

xxxxxxxxxxxxxxxxxxxxxxxxxxxxxxxxxxxxxxxxxxx

Do you know a tip that was not included in this book? If you do, I want to hear from you. And so do the thousands of parents who could read your tip in the next edition of *IT WORKS FOR US!: PROVEN CHILD-CARE TIPS FROM EXPERIENCED PARENTS ACROSS THE COUNTRY.*

Please let me know if you would like to have your name or initials and your city printed with your tip.

If you have a tip or comment about the book, write to:

> PARENTING TIPS
> 40087 Mission Blvd., Box 300
> Fremont, CA 94539
> (Please use form on next page)

or call the TIPS answering machine:

> (510) 770-1819 (24 hours)
> (FAXES also accepted)

or contact me on PRODIGY® (Interactive Personal Service) at

> SRGS42A

I am also planning a similar "Tips" book for the adolescence years (11–17). Please send me your practical parenting tips.

MY TIP IS . . .

_____

_____

_____

_____

_____

_____

I give my permission to reprint my tip(s) in all editions of the parenting books and newspaper columns authored by Tom McMahon and any derived uses therefrom or in any other manner, subject to necessary editing.

☐ Please list my name or initials, city, and state as set forth below with my tip(s).

_____
(please print clearly)

☐ Please do not print my name or initials.

_____ signature

_____ print name

_____ mailing address

_____

_____ phone number

Mail this completed form to:
Parenting Tips
40087 Mission Blvd., Box 300
Fremont, CA 94539

Use additional paper for tips if necessary

The high calling of parenthood must be more adequately recognized, respected, and honored by our society. Therein lies the future of our nation.

—NATIONAL COUNCIL OF JUVENILE AND FAMILY COURT JUDGES, 1989